THE
Outlaw
Trail

CHARLES KELLY

THE
Outlaw
Trail

A History of BUTCH CASSIDY
and His Wild Bunch

KONECKY&KONECKY

Konecky & Konecky
72 Ayers Point Rd.
Old Saybrook, CT 06475

Copyright © 1938, 1959 by Charles Kelly.

This edition published by special arrangement with
The Devin-Adair Company.

This is a revised and enlarged edition of a book privately
printed under the same title by the author in 1938.

All rights reserved.

ISBN: 1-56852-242-8

Printed and bound in the USA

Preface

When material for this book was being gathered more than twenty years ago, for its first, privately printed, limited edition, old-timers who knew the facts at first hand were very reluctant to talk about their connection with Butch Cassidy and his Wild Bunch. It was necessary to depend largely upon old newspaper accounts and second-hand stories, which were not always reliable.

After that edition was printed, a flood of letters was received, calling attention to errors and supplying new information. New records were found which added much to the story.

The new material collected during the past twenty years has been incorporated in this much-enlarged, more accurate edition for the general public.

I was fortunate to have started research for this revised edition just in time. All the outlaws who rode with Cassidy, and nearly all the old-timers who knew him, are now dead.

CHARLES KELLY

Salt Lake City
January, 1959

Acknowledgments

To Frank Beckwith, of Delta, Utah, companion of many desert journeys, is due credit for first acquainting me with the legend of Butch Cassidy. Maurice Howe, newspaperman of Ogden, lent much assistance by interviewing old-timers. Frank Swain, champion storyteller of the Uintah Basin, generously assisted in obtaining original material. Dr. R. G. Frazier, of Bingham Canyon, Utah, was the original discoverer of old "Speck" Williams, a mine of information. W. E. Gordon, old-time cowman, and Frank Silvey, pioneer of San Juan County, also furnished valuable data. Ray T. Stites, of Salt Lake City, assisted in bibliographical research.

Other old-timers who furnished source material were Albert "Speck" Williams, Pete Dillman, John T. Pope, and William Chew, of Vernal; Judge David E. Thomas, Mrs. J. H. Goodnough, and Joe Davenport, of Rock Springs, Wyoming; Dr. J. K. W. Bracken, of Salt Lake City; Charley Gibbons, of Hanksville, Utah; Matt Warner of Price, Utah; John R. Ritch, of Great Falls, Montana; Ann Bassett Willis, Montpelier, Idaho; George Searle, Duchesne, Utah; Joe LaFors, Buffalo, Wyoming; M. E. Nicholson, Wallace, Idaho; Miguel A. Otero, Santa Fe, New Mexico; John C. DeVore, Casper, Wyoming; William L. Simpson, Jackson, Wyoming;

ACKNOWLEDGMENTS

J. J. Strang, Torrance, California; and E. P. Lamborn, Leavenworth, Kansas, who furnished old photographs.

For bibliographical records I am indebted to *Outskirt Episodes*, by William G. Tittsworth; *Tales of the Old-Timers*,
by Frederick R. Bechdolt; *Malcolm Campbell, Sheriff*, by
R. B. David; *Triggernometry*, by Eugene Cunningham; *History of Natrona County*, by A. J. Mokler; *Recollections of a
Western Ranchman*, by William French; *Tombstone's Yes-
terdays*, by Lorenzo D. Walters; *Spurs and Riata*, by Charles
Siringo; *Last of the Bandit Riders*, by Matt Warner; *History
of Tom McCarty*, by himself; and two magazine articles on
Butch Cassidy, one by Arthur Chapman and the other by
Franklin Reynolds. Some of the rare old photographs reproduced are from the collection of E. P. Lamborn and the Historical Department of the Union Pacific Railroad.

Access to old newspaper files was courteously extended by
Mr. Lucas of the *Buffalo Bulletin* and by the public librarians
at Casper, Wyoming, and Salt Lake City.

Credit is also due scores of others, too numerous to name
here, who furnished various bits of information and assisted in
research. To all those named above, whose unselfish assistance
has made this story possible, I extend the sincerest thanks.

C. K.

Contents

Contents

THE
Outlaw
Trail

Introducing
Butch Cassidy

THE cowboy-outlaw period of western history has furnished fiction writers with an unlimited amount of material for stories, books and movie scripts. Although the hard-riding, gun-toting cowboy who turned outlaw has long ago disappeared from the scene, stories of his hair-raising exploits are still in demand and no doubt will be for generations to come. The principal character in most such yarns is a fearless gunfighter whose reputation is maintained by the number of notches on his gun, and before the story or picture ends, the wide-open spaces are strewn with dead men who dared challenge his infallible marksmanship.

The words "outlaw" and "killer" are generally considered synonymous, and for very good reason. But Butch Cassidy proved that this is not necessarily true, and in that respect his story is unique. In his later years he was leader of an outlaw group known as the Wild Bunch, one of whom was as desperate a character as ever pulled a trigger, and in their activities some men were shot. But Cassidy never approved of bloodshed and, so far as the record shows, never killed a man

3

until his last stand, when he was outnumbered a hundred to one.

In spite of, or possibly because of, this record, Butch Cassidy has become one of the most romantic figures of the cowboy-outlaw period. He has been called Utah's Robin Hood, not so much because of his generosity as because he was considered a "gentleman outlaw." He never drank to excess, was always courteous to women, was free with money when he had it, and extremely loyal to his friends. All old-timers interviewed for this biography, including officers who hunted him, were unanimous in saying, "Butch Cassidy was one of the finest men I ever knew."

But, in spite of his mild manner and his dislike of bloodshed, Butch Cassidy became the most famous and most successful outlaw of the intermountain country. The outlaw trail he rode extended from Canada to Mexico, crossing Montana, Idaho, Wyoming, Colorado, Utah, Nevada, Arizona, and New Mexico. He was almost universally successful and served only one short term in the pen. Among cowboys and cattlemen of the old frontier his name stood for daring, courage, resourcefulness, and a certain chivalry. His exploits have become part of the living legend of the desert country through which he rode, and his reputation as leader of the largest band of outlaws the West has ever seen is secure.

The heyday of the cowboy-outlaws was short, lasting only about thirty years, and their actual numbers were comparatively small. Yet they left an indelible impression on the pages of western history. Nearly every one of any prominence who rode the intermountain outlaw trail will eventually be mentioned in this book. Before we go further, it might be well to investigate their background and learn how they came into being.

Buckskin-clad trappers, carrying long Kentucky rifles, blazed the first trails into the Rocky Mountains, took their toll of beaver and buffalo, and left behind an almost unbelievable tradition of wild adventure and personal courage. To them, the only form of wealth in that vast wilderness was beaver fur; they never considered the land fit for permanent settlement. Their era began about 1822 and ended, for all practical purposes, in 1840, when falling prices and scarcity of fur made trapping no longer profitable.

Following these old trails, guided by mountain men of the old Fur Brigade, came long lines of covered wagons bringing pioneer families, horses, cattle, and "sod busters." Most of these early wagon trains passed on to Oregon and California, the mountain men considering the deserts and mountains of the intermountain region as obstacles to be overcome by sweat and perseverance. No attempt was made to settle in the mountains until 1847, when Brigham Young brought his pioneer band of Mormons to Salt Lake Valley. Most of these early settlers were from the New England states, accustomed to intensive farming methods. They soon discovered that, outside of a few favored localities where land could be irrigated, the desert was valueless except for grazing. In its virgin state it produced enough nutritious grasses to support a limited number of livestock, both summer and winter, with little labor expense. Cattle and horses soon became almost the only form of wealth, passing as currency in communities which saw no cash for more than a generation. Only enough sheep were raised to supply the necessary wool for clothing.

Completion of the first transcontinental railroad in 1869 ushered in a third period which marked the beginning of western development on a large scale. Millions of acres previously used only as Indian hunting grounds were soon occupied by a class of enterprising men who later came to be called cattle barons. Hundreds of thousands of Texas cattle were shipped or driven to Wyoming, Montana, Utah, and Nevada. Wealth in the form of livestock soon began roaming over vast stretches of country, unguarded and unnoticed except at roundup time, when large herds were driven to railroad points for shipment to eastern markets. Only men with large capital were able to operate on the grand scale prevalent in those days; farmers or small ranchers had no place in such a scheme.

Large numbers of cowboys were required to handle these large herds. They were recruited from among the wilder element of the frontier and had to be tough to survive. Almost as nomadic as Indians, they moved from one big outfit to another as their fancy dictated, unhampered by family or property. If some misguided cowpuncher with a few months' pay in his pocket planned to start a ranch of his own on a small scale, he found his efforts violently opposed by the large ranch owners, who had claimed all public domain, under the theory that it had been created and reserved for their special benefit. Young men who resented this attitude often retaliated by rounding up and branding mavericks with their own mark —a custom of the country also indulged in by all big outfits. From branding mavericks to genuine rustling was but a short and easy step.

Because of this attitude of the big operators, whose tactics will be described later, a generation of cattle thieves sprang up within a very short time, the like of which was never seen before and will never be seen again. While many of those early rustlers were merely trying to get a foothold on the range and never carried their activities beyond "honest" cattle stealing, a good many others became, or tried to become, genuine bandits. The cowboy-outlaw era began about 1875, reached its climax in 1897, and ended about 1905. During the '90's the largest gang of outlaws the West ever saw was organized in the Utah-Wyoming-Colorado section. Its organizer and undisputed leader was Butch Cassidy.

Intermountain topography was ideal for the operation of such an organization. Between confusing ranges of high mountains lay wide deserts often cut with deep, almost inaccessible canyons. An outlaw's greatest asset was his intimate knowledge of dim trails and widely spaced water holes. Through this rough, dangerous, and practically unexplored wilderness, cowboys who did not wish to be interviewed by the law laid out a trail extending eventually from Canada to Mexico. There have been many "outlaw trails" in various parts of the country at different times; but the trail described in this volume was the longest and wildest, was provided with better hideouts, was used by more outlaws, and continued in use for a longer time than any other. Men who used it operated on a large scale; their banditry was bold and spectacular and their hideouts practically impregnable.

Original headquarters of this gang were established in Brown's Hole, an inaccessible mountain-walled valley on the Green River in the Uintah Mountains, lying partly in Utah, partly in Colorado, and partly in Wyoming. Such a location made it an ideal hideout, since it was impossible to capture an outlaw or recover stolen stock without the cooperation of officers from all three states.

From Brown's Hole the Outlaw Trail ran north to Hole-in-the-Wall in Johnson County, Wyoming, a hideout second in importance but one which, because of its name, has received an unmerited amount of attention from fiction writers. Still farther north, in the Little Rockies of Montana, was the most northern station on the trail.

South of Brown's Hole, in the sandy San Rafael Desert of Utah, on the lower Green River, was Robbers' Roost, an isolated retreat very difficult of access. In Arizona, just south of the Utah line, the trail crossed the Colorado River at Lee's Ferry, once operated by John D. Lee, a leader of the infamous Mountain Meadows massacre. Continuing south across dangerous deserts, it penetrated the deep red sandstone canyons of Arizona, touched the western edge of New Mexico near the Mogollon Mountains, and continued into Old Mexico.

The desert and mountain country through which this trail passed was then—and still is—the least known and most isolated of any section of the West, where one might even today ride for days or weeks without meeting a living soul. Riders who passed along that trail were men of iron, accustomed to the roughest sort of life, able to ride day and night without rest over dry deserts and through dangerous canyons when occasion required. Endurance and courage were paramount requirements of their calling; those who lacked either were quickly eliminated.

Riders on the Outlaw Trail under the leadership of Butch Cassidy lived by a code of their own—a code vastly superior to anything known in the underworld of today. In comparison with modern gangsters they were all gentlemen. To shoot an unarmed man was considered the lowest of crimes, and the abuse of women and children was never thought of at any time. It is not the purpose of this volume to glorify the western outlaw or to polish his celluloid halo; yet, to give him his just due, he earned a fair share of the glamor by which he has been continuously surrounded ever since he rode the Outlaw Trail.

South Pass, famous old emigrant gateway to the Far West, lies at the south end of the Wind River range in western Wyoming. Through its wide portals, in the year 1856, passed one of the strangest processions the Overland Trail had ever seen: hundreds of men, women, and children plodding wearily toward their "Zion" in Salt Lake Valley, drawing behind them, with painful effort, two-wheeled carts in which were piled all that remained of their earthly goods. These Mormon converts, recruited principally in England, Denmark, and Sweden—too poor to purchase oxen and wagons— were compelled to walk the entire distance from the Missouri River to Salt Lake City, hitched like beasts of burden to clumsy, poorly made carts which, dried out by desert air, frequently fell apart.

The Handcart Pioneers of 1856 left their outfitting point in late August and early September, fully three months later than emigrants usually began the westward journey. They were well aware that snow begins falling in the mountains early in October; but they put their trust in promises of their prophet, Brigham Young, who prophesied the Lord would alter the weather to suit their convenience and hold off snows until all had arrived safely. Even with forced marches and almost superhuman effort, the middle of October arrived before that plodding procession reached the continental divide. They were met by deep snow and freezing blasts which always sweep through South Pass at that season, in open defiance of puny prophets. Hundreds died like sheep—many on Rock Creek, but most in Martin's Hollow, almost at the summit.

Near the head of that pitiful and deluded procession marched Robert Parker. Elder Parker was from the town of Preston, in England, where he had been "president" of the Mormon mission. Accompanying him were his wife, Ann Hartley- Parker, and family of small children. Because of his church office in England, Robert Parker became leader of the group of Saints emigrating from his section. Being one of the strongest men in the party, he was given a position well in the lead, where he helped break trail through deep snowdrifts. But strenuous exertions on behalf of his starving and freezing family finally sapped his strength, and one bitter cold morning he was found dead in his blankets, almost within sight of the warm valley of Green River. His widow and eldest son, Maximilian, then twelve years old, scratched a shallow trench in the snow, laid him away as best they could, and pushed on toward Zion, their grief dulled by cold and starvation. With assistance sent out from Salt Lake City the family succeeded in reaching its destination, where new arrivals were treated to a feast of watermelons, the first Maxie had ever tasted.

The widow Parker settled at American Fork, about thirty miles south of Salt Lake City. As a young man, Maximilian was sent by the church to guide emigrant trains from the Missouri River to Utah. He served in what is known as Utah's Black Hawk war and later helped construct the first fort at Panguitch. In 1865, after the family moved to Beaver, Maximilian married Ann Campbell and settled in Circle Valley, where he spent the balance of his life. He raised a family of seven children, the eldest of whom, George LeRoy Parker, was born in 1867.

While George Parker was still a young boy, his father purchased the old Jim Marshall ranch, twelve miles south of Circleville. This ranch, according to old-timers, had for some time been headquarters for a gang of horse thieves and cattle rustlers. It was within easy reach of a wild, broken, colorful, and almost inaccessible section furnishing a natural and easily guarded hideout for stolen stock—a place now designated as Bryce Canyon National Park.

Mike Cassidy, one of the most active members of the gang, had already made quite a reputation for himself in those parts. When Parker bought the place Mike stayed on as cowhand. Other members of the rustler outfit continued to stop there from time to time as they passed on various errands. From them young George Parker quickly obtained a first-class education in the fine points of horse stealing and cattle rustling. His particular mentor and boyish hero was jovial Mike Cassidy, from whom he learned the technique of riding, roping, branding, and shooting. Before he was sixteen, Mike's young pupil was known as the best shot in Circle Valley.

Hardened by constant riding on the open range, George grew into a stocky young man, 5 feet 9 inches in height, weighing 155 pounds, strong as a bull, tireless and fearless. He possessed a pleasant and friendly disposition and a disarming smile, enjoyed the rough give-and-take horseplay of cow camps, and was universally liked. He could be depended upon to keep his word—most of the time—and had the distinguishing characteristic of being extremely loyal to his friends.

If one believes old-timers' stories, about half the inhabitants of Circle Valley at that time were connected in some way with cattle rustling. To obtain a start in the cattle business, young men went out on the desert or into the hills and put their brand on any unmarked animals they found. It was an easy matter to separate a calf from its mother, when it became technically a maverick. Branding calves was a sort of game played by all cattlemen, the winner being the one who got his mark on the largest number.

Many stories have been told to explain George Parker's outlaw career. Parley P. Christensen, for thirty years sheriff of Juab County, who knew him well, says that while still a young boy he was arrested—presumably for the theft of a saddle—and thrown in jail, where he was mistreated by the sheriff of Garfield County. Resentment for what he considered unjust treatment caused him to swear vengeance against all representatives of the law. This incident may have had some bearing on his future acts, but his early association with the outlaw element then dominating southern Utah was undoubtedly a deciding factor. Even before his first arrest he had probably determined to follow an outlaw career. If so, his ambitions were fulfilled beyond his wildest dreams.

At odd times during his employment by Jim Marshall and Maxie Parker, Mike Cassidy had gathered a considerable number of cattle on his own account. When the herd could no longer be held in the breaks of Bryce Canyon without exciting suspicion, he moved it to the Henry Mountains near the Colorado River. Needing assistance, he hired George Parker, who herded Cassidy's cattle in that section later famous as Robbers' Roost. If there were any tricks the young Mormon boy did not already know, he soon learned them under the capable tutelage of Mike Cassidy during this employment. Within a short time Mike got into difficulties with the law and left for Mexico. After his departure George Le-Roy Parker appropriated the name of his mentor and became known to his outlaw friends as George Cassidy. Later, "George" became "Butch."

George's second unlawful act of record, in which he attempted to uphold the reputation of the name he had assumed, was the theft of a small bunch of horses from Jim Kittleman somewhere near Circleville. The owner began searching for his animals almost immediately, trailed the thief, and returned to swear out a warrant. Two officers took up the trail, found young Cassidy in possession of the horses, placed him under arrest, slapped on a pair of handcuffs, and started for the county seat.

Mike Cassidy's young pupil had offered no resistance. He seemed docile—even cheerful—on the return trip, a full day's ride. At noon the officers stopped under some cottonwoods near a stream for lunch. Still shackled, George dismounted, but of course took no part in the preparations. One of the officers went to the creek, some distance away, for water, while the other began gathering firewood. Neither paid any attention to their prisoner, who lazily watched the man kindling a fire. Just as the officer with the bucket stooped to dip it in the stream, George gave the man squatting by the fire a quick push with his foot, grabbed his gun, and covered the other returning from the creek. In less than a minute he had disarmed both men, secured their keys, unlocked the handcuffs, mounted his horse, and ridden away, taking the stolen horses and the officers' mounts.

The two deputies found themselves unarmed and afoot, thirty miles from town, with their prisoner out of sight. George had ridden only a short distance, however, when he noticed that all canteens were still on the saddles; so he returned and gave each officer his own canteen. He knew what it was to be without water on the desert.

During his subsequent career George Cassidy was arrested four times, but served only one term behind bars. His escape in the instance told above was due to quick thinking, cool planning, and the ability to take advantage of opportunities at the right moment, rather than to his ability with a six-gun or an itching trigger finger. It was a good illustration of his methods in later years and in tighter places. His humanity to the officers in returning their canteens, thus perhaps saving their lives, was also a typical circumstance. He held no grudge against them for his arrest and made no move to do them physical injury when they were in his power.

George Cassidy never lacked courage to take a chance, and when his mind was made up he acted without hesitation. But he was never vengeful and never killed a man during his entire career as an outlaw, until his last stand in South America. The friends he made, his temperance in the matter of liquor and women, and his ability to keep cool in an emergency kept him one jump ahead of the law.

Having been caught with stolen horses and having escaped from the officers, George Cassidy decided to leave Circle Valley for a time. Many Mormon boys had found profitable employment in the mines around Telluride, then on the boom, so he decided to try his luck in that mining district. On his journey he was accompanied by Heber Wiley and Eli Elder, two young men about his own age. The latter had just escaped from jail after being arrested for chewing off a man's ear in a fight, and was just as anxious as Cassidy to raise a dust in the direction of Colorado. The three young fellows found work packing high-grade ore down the mountains on mule-back. After a few months of this employment Wiley and Elder tired of the job and drifted back to their own range; but Cassidy stayed on.

In Telluride, as in most pioneer communities, horse racing was the most popular form of entertainment. Money circulated freely and people came for miles to watch the sport. One day Matt Warner, whose story will be related later, arrived in Telluride with a fast horse which happened to be better than the local favorite. At this race Matt first encountered George Cassidy, who had bet his entire outfit on the local horse. But George was such a good loser that he and Matt became friends and finally partners in racing horses all over that part of Colorado.

According to Matt Warner, Cassidy obtained his nickname in the following manner: Matt owned an old needle gun with a terrific kick, which he called "Butch." One day he maneuvered Cassidy into firing this gun while seated with his back to a waterhole. The recoil knocked him sprawling into the water, and from that day he was called Butch instead of George.

At Cortez, a wild Colorado town, Matt and Butch met Tom McCarty, Matt's brother-in-law, who had been operating as an outlaw for some time. And since these three worked together several years, it will be necessary to pause long enough to introduce Matt Warner and the McCarty gang.

The McCarty Gang

Old Doctor William Mc-
Carty, from Tennessee, had been a surgeon in the Confederate army. With his family of three sons and four daughters he
emigrated to Montana shortly after the Civil War. In that new
territory his services as a surgeon were not much in demand,
so he went into the business of buying and selling horses and
cattle. With his sons he made annual journeys south into Utah
where cattle could be bought at reasonable prices from Mormon ranchers who had come west with Brigham Young
twenty years before. Cow-critters brought good prices in
Montana in those days, and he made a nice profit. The northern range was marvelous in summer, but blizzards sweeping
down from the Canadian Rockies played havoc with range
stock during winter; so it was not many years before Doctor
McCarty—like hundreds of other western pioneer cattlemen
—began looking for "cow heaven," a place where cattle could
range the year 'round without attention.

Southern Utah at that time seemed to fulfill every require-
ment. There was plenty of good feed on the range and in the

15

mountains; winters were very mild. Traveling in covered wagons, the McCarty family moved south. When next heard from, Tom and Bill were located in Grass Valley, north of present Antimony, Utah, with three or four others, including the famous Mormon Danite, Porter Rockwell. In the fall of 1874, four young Navajos came to Grass Valley to trade with Piutes and are said to have killed a calf belonging to the McCartys. They then entered the cabin, forced the two whites out, helped themselves to breakfast and left with a horse belonging to James Clinger. The McCartys followed them and killed three. The fourth, shot through the body, somehow lived to return to his family. When he reported the death of his comrades, the Navajos declared war on all whites in Utah and began raiding Mormon herds around Kanab. To settle this affair, Jacob Hamblin, missionary to the Indians, visited the Navajos in their own territory, was threatened with death, but finally talked his way out by declaring that the men who did the killing were not Mormons. To prove his point, he later took a group of Navajos into Utah to listen to evidence. This conference, says Hamblin, was the most difficult of his life and incurred the greatest danger.

The McCartys seem to have left Grass Valley after this affair. They then went to Nevada, perhaps following some mining excitement, where they became acquainted with the Jack Wade family. Wade's daughter, then a young girl, who later became Mrs. John Wetherill of Kayenta, Arizona, hints that Bill had already acquired an outlaw reputation.

After about two years the whole McCarty family were reunited at Mount Pleasant, Utah, where they met Thomas R. Ray and family, former acquaintances from Tennessee, who had just arrived in Utah after a few years spent at Chico, California. Rumors of a perfect unoccupied range in the LaSal Mountains had drifted in to Mount Pleasant, so the McCartys and Rays, joined by the Philander Maxwell family, decided to investigate. After many difficulties in crossing rivers and deep canyons, the three outfits eventually landed at a point south of present Monticello, Utah, which they decided was the answer to every cowman's prayer.

These three families pioneered what is now San Juan County, Utah, in 1877, two years before the celebrated "Hole-in-the-Rock" expedition to Bluff on the San Juan River. They blazed the way for Highway 450, leaving their names on a cliff beside the road. By 1882 they had a post-office at LaSal, named after the range of mountains they occupied. Only two men had previously penetrated that section— one a Negro, the other a Frenchman. It was, and still is, a beautifully isolated spot, bounded on the west by the Colorado River, on the south by the San Juan River, on the north by the Grand River, and on the east by the Mesa Verde country. The mountain uplands furnished a perfect cattle range and they had the whole country to themselves.

Within a few years old Dr. McCarty and son George moved to Haines, near Baker, Oregon, leaving the ranch to his sons, Bill and Tom. Bill had already married Letty Maxwell, a young widow; Tom soon married Teenie, a sister of Willard Christiansen (Matt Warner), while George found an attractive French-Canadian girl in Marysvale named Nellie Blanchett.

The McCarty brothers were rather well fixed for those days, with fine herds of cattle and horses, located on the best range in Utah. If they had remained in the stock business they would eventually have become wealthy. But for some reason they sold their holdings at a price reported to be $35,000. Both brothers then turned outlaw.

Thomas L. McCarty, a resident of Los Angeles and a grandson of Tom McCarty, has recently furnished this writer with the only known copy of his grandfather's autobiography, *History of Tom McCarty*. This interesting document, which for obvious reasons omits all names and dates, furnishes valuable firsthand information on the later activities of the author, elaborating on some of the stories recorded by his brother-in-law, Matt Warner. But it fails to furnish any clue as to why he turned outlaw, except for the following paragraph:

The fore part of my life I will say little about. I was born and raised by as good parents as anyone can boast of, but fortune never seemed to favor me, which I suppose was my own fault. My downfall commenced by gambling. Horse racing was the first, then other gambling games; and as we all know the company one comes in contact with was of the wrong kind for teaching honesty. . . . After losing about all I had I commenced to cast around for something else.

That "something else" was cattle rustling, an occupation he followed for some time, apparently with his base of operations in Brown's Hole, where he is remembered by old-timers. In the meantime Bill McCarty had gone to Missouri and joined the Cole Younger gang, according to a story told by a girl he married in the East. While his name is not mentioned in the known records of this famous outlaw gang, his eastern wife knew enough about Bill, Tom, and Matt to make her story plausible.

Little is known of Bill McCarty's operations with that outfit until his arrest for the murder of O'Connor, his partner, in a quarrel over the loot from some holdup. For this offense he was sentenced to the pen at Stillwater, Minnesota. About that time, friends of the Younger gang succeeded in having a law passed allowing the governor to pardon criminals who promised to leave the state. On that promise Bill was released after a short term.

Just previous to his arrest, and in spite of his former marriage, Bill had married Anne Perry, a 16-year-old girl who had run away from home to join a traveling show troupe—as girls used to do before the days of Hollywood. Taken sick at Muncie, Indiana, she was abandoned by her troupe. Bill Mc-

Carty, posing as a prosperous businessman, wooed and married her.

Upon his release from the pen he left the state of Minnesota, according to promise; but within a few weeks his young wife was again taken seriously ill, believed she was dying, and sent for Bill, who violated his parole by returning and was rearrested. Having some funds remaining from previous operations, he took his case to the supreme court, where he was finally freed on a legal technicality. His young wife seems not to have cared for the life of a "gunman's moll" and left him within a short time. Deciding that the East was a little too civilized for his talents, Bill soon returned—a full-fledged bandit—to his old range and his first wife in the LaSal Mountains.

The two brothers seem to have operated together for a while in Utah, stealing horses and cattle in some of the older settlements, particularly Nephi and Manti. On an expedition to Nephi, Tom was caught with a stolen herd and placed in jail. When his relatives (probably Chris Christiansen, Matt Warner's father) posted $2,000 bail he promptly jumped bond and went back to the Blue Mountains, south of the La-Sals, where no officer cared to follow.

It appears that within a year or two Bill left Tom and went to Oregon. There he bought a ranch near where his brother George had located. So far as is known, he quit the outlaw trail temporarily but was later lured back to it and to his death by Tom and Matt.

Tom McCarty then went to Arizona and New Mexico, where he and various unnamed partners operated as large-scale cattle rustlers. With some of the profits from these operations Tom went to Iowa, where he purchased for $1,000 three of the fastest horses he could find. These were used in all his later operations and enabled him to outdistance any posse.

His autobiography lists in detail many raids and gunfights, only one of which is pertinent to this story. Before telling it, however, it is necessary to introduce another notorious character who joined the McCarty gang at about this time (1884 or 1885) and soon became, under Tom's instruction, one of its most daring operators.

Willard Erastus Christiansen was the son of Christian Christiansen, a Mormon convert from Denmark who had settled at Ephraim, where Willard was born in 1864. His mother was Bishop Christiansen's fifth and youngest wife, a German convert. The family later moved to Nephi and eventually to Levan in Millard County. One of Willard's older sisters, Teenie, had married Tom McCarty.

Like his friend, George LeRoy Parker, young Willard was raised in a wild frontier atmosphere, made even wilder by the peculiar "blood atonement" doctrine of the Mormon church. Half his neighbors were cattle rustlers or horse thieves, and his brother-in-law, Tom, had already made a wide reputation for himself as leader of the "Blue Mountain Gang." The Christiansen boy was stockily built and bubbled over with uncontrolled energy. When in good humor he was a pleasant, likable boy; when in a fit of temper he was a wildcat.

At the age of thirteen Willard got into an argument with one of his chums, Andrew Hendrickson, at Levan, over a girl named Alice Sabey. During the fight which followed, Willard hit the Hendrickson boy over the head with a heavy rock, knocking him senseless. Believing he had killed his chum, he saddled a fast horse and within a few minutes was headed for Brown's Hole, then headquarters for a gang of rustlers. The Hendrickson boy regained consciousness a few hours later but was always afterward "a little queer in the head." He died in an asylum.

Having previously helped drive cattle into the Uintah Basin, Willard knew the trail and headed in that direction, eating at various cattle camps along the road. To those who asked, he gave his name as Matt Warner in order to hide his identity. He didn't stop until he reached the ranch of Jim Warren on Diamond Mountain, just south of Brown's Hole.

Warren gave him a job. It wasn't long until he discovered his boss was a cattle rustler, and Warren, by giving him a few head of stolen cattle, made the boy a rustler also. He worked a little over two years and by that time had accumulated enough stolen stock to start a ranch of his own on Diamond Mountain. After a gunfight in which he shot a Mexican horse thief, he considered himself a full-fledged bad man.

Then one day Moroni Hendrickson, brother of the boy he thought he had killed, rode into camp. When he explained Andrew wasn't dead, Matt wrote to his parents for the first time since leaving home. As a result of that letter Lew Mc-Carty, son of Tom, came to visit Matt and stayed for some time. Together with Elza Lay, whose story will be told later, they planned the first holdup in which any of them had taken part.

In those days it was customary for peddlers to travel through isolated sections with clothing, tinware, jewelry, and supplies needed by ranchers. A peddler had come to Brown's Hole with a wagonload of goods, and started to cross over Diamond Mountain, when he was held up by three masked robbers, Matt Warner, Elza Lay, and Lew McCarty. While one held the horses, the other two took the man's money, emptied the wagon, and scattered goods all over the canyon of Pot Creek. Then they turned him loose to find his way to Vernal on foot, a distance of fifty miles. William Preece, who later became sheriff of Uintah County, offered to trail the robbers, but the peddler declined this offer with the wise observation that it would do no good, since all officers were in partnership with the outlaws. The story of this holdup is still told among old-timers, with many a chuckle over the peddler's story. After the victim had been sent on his way the boys, not knowing what to do with their loot, gathered up the stuff, packed it to Brown's Hole, and distributed it among various ranchers.

Looking for more excitement, Matt Warner then joined up with Cherokee Bangs, who planned a cattle-stealing raid into the Wind River country. They rounded up 2,100 head and sold them, but were caught by the sheriff while dividing the money. Bangs disarmed the sheriff and both men got away with their money but lost their horses and outfits.

To avoid pursuit after this job, Matt went to Arizona with a wagon train. After his arrival, he and his partner, Joe Brooks, decided to hold up a store at St. John's. They took $837 in cash, then rode 250 miles to hide out in Robbers' Roost.

The St. John's holdup netted much less than expected, so, after resting a few days, Matt sent Joe Brooks to Diamond Mountain and then headed for Arizona to find his brother-in-law, Tom McCarty. He found Tom at Fort Wingate, where he and a partner, Josh Swett, from Panguitch, were about ready to go on a cattle-stealing expedition into Old Mexico. Matt joined up and from that time on was an accepted and prominent member of the McCarty outfit.

In Mexico the men had no trouble in rounding up a large herd of cattle. But just after crossing the line back into New Mexico they were jumped by the border patrol. In the fight which followed Josh Swett was shot three times—through the lungs, one arm, and one leg. Tom and Matt thought he was finished, but he kept firing until the federal officers retired, then insisted on mounting his horse and trying to make his escape.

For days the three outlaws rode north, just ahead of the posse, exchanging shots when things got too tight. Each morning Tom and Matt expected to find Josh dead, but somehow he stayed alive and rode with them after being helped onto his horse. At Lee's Ferry the officers almost overtook them, but they managed to get across and gain a lead, hiding in the rough country along the Pariah River. In a few days they passed near Kanab, the first settlement, where they left their wounded partner to be cared for by friends. Josh Swett was made of tough stuff, and lived out his allotted span, after one of the most cruel rides any man ever made.

Tom and Matt, having lost their pursuers, rode on to Frisco, a wild mining town west of Milford. In Tom's autobiography he says that at this time he decided to quit the outlaw trail and make a new start. Having a little money, he and Matt bought a small herd of steers and drove them to Frisco to sell, there being a good market in that booming town. As they were eating supper in a restaurant, they were warned that Billy Sackett, town marshal, was looking for them, having read a recent account of their flight from New Mexico. Before they could escape, Sackett appeared and put them under arrest, lodging them in the Frisco jail. Later they were transferred to Milford. There a trial was held and they were released on testimony of the man from whom they had bought cattle. But Sackett, according to Tom, was determined to hold them on some charge, having suspicions of their identity. He made them walk back to Frisco, where their horses had been left. That fifteen-mile hike made Tom more bitter than the "false" arrest.

Tom and Sam Ketchum, a pair of brothers whose names will appear prominently in later pages, maintained a "ranch" in Snake Valley, about forty miles west of Milford, a spot so isolated and desolate that no one but horned toads and outlaws could exist. It was a blind for their horse-stealing and cattle-rustling activities. It has been impossible to uncover any of their earlier history, but their "ranch" seems to have been known already as a safe hideout for outlaws, and apparently the place was known to Tom McCarty.

As soon as they reached Frisco, after their long, dusty hike, Tom and Matt mounted their horses and made a dust for the Ketchum ranch, where they felt perfectly safe.

A few days later two men arrived at Ketchum's in a buckboard, posing as prospectors; but Tom noticed they were not equipped with the familiar prospecting tools and immediately suspected them of being officers. They stayed at the place that night, but in the morning Tom entered their room, with gun drawn, and found two pairs of handcuffs in their clothes, revealing their identity as officers.

Remembering his long walk of a few days before, Tom handcuffed the men with their own irons and ordered them to start walking to Milford, forty miles away, across a dry desert crusted with alkali. He thought it a fitting penalty for the treatment he had received.

One of the officers was a short, heavy man, the other tall and thin. After they had been gone for an hour or two, Tom began worrying. The thin man might make it back to town but he doubted if the fat one could survive on that desert. So he mounted his horse, filled two canteens with water, and followed. When he overtook them, the two thought he had come out to kill them and begged for their lives. He unlocked the handcuffs, gave them the canteens of water and bade them a courteous goodbye. Later he learned that the fat man did give out, but the lean one reached town and sent a horse back for his partner. Tom writes: "I have no ill feeling toward those two men and had we not been treated in such an unjust way at the little town of M— we would not have felt so bitter against the two officers."

This incident is told by Tom McCarty and Matt Warner with variations. Since Matt was writing from hazy memory at least fifty-five years after the event, Tom's version appears more reliable. McCarty's book was published in Manti, Utah, around 1898, by Matt's father, Christian Christiansen.

After resting a while at Ketchum's, Tom and Matt decided to part company for the time being. Tom rode to Ely, Nevada, but got caught in a bad storm and nearly died of pneumonia, being laid up several months. When he was able to travel again, he bought an outfit of "dude" clothes and returned to Milford to get even with Billy Sackett. The officer had moved to Richfield. Tom followed and succeeded in stealing his valuable riding stallion, leaving a derisive note. On this animal he rode to the Colorado River, probably at Hite, where he did a little placer mining without much success. Within a few months he continued east to the vicinity of Cortez, Colorado, where he says he lived quietly, "having no adventures of any consequence."

After parting at Ketchum's, Matt Warner rode back to Diamond Mountain, just south of Brown's Hole, where he had previously started a small ranch. (His roofless cabin still stands.) He had been there only a short time, however, before word came that officers were looking for him because of some cattle he had stolen in Wyoming, and he thought it best to leave. Driving his horse herd to a good location on the White River, he tried to start another ranch. Within a short time his whereabouts became known, as he thought, and he moved on into the LaSal Mountains near the McCartys' former ranch. Here he trained some fast horses for racing and later went to Telluride, Colorado, to pick up some easy money. In Telluride he met Butch Cassidy, who became his partner in the horse-racing business. Together they traveled around Colorado, sometimes winning, sometimes losing, but always having one hell of a time.

Near Cortez, Matt again met his former partner, Tom McCarty, and they celebrated their reunion by getting gloriously drunk. This, so far as is known, was Tom's first meeting with Butch Cassidy, third member of the triumvirate which was to become famous as the "Invincible Three."

In his book, *Last of the Bandit Riders*, published after his death, Matt Warner tells about many of his exploits—with a fair degree of accuracy, considering the lapse of time. But he admits he "only hit the high spots," and his record does not contain a complete account of his activities. Tom McCarty's story, while more accurate as to details, also omits certain exploits.

One of these, credited by officers to the McCarty gang, was the holdup of a train five miles east of Grand Junction, Colorado, on the night of November 3, 1887. At the place chosen for the holdup the Denver & Rio Grande tracks run along a narrow roadbed between the Gunnison River and a 200-foot cliff. A pile of boulders placed on the track forced the engineer to stop. One of the outlaws boarded the engine and forced the engineer out of his cab. Two of the gang stationed themselves on each side of the express car, while two others took charge of the mail car, pounding on the doors and ordering the clerks to open up. Mail Agent Grubb had dropped to sleep after leaving Grand Junction; when he heard the pounding he supposed the train had reached its next stop. On opening the door he was confronted by two guns and ordered out of the car. Two robbers then entered and rifled twenty-two packages of mail without finding anything of value. They then joined the other two who were trying to force an entrance into the express car.

Messenger Williams suspected something was wrong, so he put out all lights and grabbed his shotgun. When the robbers demanded admittance he told them to go to the opposite door, as the one on their side was obstructed by a pile of trunks. They ordered him to move the trunks. To stall for time, he pretended to comply by rolling a trunk about the car, meanwhile trying to find out how many were in the gang and what his chances might be in a fight. He was unable to distinguish anything in the darkness and, knowing there was nothing of value in the car, decided to open up. The robbers then climbed in and ordered him to open the safe. When he told them he did not know the combination, one bandit held a gun against his head and asked the leader if he should shoot. Receiving a negative shake of the head, he put up his gun. No further attempt was made to open the safe. The proposition of robbing the passengers was discussed but voted down.

A brakeman and a passenger had started forward from the rear to investigate the delay. Their curiosity seemed to unnerve the four robbers in the express car, who immediately jumped out. Before riding away the bandits thoughtfully walked forward to remove the obstruction and bid the engineer goodnight. Nothing of value was obtained.

According to Engineer Malloy, two of the men were cool and possessed, while the others were apparently green at the business. Investigating officers were certain that Tom, Bill, and George McCarty, with some raw recruits, were responsible for this job. It is more likely that the leaders were Tom McCarty, Matt Warner, and Butch Cassidy, since Bill and George McCarty are believed to have been in Oregon at this time.

Later that year (1887), however, according to Mrs. John Wetherill, Tom and Bill were hiding out in the vicinity of Mancos, often stopping at the home of Martin Rush, whom they had befriended in Nevada and the LaSals. One day, when Tom found young Jim Wade hunting with a new rifle, he forced the boy to trade for an old one. Because of past favors this matter was kept a family secret.

On March 30, 1889, a man walked into the First National Bank of Denver, asked to see the president, Dave Moffatt, and carelessly exhibited a vial filled with a colorless liquid which he claimed was nitroglycerin. He demanded $21,000, which Moffatt obtained from the cashier and gave him. The robber then coolly walked out, handing the money to a confederate standing just outside, who instantly disappeared in the crowd. The robber was said by newspaper reports to be Tom McCarty, and his confederate Matt Warner.

Matt makes no mention of this robbery in his book, and Tom, in his own story, denies being the robber of Moffatt's bank. But Mrs. John Wetherill, who knew the McCartys well, repeats the story as fact in *Traders to the Navajos*. Certain other incidents offer circumstantial evidence, although nothing can be definitely proved. In any case the McCartys were by this time so well known, through their recorded and unrecorded exploits, that every unsolved robbery was credited to them.

Telluride
Bank Robbery

AFTER remaining more or less quietly on his ranch near Cortez, Tom McCarty began looking about for some excitement to relieve the monotony. In his autobiography he naïvely leads up to the next exploit in this manner:

In that part of the country were men of all grades, and I soon joined up with some that longed for excitement of any kind, and having been quiet for so long a time, my restlessness began to annoy me. Times being now rather dull and becoming acquainted with men that had no more money than myself, we thought it time to make a raid of some sort. Our plans were accordingly laid very carefully to go to a certain bank and relieve the cashier of his ready cash.

His companions on this venture were Matt Warner and Butch Cassidy. The bank they planned to rob was the San Miguel Valley Bank at Telluride, Colorado, which was known to handle large mine payrolls.

Butch Cassidy, who had worked in Telluride and knew the

town well, was to be a full partner in this job. He was known to many townspeople, some of whom were from Utah. Mrs. John Hancock, a daughter of John D. Lee, from Torrey, Utah, remembered that Butch arrived in Telluride a month before the holdup and spent his time training one of Tom's fast horses. Butch taught it to stand motionless while he approached at a full run and vaulted into the saddle, galloping a full mile before stopping. Miners in the camp thought this just another crazy cowboy stunt and paid no attention.

While Butch was thus occupied, Tom and Matt visited the Carlisle ranch near Monticello, Utah, where Latigo Gordon, foreman, remembered seeing them making buckskin bags in which to carry the loot. Another reason for this visit was probably to scout the line of retreat and arrange for relays of horses at necessary intervals. Dan Parker, a younger brother of Butch, was working there at the time, and they decided to take him along as horse wrangler.

Returning to Tom's cabin, eight miles from Cortez, Colorado, the McCartys posed as placer miners while training their imported horses for the business in hand, as Butch was doing in Telluride. In Mancos they contacted Bill Maddern, a saloon keeper, whose half brother, Bert, was looking for excitement. At the end of a month they all rode into the hills with the announced intention of looking for strayed horses. They rode directly to Telluride, contacted Butch Cassidy and learned when the mine payrolls would arrive at the bank.

At ten o'clock on the morning of June 24, 1889, the bank's cashier stepped out to make some collections, leaving only the bookkeeper in charge. Tom McCarty, Matt Warner, and Butch Cassidy then entered, leaving Bert Maddern in charge of the horses. With guns drawn they covered the bookkeeper and helped themselves to all money in sight, amounting to $10,500. Backing out, they mounted their horses and were off in a cloud of dust before anyone in town was aware of their presence. The whole thing was done so quietly and smoothly that considerable time elapsed before the alarm was spread and a pursuit organized. Sheriff Wasson never had a chance to overtake the fast McCarty horses, and the robbers were soon lost in the brushy hills between Dolores and Mancos rivers, where the posse found it impossible—or inadvisable—to follow.

After it was all over, Sheriff Wasson remembered the peculiar antics of Cassidy and his trained horse. He surmised there might be others in Telluride who knew the robbers, so he kept a close watch on everyone leaving town. Six days later he observed Bill Maddern leave camp with a loaded pack horse. Wasson followed the Mancos saloonkeeper until Maddern turned the packs over to another rider, then arrested both men. On Maddern he found a letter from his half brother, Bert, asking for supplies and giving the location of McCarty's camp. A posse was immediately organized and with it rode L. L. Nunn, president of the Telluride bank. These men followed the trail several days, but by that time it was cold. At one place they found a note warning them not to follow, and finally they gave up when the outlaws padded their horses' feet with gunny sacks and rode across slick rock. At least that was the story given to newspapers after the posse returned.

Tom McCarty gives a somewhat different version of his movements after leaving Telluride, and I am inclined to accept his story. After leaving the bank, he says, they rode about five miles when one of their horses showed signs of failing. Meeting a rancher with a team, they traded for his best horse, changed the saddle, and continued. This delay, so they thought, allowed the posse to approach almost to within pistol shot. In order to lose them, the outlaw riders headed for a high mountain covered with dense timber. Reaching the top after great difficulty caused by fallen trees, they found, in an open spot, an Indian pony. This gave one of the party, probably Matt Warner, a brilliant idea. Roping the pony, he tied

a large brush to its tail, then started it down, riderless, toward
the posse, which was slowly fighting its way upward. Tom
says:

The noise caused by the breaking and snapping of dry timber
and the speed of the horse made it sound as though we had an
army of men and were all making a charge at the posse. This
caused all the men to stampede; also their horses. Down the hill
they all went pell mell, and it has been told that some of the
stampeders did not stop until they fell exhausted.

Continuing down the opposite side of the mountain, where
it was thought impossible to go with horses, the outlaws
threw off all pursuit and felt comparatively safe.

Bill Maddern, who was well known in Mancos, talked himself out of his jam and was soon released. Dan Parker, Butch's
brother, who had previously held up a stage in Wyoming with
a man named Rogers, was turned over to Wyoming authorities and finally sentenced to a reformatory in Michigan on the
charge of robbing United States mail. He was eighteen years
old. He was pardoned after two years, through the efforts of
a friend, and returned to rejoin the gang; but his application
was turned down cold. "You're too damned easy to catch,"
Butch declared.

After losing the posse Tom, Matt, and Butch continued on
to the Carlisle ranch near Monticello, where they showed
Latigo Gordon the proceeds of their exploit. It was considerably less than expected, because the big mine payroll had left
the bank just before their arrival.

Although the Telluride posse had given up the chase, the
"Invincible Three" were jittery. Every rider they saw looked
like an officer and every swirl of dust suggested a posse in
pursuit. In order to avoid these imaginary followers, they
made one of the wildest rides in their history. Having already ridden from Telluride to Mancos to Monticello, they

continued north to Moab, crossed the Colorado River, and went on to Thompson and the Hill Creek country, then on to the White River and finally to Brown's Hole, where they stayed in one of Charley Crouse's cabins. After a rest of only three days, more rumors of officers sent them flying south to Robbers' Roost. When Butch rode fifty miles to Greenriver, Utah, for supplies, he was recognized and Sheriff Fares went out to arrest the gang. According to Matt, they took his horse and guns away from him, stripped him of his pants and sent him back with his shirttail flying.

After a few days in the Roost, the three outlaws felt an urge to hit the high spots and spend some of their loot, so they headed for Lander. They entered a saloon and had taken only a couple of drinks before they were warned by a friend to hit the trail quick. Ducking out the back door, they started riding again, followed for some distance by bloodhounds, according to Matt Warner.

Star Valley was then and still is an isolated section surrounded by mountains and well off main routes of travel. It lies partly in Wyoming and partly in Idaho, just south of Jackson Hole. The place had recently been settled by Mormon polygamists hiding from the law, and guards were posted in the passes to warn polygamists of approaching officers. In the long, deep valley of the Salt River, fugitives from the law, whether polygamists, cattle rustlers, or bank robbers, felt perfectly safe. It is not known whether any of the "Invincible Three" had been in Star Valley previously, but either by accident or design they chose it as their winter hideout, arriving probably in late August. Early winter snows soon closed all passes, and settlers and outlaws were marooned until spring.

In relating their experiences of that winter (1889-1890), neither Matt Warner nor Tom McCarty mentions Butch Cassidy, although the three had been together in the saloon at Lander and made their escape together. Other evidence indicates that Butch separated from the other two at Wind River, later returning to the general vicinity of Lander to spend the winter.

Tom and Matt still had their share of the Telluride loot, amounting to about $3,500 each, a small fortune in those hungry days in Star Valley. They told the settlers they were cattlemen, had just sold their ranch, and were looking for a new location, a story no one questioned. Matt was then twenty-five years old and Tom somewhere near fifty. They gave their names as Tom Smith and Matt Willard.

Purchasing a log cabin on the outskirts of Afton, the valley's only town, the two outlaws prepared for the long winter by buying several fat cattle and a large stock of groceries. In one end of the cabin Matt fixed up a small bar and began serving drinks to all his friends, which included everyone in Star Valley. The wall back of this bar, according to old-timers in Afton, was papered with greenbacks, among them a $10,000 bill.

All stories seem to agree that the denomination of that large bill was $10,000 and that it was pasted on the wall because the robbers were afraid to spend it or present it to any bank for bills of smaller denomination. If this is true, then it would seem to prove that Tom McCarty, and perhaps Matt Warner, had perpetrated the Moffatt bank robbery in Denver, where $21,000 was taken. The Telluride robbery had netted only $10,500, so the large bill did not come from that source. Although those who saw it stick to their story, it is probably a fact that intervening years have added an extra cipher to that famous bill and that it was actually only $1,000. Even so, it would have been very difficult to spend.

With more cash in their pockets than Star Valley had ever seen before, it is not strange that Tom and Matt soon became the most popular men in Afton, and were invited to the homes of all their neighbors. Nearby lived the Rumel family, consisting of Mr. Rumel, his wife (formerly Mrs. Morgan), a daughter, Rosa Rumel (fourteen years old), and her half sister, Sadie Morgan. In a short time Matt was sparking Rosa, and he must have made quick progress, because they were married in Montpelier, Idaho, on September 4, 1889.

Matt Warner, in his later years, was one of the best storytellers I have ever met; but he never told a story the same way twice, and over the years his memory got a little tangled up. One would think he would accurately remember the facts of his marriage, but in his book the story is considerably garbled. He claims he was married in the spring, as soon as the passes were open, but records show this was not the case. He says Tom McCarty also married Sarah Lemberg at the same time. If county records are correct, they were both living with their wives all during the winter of 1889-1890, in the log cabin at Afton.

That winter was one of the most severe ever known in Wyoming. Star Valley settlers, always poor, ran out of supplies before the winter was over. The only store in Afton was owned by Burton, who refused to sell groceries except for cash. This state of affairs seemed to call for action; so Tom and Bill held up the storekeeper, told the settlers to help themselves to anything they needed, and then paid Burton, according to Matt, half the retail price of the goods, amounting to $1,150.

In the spring two officers arrived with a warrant for Tom and Matt, probably on account of the store robbery. Tom ran them out of the valley with a rifle; but it became evident Star Valley was no longer a safe place, so the two men put their wives in a buckboard and headed for Jackson Hole, over Stump Creek pass, still deep in snow. Camping out, however, was too uncomfortable at that time of year, so the four headed for Butte, Montana, where the balance of their Telluride loot was soon spent in high jinks.

When they found themselves almost broke again, Tom and Matt gave their wives $100 each and sent them back to Star

Valley, with the excuse that they had to go to "British Columbia" to look after some gold mines and would send for
the girls later. To supply their immediate wants, the two men
held up a gambling joint in Butte, taking $1,800, then rode to
a hideout near Big Hole, Montana. Since this small change
would not last long, they decided to pull a really big job before sending for their wives. After studying several possibilities they agreed to ride to Haines, Oregon, where George and
Bill McCarty had located after leaving the LaSal Mountains.

Oregon Bank Robberies

Bill McCarty, his wife, and 17-year-old son, Fred, had left Utah with considerable money; but times had been tough for him in Oregon, and when Tom and Matt arrived he was about broke. It took very little persuasion to induce him to join his brother and Matt as a member of the outlaw trio, replacing Butch Cassidy, who remained in Wyoming.

Their first job was the robbery of a mining-camp store at nearby Sparta, where they got only $600. With this small stake they sent for their wives. Tom's wife refused to come, but Rosa soon arrived and joined to some extent in their activities, since it was useless for Matt to continue the pretense of being a wealthy cattleman. To hide his identity in Oregon, Matt changed his name to Ras Lewis.

Officers began to suspect the McCartys, so the family left the ranch at Haines and bought a small, isolated place called the 7 U, twenty-seven miles from Cooley, Washington, at what was known as Seventeenth Crossing. Here, according to Rosa, she cooked for construction crews on the Northern

Pacific Railroad while her husband was absent on raids. She claimed Matt often mistreated her and, on one occasion after she became pregnant, made her dance for the amusement of her boarders until she fell exhausted.

While located here, the McCarty gang pulled off an amazing number of robberies within a comparatively short distance of their headquarters. Only a few will be detailed here. On October 8, 1891, they robbed the bank at Wallowa, Oregon, taking $3,450. Less than a month later, on November 3, they took $5,000 from the Farmers Mortgage and Savings Bank at Summerville. They also planned to rob a bank at Walla Walla, but had to call it off when post-office detectives intercepted Matt's message to Tom. They tried to rob a circus at Moscow, Idaho, and only escaped capture because officers were afraid to fire into the crowd.

Their next job, and one which caused them serious trouble, was the robbery of a bank at Enterprise, just over the mountain from Sparta and within twenty-five miles of Bill's home ranch at Haines. Tom was posted outside while Bill and Matt went in to scoop up the cash. No one was in the bank except the cashier, and they had no trouble in gathering up $9,000 and putting it in three bags. Just as they were leaving, Tom fired a shot outside at a man who attempted to go into the building. This caused some excitement on the street and a crowd began to collect. To make matters worse, Matt's horse started bucking when he tried to mount and nearly threw him off. He says, "I never tried harder in my life to stick to a bronco, for if he throwed me he would throw me clear into jail." Before they finally headed out of town, citizens had grabbed their rifles and were shooting, but they got away without being hit, lost their pursuers, and arrived at Bill's ranch with their loot. After a few weeks they thought it safe to ride to their other hideout, the 7 U ranch.

When Matt got back, his wife complained about being left alone for such long periods without knowing whether he was dead or alive. He promised her he would save his winnings and buy a ranch, stock it with cattle, and quit the outlaw trail. He buried part of his loot in a tin can and added to it from time to time toward that end. He also sent for Rosa's sister, Sadie Morgan, then living in Salt Lake, so that she would not be lonesome while he was away. When Sadie arrived, she soon found out about the McCartys' outlaw activities and seemed to go along with them; but she did not approve of what she saw, and later she offered to testify against them.

Shortly after the job at Enterprise, the boys held up a train on the Northern Pacific between Union and North Powder, Oregon. On that occasion Rosa made the masks, and she and her sister rode with the men, starting from the 7 U ranch. Five young men were later sent to the pen for that job; the girls felt sorry about that but kept their mouths shut.

In all the cases mentioned, including many minor robberies not listed, the gang had managed to escape to their hideouts without too much difficulty, either at their outlaw ranch or at Bill McCarty's place. It seems rather odd that so many jobs could have been pulled within such a short time, all in approximately the same vicinity, without some suspicion being attached to the McCartys, who were mysteriously away from home most of the time but always had plenty of spending money.

Finally, however, they got a little reckless and robbed the bank at Baker, only a few miles from Bill's ranch. Closely pursued, they hid in Bill's haystack while Letty, Bill's wife, led the officers to believe they were in the house and would put up a desperate fight. The posse surrounded the house, guarded it three days, then threatened to blow it up with dynamite. Bill's wife then admitted them, and while they were searching the empty premises the outlaws made their escape from the haystack and disappeared.

Things were getting a little hot around Haines, so the gang decided to disappear for a while. They rode to Lander, where they found Butch Cassidy running a "horse ranch." About that time, news came of the Johnson County war, which will be described later, and all four decided to get in on the excitement. Apparently arriving too late for the shooting, they went into the country around Belle Fourche, South Dakota, to round up a herd of cattle. Since they wanted to travel fast and light they left their rifles behind, taking only six-shooters. Before they had succeeded in gathering more than a few head they found themselves almost surrounded by a posse of cattlemen carrying rifles. There was nothing to do but run, which they did, in different directions. Matt finally eluded his pursuers by swimming his horse across a raging river.

Matt did not see his partners again until he arrived at the 7 U ranch several weeks later. Because Tom and Bill and Butch had about given him up for dead, there was a hilarious reunion. Butch Cassidy had returned to his "ranch" near Lander.

When Matt got back, Rosa told him she was going to have a baby and didn't want to raise it to be an outlaw. He promised her that after one more raid he would have enough to quit and settle down. He wanted this last one to be a real haul, so he and the McCartys picked the bank at Roselyn, in central Washington, as their final victim, where they expected to get at least $100,000.

Matt Warner indicates that only he and Tom and Bill were implicated in this job; but newspaper stories printed at the time say that George McCarty, the third brother, was present and that his French-Canadian wife, Nellie, held the horses. The date was September 24, 1892. According to Matt, Tom stood outside while he and Bill went after the cash. This time the cashier was slow in getting his hands up, so they hit him over the head to keep him quiet. Just as they were gathering up the money—$20,000—they heard a shot outside. Tom had shot a Negro who got too close.

The shot brought a crowd, some of them armed; but the

robbers succeeded in getting out of town without being hit. They headed for high timber, but were outguessed by a smart sheriff, who opened fire. Changing their planned route, they headed for a crossing of the Columbia River near Wenatchee, closely followed by the posse. While the others scattered in dense brush, Matt led his pursuers straight to the river bank, which was about twenty feet high. Throwing away everything but his money belt, he pushed his horse off into the Columbia, which looked to be a mile wide at that point.

When he came to the surface he was half drowned and almost ready to give up. Then the officers started shooting at him in the water. He thought they were taking unfair advantage of a helpless man, and it made him mad. Soon his head cleared and he slipped off the saddle into the water to give his horse a better chance. It is difficult for anyone to hit an object floating on water, so he knew he was in no great danger except from an accidental hit. Before long he was out of range, but his horse was tiring. He tried to throw away his money belt, containing $10,000, partly in gold, but couldn't loosen the wet straps. He was sucked into a whirlpool once or twice and almost drowned, but his powerful horse kept on swimming. At last they reached quieter water and finally pulled ashore. This, Matt told me, was his most terrifying experience, and he promised the Lord he would never rob again if he got out alive. After a two-hour rest on the sandy banks of the Columbia River he thumbed his nose at the officers watching him from the opposite shore and rode off. He returned to the 7 U after a safe length of time had passed.

When Matt got back he found himself the father of a daughter only a few days old, born December 30, 1892. As soon as his wife was able to travel he planned on digging up his buried gold and leaving the outlaw trail to make a new start where he was not known. A few days later some men posing as cattlemen looking for strayed stock stopped at his cabin and asked for breakfast. They appeared to be unarmed, so he invited them in. While he was carrying some water they seized him and after a furious fight finally subdued him. One of the men was Sheriff McNeil, from Ellensburg, who arrested Matt, known to them as Ras Lewis, for the Roselyn bank robbery. Matt believed Sadie Morgan had disclosed his whereabouts; later McNeil showed him a letter she had written to a detective in Salt Lake, implicating Matt, Tom, and Bill. She had betrayed them, she said, to protect Rosa and her child.

A few days later George McCarty was apprehended and thrown into the cell with Matt. Tom and Bill had not been found. The two prisoners spent all their waking hours planning a jail break. It was the first time either had been inside looking out. Another prisoner in the next cell, who had often been in trouble, advised them to get a lawyer, and they finally consented. The lawyer, Brice, said he could get them out if they had enough money. Matt said he had plenty, but it was buried on his ranch. After the lawyer had made many promises, Matt gave him a map of the location and the lawyer dug up his gold, which Matt says amounted to $41,000.

But the wheels of justice grind slowly, and when no immediate action occurred, Matt and George got restless, believing they had again been betrayed. They arranged with another prisoner who was about to be released to slip them some saws, and with these they cut the bars of their cells and dug through a wall. Their pal had also brought them two six-shooters. They had hoped to escape during the night, but when they crawled through the hole they found it was broad daylight and in a few minutes were discovered. A gunfight followed in which George was hit by buckshot; in a few minutes both men were back in jail.

On the next day lawyer Brice came to see them, saying that their trial was to come up within two days but that, on account of their attempted break, he might have difficulty in getting them off. It would cost more money. But certain palms had been well greased, and when the two men appeared in court, the prosecuting attorney moved the case be dismissed, "since he did not have sufficient evidence to convict." Matt and George were free! The date was July 24, 1893.

"How much do I owe you?" Matt asked lawyer Brice when it was all over.

"Forty-one thousand dollars," Brice replied coldly.

"But, my God, that's all I've got!" Matt said. "How come it cost so much?"

"Certain parties had to be taken care of," Brice said, "and there were contingent expenses. Would you rather have the money and go to the pen?"

"No," Matt admitted, "but I had planned to use that money to buy a ranch and go straight. Now I'm broke again."

"Here's $500," said Brice. "Don't ever say I took your last cent."

There was nothing he could do about it. "I was so damn mad," Matt told me many years later, "that I had a good notion to go back and hold him up to get my money back. The only reason I didn't was because I thought I might need him again some day."

Unknown to Matt, Sadie Morgan had been in Ellensburg waiting to testify against him. Possibly she received some of the money spent for "contingent expenses." When the two men were freed she went to the 7 U and took Rosa and her child to Salt Lake City.

A clever young reporter found Rosa, Sadie, and their mother in a cheap hotel next day. He met them in a dark hallway and found himself looking down the muzzles of two guns. They thought he was Tom McCarty and that he had come to kill them. When they learned his identity the women talked freely. Mrs. Rumel and Sadie painted a black picture of the cruelties Rosa had suffered, and their terror of the gang was not simulated; they expected to be followed and killed. Rosa, however, still insisted Matt Warner was a brave, generous man when sober, "good for twenty men in a fight."

Said she, "Matt is no petty thief. When he steals he takes thousands. He robs train and banks, not individuals. He is generous with his friends and likes to make a show of his money when he has it. He is leader of the gang now; the others follow him."

The same enterprising reporter also located Bill McCarty's young eastern wife, in Ogden, Utah. The former Anne Perry told of her life with Bill but stated that they were separated by mutual consent. Anne was a pretty woman about twenty-eight years old. She said the boys all had secret names: Bill was "Firefoot," Tom was "Waluka," and Matt Warner was "Crapo." She furnished the details of Bill's connection with the Younger gang in Minnesota. After telling her story she began packing. "I'll have to leave town," she explained, "after you print that story. The gang will kill me."

In the meantime, officers had not given up their hunt for Tom and Bill McCarty. Sheriff Conde of Baker County had suspected them for some time, since they had been spending gold quite freely. He set out to capture them, accompanied by ex-Police Chief Farley of Denver, who had already spent $2,000 trying to track down the Moffat bank robbers.

Sheriff Conde wanted to have the credit for capturing the desperadoes single-handed, so he slipped away from Farley and approached the McCarty house alone. Bill McCarty answered his knock.

"Consider yourself under arrest!" said the sheriff.

"What's the charge?" asked Bill.

"Carrying concealed weapons."

"All right, Sheriff. Step inside while I tell my wife and change my clothes."

The sheriff stepped through the door to find himself facing a Winchester rifle in the hands of Tom, who was being theatrical, acting like a crazy man. The sheriff was scared out of his wits.

Leaving Fred, Bill's 18-year-old son, to guard Conde, Tom

and Bill saddled three horses. When everything was ready the three calmly rode away, warning the sheriff they would never be taken alive. By attempting to arrest the entire gang single-handed, Conde had pulled a boner and lost them all.

With the $500 lawyer Brice had so generously given him, Matt rode back to his 7 U ranch, after being released in Ellensburg. He found the place turned upside down by men searching for more buried treasure. Rosa was gone. So he traded the ranch for a saddle horse and outfit and headed for his place on Diamond Mountain, where he found his old partner, Butch Cassidy, and Elza Lay, who was later to become Butch's partner. Within a few months he heard from Rosa, who had gone to Boise, and persuaded her to join him.

Delta
Bank Robbery

After his discharge in El-
lensburg, Matt Warner lived in comparative quiet at his ranch
for about two years. Tom and Bill McCarty, with Bill's son,
Fred, realizing the close shave they had had at Bill's ranch,
made one of their long rides—from Oregon to Nevada, then
to Manti, Utah, where they rested for a time, and finally east
again to Robbers' Roost. Here they planned another bank
robbery. The victim this time was to be the Farmers and
Merchants Bank in Delta, Colorado.

Tom and Bill rode into Delta on September 6, 1893,
registering under assumed names at a hotel. On the morning
of the seventh Fred came in with their horses, which he tied
in an alley behind the bank. At 10:15 Tom and Bill stepped
into the bank. A. T. Blatchley, cashier, and H. H. Wolbert,
assistant cashier, were at their windows. W. R. Robertson
was in his law office in a room at the rear. While Tom and Bill
stuck up the tellers, Fred came in from the back and held a
gun on Robertson.

Blatchley and Wolbert surprised the robbers by refusing to

hand over the cash. Tom and Bill then jumped over the low partition separating the cages from the lobby. Wolbert reached for his gun but raised his hands when Bill stuck a six-shooter in his ribs. Inside the cage Tom began grabbing all money in sight. Blatchley shouted for help. Tom cursed him, warning him to be quiet, but the cashier shouted again. Tom shot him in the head, killing him instantly.

A gale that was blowing that day had made the cashier's shouts inaudible on the street. Tom's shot, however, attracted the attention of several men outside, who shouted the alarm. The robbers had secured only $700 but were afraid to delay longer. Fred rushed to the horses, quickly followed by the other two. Without further delay they all mounted and started to leave town.

Across the street was a hardware store operated by W. G. Simpson & Son. W. Ray Simpson, junior member of the firm, hearing a shot in the bank, suspected a holdup. Grabbing a repeating Sharps rifle and a handful of shells, he rushed into the street just as the McCartys were mounting. Instead of joining the crowd in front of the bank, Simpson ran a hundred yards down the street, loading as he ran, to intercept the robbers as they emerged from an alley. Since this was Tom McCarty's last exploit, it might be well to let him tell what happened next.

As we passed the first street I heard the sharp crack of a rifle, and looking for my partners, I saw one of them (Bill) fall from his horse; my other companion (Fred) being a little ahead, then partly turned his horse as though he wanted to see where the shot came from. I told him quickly to go on, but as I spoke another shot came which struck his horse, and before he could get his animal in motion another shot came which struck him and he fell dead. His horse started to run back toward the place where the shots had come from. This was the last I saw of the horse. I was now going at full speed, but looking back I saw a man standing by the corner of a building having what I supposed was a

Winchester and shooting as fast as possible at me, after having killed my relatives. The first man he killed could not have been more than twenty-five yards from him when he fell; the other about one hundred and fifty feet. He must have been a very good shot, for several bullets passed so near me that I felt the force of the balls as they passed; one of his bullets struck my horse in the hind leg near the heel, which crippled him, but having other horses stationed on the outskirts of town, I was not long in being again well mounted, and had no trouble in keeping ahead of anyone that wanted to follow.

This story, from comparison with the local newspaper accounts, is an accurate description of what happened at Delta. The local reports also add a few details. Simpson's first shot hit Bill McCarty in the hatband and tore off the top of his head. Ignoring Tom's orders, Fred McCarty dismounted and was leaning over the body of his father when Simpson's next shot entered the base of his skull and came out his forehead. All but $100 of the loot was recovered. A posse was organized within ten minutes, but was never able to overtake Tom's swift mount.

An inquest was held over the bodies of the two dead robbers. Bill McCarty was described as being 5 feet 10 inches in height, with dark, curly red hair, brown moustache and gray eyes. He was thickset, weighing about 160 pounds, and appeared to be between 40 and 45 years old. Newspapers reported the older robber to be Tom McCarty, but on September 10 Ed Taylor of Moab, Utah, a relative by marriage, arrived in Delta and identified the two dead men as Bill McCarty and his son Fred. Shortly afterward Sheriff Conde and ex-Police Chief Farley arrived and identified them as two of the gang which had been terrorizing eastern Oregon for several years. The bodies were exhumed and photographed.

The killing of Bill and Fred was the first serious setback the gang ever had. They believed themselves bulletproof; but one resolute man had put an end to their organization. George remained in Oregon, but Tom returned to his old hideout in the Blue Mountains to quiet his shattered nerves. The more he brooded over what he considered a dastardly trick, the angrier he became. Three years later, in the fall of 1896, he announced his intention of going to Delta to kill Simpson. Several cowboys reported seeing him in the vicinity.

In the meantime Simpson had been appointed postmaster at Delta. A government detective was sent to trap the outlaw if possible. To this operative Simpson presented his "card," with instructions to deliver it to McCarty at the earliest opportunity. It consisted of a small piece of black cardboard perforated with ten holes, all within the circumference of a half dollar. Simpson's "signature" had been written with his new Winchester at a distance of 225 feet. This card was later given to a reporter on the Salt Lake *Herald,* who wrote a description of it in the issue of January 29, 1897, concluding with the following words:

Utah officers are inclined to the opinion that McCarty does not possess his old-time spirit and will therefore never seek to molest the redoubtable Colorado postmaster. It is quite well known that McCarty has been living for some time past in San Juan County, this state, under the name of Nels Oleson, and that Cassidy, another familiar figure in many western holdups, is with him.

After the fiasco, which ended all activities of the McCarty gang, Tom says he went to northern Wyoming and engaged in trapping for several months. Then he rode to the Black Hills, where he was arrested on a charge of horse stealing. Escaping by a clever trick, he went north, "almost to the Canadian line," where he was engaged in the cattle business until the winter of 1895-1896. Then, closing his narrative, he says: "Wanting something of a more exciting nature I have drifted back a little further south, and having taken up my headquarters in an out of the way place, I have dictated some of my principal adventures, and will have them sent to friends."

This is all the information we have on Tom McCarty. No one, not even his family, knows where, when, or how he died. He was about fifty-five years old when his autobiography was written. For at least fifteen years he had terrorized the West, escaping every trap set for him. He was the mentor of Matt Warner and of Butch Cassidy, who was soon to become more daring and famous than his nervy teacher had ever been.

Cassidy Meets
the Law

Matt Warner once said to me, "I taught Butch Cassidy everything he knew about bank robbing." But that was one of Matt's exaggerations. As a matter of fact, both Matt and Butch were amateurs when they assisted Tom McCarty in the Telluride affair. Tom was a cool, clever, bold outlaw who was never caught by the law. Matt was brave but reckless, with an uncontrollable temper which often got him into trouble. Undoubtedly Cassidy learned from both; but he was more cool and calculating than either and apparently believed that sooner or later Matt's dashing recklessness would bring disaster. For that reason, I believe, he ceased operations with the McCarty gang and started out on his own. He was more careful with money, and when he left Tom and Matt on the Wind River, he is believed to have had most of his share from the Telluride bank robbery.

In 1890, a year after the Telluride affair, Butch went to work as a cowhand for Pat Ryan, a cattleman of southern Utah. Ryan says he was a good worker, although hard on horses. For the next three years he seems to have worked on various ranches, mostly in Wyoming.

He spent part of one winter in Rock Springs. One night a drunk was "rolled" and relieved of his cash in one of the saloons frequented by Butch. Cassidy had been seen drinking with the man during the evening, and for some reason was accused of the robbery, arrested, and thrown in jail to await trial. There is little doubt of his innocence, for during his whole career he never stooped to petty thievery. When the case came to trial no evidence could be produced against him and he was acquitted. But the circumstances surrounding the case, his confinement in jail, and the injustice of his arrest for the lowest of crimes made him so bitter that when he left the courtroom he cursed the officers, the judge, the town of Rock Springs, the county of Sweetwater, and the entire state of Wyoming. He swore they would sooner or later feel the sharp edge of his vengeance. Men in the courtroom paid little heed to the angry cowboy at that time but were often reminded of his threat in after years. Cassidy never forgot that day.

He went back to the cattle ranches, where his skill with a rope and branding iron was appreciated. In a very short time he was known as leader of the rustlers and for that very reason big ranchers were anxious to have him on their payrolls. They knew that as long as he took their money their herds would not be molested. It was cheap insurance against cattle stealing. The late Tom Beason, of Ogden, formerly owner of a big ranch east of Opal, Wyoming, once hired Cassidy as foreman and said the outlaw was the best man he ever had on the ranch. George C. Streeter, of Ogden, once worked for the 2-Bar Cattle Company, which owned 160,000 head of cattle and used most of the state of Wyoming for its range, wintering in Bates Hole near Casper or on Horse Creek. Says Streeter:

One day I was trying to throw my roll of bedding up onto the four-horse wagon that accompanied the roundup. A short, thickset stranger came up and said, "Buddy, let me throw that in for you." He hoisted the heavy roll into the wagon with one hand and then turned to me and said, "Let's bunk together from now on. I am going to work for this outfit."

I replied, "All right, where is your bedding?"

"I haven't any. We will have to use yours," said the stranger. So we bunked together for two years. That man was Butch Cassidy, who later became the famous outlaw.

Butch was the best-natured man I ever saw and he would never stand for anyone molesting me. He was a crack shot, and the best there was with a rope. He was top cow hand, and it wasn't until some years later that he started his bandit career. He could ride around a tree at full speed and empty a six-gun into the tree, putting every shot within a three-inch circle.

The last time I saw him was over thirty years ago here in Ogden. At that time there was a price of $50,000 on his head. I spoke to him on the street but he did not turn around. He said quietly to meet him in the Broom Hotel, and I went to his room and had a long talk with him. He never was much of a hand to drink and used less liquor than the average.

The occupation of cowboy, however, did not promise much in the way of financial returns, so Cassidy decided to become a "horse dealer." He had saved his wages and may have had something cached away from his share of the Telluride robbery. Somewhere in Wyoming he picked up a partner, Al Hainer, and in the fall of 1892 the two men went to the Wind River country near Lander to start their "ranch."

The Wind River country in those days was as wild a section as could be found outdoors. Its immense ranges were dotted with cattle and horses which could be taken with little trouble and in almost perfect safety. To their scattered neighbors the men represented themselves as horse traders. Neighbors failed to note that they always sold—never bought.

Christian Heiden, of Salt Lake City, emigrated to Wyoming from Germany, in 1892, at the age of fourteen. His father located a homestead not far from the "ranch" of Cassidy and Hainer. He knew both men well. In an interview with Jack Plane in the *Labor Broadcast* of December 25, 1937, Mr. Heiden said:

I was fifteen years old when I first met Butch Cassidy. I was living with my folks, the first homesteaders in the Big Horn Basin, 75 miles north of Lander, near the M-Bar ranch. My uncle ran a saloon near the M-Bar and I can well remember my first glimpse of Butch when, with his pals, Jakie Snyder and Al Hainer, he came galloping up to the place. He was dragging a mountain lion he had roped that day and tied him to the hitching rail, where the lion snapped and spat at the assembled cowpunchers who had piled out of the saloon to tease him.

I drove stage the following year from the M-Bar to Meteetse, 60 miles north, on the Gray Bull River. It was an open rig, and the route lay through one of the wildest spots of the last frontier. It was then that I became really acquainted with Butch. He used to ride with me sometimes on the stage coach after tying his horse to one of the wheelers. He was full of entertainment and usually had a bottle on his hip.

Butch was not the only outlaw in that district, and sometimes Tom O'Day's gang from the Hole-in-the-Wall, about fifty miles distant, would waylay me and have me bring them tobacco, whiskey, newspapers, and so on. I made my deliveries in some mighty wild sections. Sometimes they would throw a quarter of beef on the stage, telling me to take it home to Uncle George at the M-Bar saloon. There were several cowpunchers from Texas, most of them apparently traveling for their health. They were a wild bunch and some of their dare-devil performances would put the present-day drug-store cowboys of the movies considerably in the shade. I remember three of them roping a grizzly bear not far from the Padlock ranch, six miles east of the M-Bar.

Butch and his pal Snyder rode with me one time up to Meteetse. We stopped at Rose Williams' log cabin for a meal. Rose was a widow and served meals and sometimes whiskey.

That day she served us a somewhat meager meal of jackrabbit, and Butch asked me if that was the usual bill of fare. I told him it often was. Butch suggested that we go hunting and we started out on horseback. We ran on to a few buffalo, the last I ever saw, and then some deer. Butch wouldn't bother with them and later shot a two-year-old calf. "What's the brand?" I asked, as he examined the kill.

"Never mind the brand," he said, "it's meat we're after." We took it back to the widow Williams.

I never saw Butch shoot anyone, but he always packed a wicked-looking Colt .45 with a big wooden handle on it. He was very quick in his actions and quick-witted.

The winter of 1892-1893 was extremely severe—almost as bad as the terrible winter of 1886-1887. Thousands of head of stock froze to death or starved because of the deep fall of snow. To make matters worse, almost everyone in that section was stricken with the epidemic now known as flu, leaving no one to look after the stock or care for the sick.

According to a story circulating in Lander, during this epidemic Butch Cassidy obtained home remedies from Mrs. Simpson, who lived on a ranch four miles distant, and ministered to his sick neighbors. However, William L. Simpson, a son, who owned the ranch, denies this and says Cassidy had no other neighbors.

In the spring of 1893 the two partners sold their ranch and made their headquarters in Lander. Will Simpson knew them both well during that time. They were often seen in the saloons and gambling houses of that wild frontier town, and their pockets were always full of money. Apparently their "trading" operations were quite successful. There were plenty of other "horse traders" in Lander who were not in a position to ask embarrassing questions.

The hard winter of 1892-1893 had greatly reduced the number of animals on the range. Cowboys no longer needed were discharged, most of them becoming rustlers. Because of their losses stockmen were careful to count all surviving animals, and thefts were more easily detected. To put a stop to the increased activities of rustlers, stockmen had formed an association with the purpose of making an organized stand against stealing.

Some frontier sheriffs had formerly been rustlers and did not exert themselves to curb the activities of their friends. Sheriff John Ward, of Uintah County, Wyoming, with headquarters at Evanston, was not of that breed, however, and entered into the campaign of extermination with enthusiasm, backed by genuine ability, in cooperation with Governor W. A. Richards. He was fortunate in having for his chief deputy a Texan named Bob Calverly. These two men did more to break up organized rustling than any other two officers in the state. They were both big, fearless men who commanded respect from the outlaws for their honesty and courage.

In June, 1893, Butch Cassidy and Al Hainer were arrested for the theft of some horses, probably stolen from the Padlock ranch. Unfortunately we have no details of this arrest. On June 22, both men were acquitted, according to court records.

One day in 1894, Sheriff Ward received a request to trail down a bunch of sixty horses stolen the previous fall from John Chapman. Bob Calverly started out to locate the stolen animals in company with a sheriff from Montana on a similar errand. From clues picked up here and there the horses were finally located in Star Valley, where the McCartys had hidden out in 1889. Calverly discovered that the thieves were receiving mail from the post office at Afton, Wyoming. Their mail was called for once a week by Kate Davis, daughter of a rancher near Afton. With that information Calverly was ready to act.

When the girl next came to town she was pointed out by the postmaster. The two officers quietly followed her trail as she rode back to the ranch. Before she reached the cabin they intercepted her, disclosed their identity and asked her where the two thieves could be found. The girl replied one was working at a small sawmill some distance away; the other was resting on a cot just inside the cabin door.

Taking the girl with them, the two officers rode to the sawmill where they had no difficulty in arresting Al Hainer. They tied him securely to a tree and went to the ranch for his partner, Butch Cassidy. Both officers knew Butch was an expert with a gun, and the girl had told them he was armed. Neither hesitated, however, and both stepped through the cabin door at the same time, guns drawn ready for action. Cassidy was lying on a bunk near the door, but had hung his gun belt over a chair within easy reach. He was expecting the girl to return with the mail. When he heard unfamiliar footsteps he was instantly alert and reached for his gun just as the two sheriffs stepped into the room.

The Montana officer, in his anxiety to capture the outlaw, stepped ahead of Calverly just as Cassidy fired. The bullet went wild. Calverly attempted a shot but Cassidy shielded himself behind the Montana officer. Cassidy tried two more quick shots but, being jostled by the Montana man, missed both times. Then Calverly lunged, pulling the trigger as he did so. The end of his gun barrel struck Cassidy's forehead, and the bullet plowed a deep furrow in his scalp. Cassidy was stunned for a moment, and Calverly slipped on the handcuffs.

The whole action had taken but a few seconds. Butch Cassidy, cleverest outlaw on the range, was a prisoner. It was the fourth time he had been arrested. It was also the last. Witnesses to this arrest, says Mr. Simpson, were John Chapman, from north of Cody, who had lost some horses, and Charlie Davis, brother of Kate, who afterward became sheriff of Park County, Wyoming.

Cassidy and Hainer were taken back to Lander, where

charges were filed against them. The case came up before
Judge Jesse Knight, later of the Wyoming supreme court,
and was prosecuted by William L. Simpson, who had just
been admitted to the bar. For his defense, Cassidy hired Douglas A. Preston, a famous criminal lawyer, afterward attorney
general of Wyoming, who handled all Cassidy's legal affairs
from that time on.

Butch had been a good fellow in Lander, had spent his
money freely and made many friends, none of whom wanted
to see him sent to the pen. He and Hainer had been found in
possession of stolen horses; it looked like an open-and-shut
case. But Cassidy's friends promptly came to his rescue by
writing a bill of sale for the horses, signing the name of a
prominent rancher in a distant part of the state. Everything
looked set for acquittal.

Unfortunately for the prisoner, existence of this forgery
leaked out. On the day of the trial the defense was con-
founded by learning that the man whose name they had
forged was present in the courtroom, so this document was
never presented in evidence. The verdict of the jury was
reached on July 4. Cassidy was found guilty and was sentenced to the pen for a term of two years. Al Hainer was
acquitted. Butch Cassidy entered the Wyoming state prison
as No. 187, on July 15, 1894. He was twenty-seven.

Of the circumstances following this conviction the prosecutor, William L. Simpson, wrote in 1939:

The jury found Cassidy guilty on a Saturday and returned a
sealed verdict to the clerk of the court. On Sunday morning
Cassidy, who was in custody of Virgil Rice, a deputy sheriff,
at the courthouse horse-whipped one of the witnesses, Arapahoe
Dave, for his giving testimony to the effect that he had seen one
horse in his possession on the Owl Creek mountains.

This same Sunday morning an attempt was made upon my life
by Hainer, a Mexican by the name of Armento, and a half breed
by the name of Lamareaux, who jerked me off my horse in front

of the livery stable about sunup and attempted to get me inside the stable. They were all drunk and all defendants being tried at that term of court except Lamareaux. I was riding a rather wild horse and as I was jerked off the horse by Lamareaux I held to the bridle and turned the horse around, and he kicked Lamareaux up against the stable. This gave me an opportunity to get my six-shooter, which was between my overalls and my other clothes, and they all disappeared into the barn.

Charles Stough was sheriff and rode up to the barn horseback and asked me what had happened and I told him. We rode down to the Fremont hotel, went up and had a talk with Judge Knight and he ordered Cassidy and the other three to be placed in jail, which was done. My wife was diagonally across the street and observed what was going on and was screaming. It was pretty well known among Cassidy's friends, especially Matt Warner and his outfit, that Cassidy would probably be convicted, and there were at least eight or ten strangers in Lander, camped about a mile from town on a little stream.

Sunday night after the assault and the horse-whipping of Arapahoe Dave, the citizens of Lander got together in the jewelry store of F. G. Burnett intending to have it out with the outlaws. I heard of this and went into the meeting and told them to break it up. However, on Monday when the court opened, the courtroom which was upstairs was strictly guarded by the sheriff and deputies, and no stranger was permitted in the court-room until after verdict of the jury had been returned. The mayor, councilmen and numerous businessmen went to the courthouse armed. Judge Jesse Knight, the presiding judge, was also armed and all of us interested in the courts were armed. No effort was made by Cassidy's friends to get into the courthouse after being warned.

After Cassidy was sentenced to two years in the penitentiary he sent for me in the jail and told me that he did not blame me at all; that I had done my duty and that he wanted to be friendly and this was understood as we had always been friends on the range during the time we were on Wind River.

At the time he was taken to the territorial penitentiary at Laramie City he made a request upon Charlie Stough. He told the sheriff that he did not wish to be manacled with handcuffs; that he would go to the penitentiary alone; that he intended to serve his sentence and take his medicine. I know of my own knowledge that when Charlie went with him to the penitentiary he didn't even have a gun on him.

For an active man such as Cassidy had been, two years' confinement was a long time. At the end of a year and a half he applied for a pardon and was given a hearing before William A. Richards, who had been elected governor and was already being criticized because of the number of pardons he had issued.

"My time is three-fourths done," argued Cassidy, "and a few more months won't make much difference. I've got some property in Colorado that needs looking after, and I'd like to get a pardon."

"If it is your intention to go straight after you get out, perhaps it could be arranged," said the governor. "You're still young, and smart enough to make a success in almost any line. Will you give me your word that you'll quit rustling?"

"Can't do that, governor," replied Cassidy, "because if I gave you my word I'd only have to break it. I'm in too deep now to quit the game. But I'll promise you one thing: if you give me a pardon I'll keep out of Wyoming."

The outlaw's frankness appealed to the governor. He knew a man like Cassidy could do a lot of damage in the state, and believed he would keep his pledge. It was worth the chance.

"Give me your word on it?"

"Sure thing."

The pardon was signed and Butch Cassidy walked out of the Wyoming pen a free man, on January 19, 1896. He never saw the inside of another penal institution.

Brown's Hole—
Early History

To TRAPPERS of the old Fur Brigade who first penetrated the fastnesses of the Rocky Mountains, a "hole" was any valley completely surrounded by mountains. The place they called Brown's Hole answers that description perfectly. Approaching from either the north or the south, one rides to the brink of a precipice and views far below a deep "hole" to which one can descend only over a steep, rocky trail. The valley constituting Brown's Hole extends in an east-west direction for thirty miles, with an average width of about five miles. Along the foot of Diamond Mountain, southern wall of the Hole, runs the Green River, a stream of considerable volume and in early summer a raging torrent.

Geographically, Brown's Hole surrounds the point where the eastern boundary of Utah and the western boundary of Colorado join the southern boundary of Wyoming. Parts of it lie in all three states. The valley floor consists of ancient river terraces lying at various levels above the present river bed. In earlier days those flat acres furnished rich grazing for innumerable herds of deer, antelope, and mountain sheep which once made the place a hunter's paradise. A few acres of bottom land along the river are under cultivation, with an occasional orchard or garden patch at the base of Cold Springs Mountain, northern boundary of the Hole. The eastern end terminates at Vermillion Creek, an alkali-laden stream running along the base of the Douglas Mountain foothills. Two creeks of fresh water flow from Cold Springs Mountain to lose themselves in the muddy current of the Green River. Those two streams furnish the only supply of irrigation water.

The Green River enters the Hole from the west through a deep, rugged canyon and follows the base of Diamond Mountain, seeking an exit through the Uintah range. Tiring of its search after thirty miles, it plunges frantically through the highest mountain in its path and goes roaring through Lodore Canyon, a narrow, deep, and dangerous slit in the red-sandstone cliffs.

In 1824 the Fur Brigade first penetrated to Green River Valley through South Pass, a hundred miles north of Brown's Hole. Thousands of beaver pelts were taken during the season of 1824 as trappers explored the river and its tributaries. In the spring of 1825 General William H. Ashley, leader of the trappers, conceived the idea of exploring the lower course of the Green River, hoping to find new tributary streams rich in fur. With a few picked men he began his memorable journey in bull-boats made of buffalo hide. He had no maps, no guide, and no information of what he might expect below, except vague stories of Indians who had seen the river at various points.

Starting near Fontenelle, Wyoming, Ashley and his men drifted down stream in comparatively quiet water until they reached Flaming Gorge, where the stream enters the jaws of a deep and highly colored canyon. Some distance down stream, at a point now called Ashley Falls, the general left his name and the date of his passing on a rock above high-water mark, in paint which remained partially visible as late as 1912. About one day's run below that place the river entered the western end of Brown's Hole, where for thirty miles the boats drifted quietly with the current. But this beautiful valley was only a breather between two canyons.

Suddenly the river made a right-angle turn south and without warning dashed headlong into what is now called Lodore Canyon, where the narrow channel and rapid descent churned the water into foam. Still farther down, at what Major Powell called Disaster Falls, the boats were swept over a sharp drop of twelve feet. At this place some equipment had been abandoned by the W. L. Manly party of 1849, leading Powell to the conclusion that Ashley had met disaster there. Ashley's record states he continued with the skin boats to the mouth of the Uintah River, explored farther down the canyon on foot, then returned to the Uintah and followed it to its source and so back to his appointed rendezvous.

Records of that expedition are scant, and if Ashley left any description of Brown's Hole it has been lost.

M. Wilson Rankin, in *Reminiscences of Frontier Days*, tells how the place got its name:

One of the first white men to inhabit Brown's Hole as a trapper was Baptiste Brown, according to reminiscences told by Jack Robinson, a reliable man who in his declining years was known as Uncle Jack.

Brown, a French-Canadian, had been employed by the Hudson Bay Company. . . . After a disagreement with officials of the company, Baptiste, with a squaw companion, drifted to Green River in 1827. Moving down the river, he located in a small valley which, because of his early occupation, was named Brown's Hole.

Baptiste had a fondness for drink. When accumulated furs had been disposed of for cash, he imbibed freely in "trapper's delight." During one of his jamborees at Jim Bridger's rendezvous on Henry's Fork in 1842, he met a young man of twenty years who had recently come to Bridger's Fort and who longed to be a trapper. This young man had left the Missouri River driving a team and wagon loaded with supplies for Ft. Laramie. From there he joined an emigrant party that was on the way to Oregon. At the crossing of Green River he met and joined Jack Robinson and a party of trappers who were on their way to Bridger's trading post with furs. During the several days of Baptiste's celebrating, he became interested in the young man. Bridger interceded with friendly advice; he also furnished the young man with a pony so he could go with Baptiste to his tepee in the Hole, where he made his home for three years. Through Baptiste's direction he became a successful trapper. Baptiste, with his "Canuk" accent, could not speak the young man's name intelligibly—nor did it matter. The many trappers with whom he mingled at Bridger's trading post soon supplied a name. Because of his pious or quiet disposition, his stooping shoulders, and his living at Baptiste's camp, he was named "Bibleback Brown."

In 1843 Rufus Sage wrote that a trapper named Brown had entered the Hole "some six or seven years since." Jack Sumner, who accompanied Major Powell in 1869, also speaks of a "Cutbanks" Brown. Both of these may refer to "Bibleback."

Baptiste Brown, according to Inman's *Santa Fe Trail*, later went to Santa Fe and was selected as a juror in the trial of Indians who massacred Charles Bent and others in 1847. It is said he was very impatient with legal procedure and was strongly in favor of hanging all the Indians without wasting time on evidence. He does not appear further in the records.

The isolated valley to which trapper Brown gave his name proved to be an ideal winter camp for two reasons: First, being surrounded by mountains it was protected from winter's cold blasts; second, it was teeming with game animals which came down from the mountains to feed in the valley.

So many trappers were making their winter headquarters there in 1837 that Philip Thompson and William Craig decided to establish a trading post. A cabin was built inside a rude stockade of cottonwood logs and the place was named Fort Davy Crockett. It never was a fort—only a trading post. Most of the trappers had taken Indian wives and were on good terms with their dark-skinned relatives. The establishment, spoken of by several who visited it as the "meanest fort in the west," was built on Green River bottoms in a large grove of cottonwoods two miles above the entrance to Lodore Canyon, just below the present 2-Bar ranch. Joe Meek, famous old trapper, has left a vivid account of the doings at Fort Davy Crockett in Mrs. Victor's *River of the West.*

Thompson soon sold his interest in the fort and built an establishment at the mouth of the Uintah River near what is now the town of Ouray, Utah. Needing horses, he proceeded to steal them from the Snake Indians, peaceful neighbors of the Utes. The Snakes immediately went to Brown's Hole, where they protested to the whites at Fort Davy Crockett. To restore peace, Joe Meeks, Joe Walker, Kit Carson, William Craig, and Robert Newell formed an expedition to take the stolen animals from Thompson. They traveled down the Green River on ice to Thompson's fort, seized the horses, returned them to the Snakes, and moved back to Brown's Hole in time to celebrate Christmas in mountaineer fashion with several kegs of whiskey brought from Fort Hall on the Snake River.

After 1840, because of scarcity of beaver, the Fur Brigade began to abandon their former haunts. Fort Davy Crockett soon fell into decay, and Brown's Hole was no longer a great winter gathering place of mountain men. Some trappers with Indian wives, like Jim Baker, finding an easy living there, made it their permanent home, leaving behind a numerous progeny of halfbreeds. A few picturesque old mountaineers survived until after arrival of the first settlers in the early 1870s. One was Uncle Louis Simmons (or Simonds), son-in-law of Kit Carson, who first saw Brown's Hole in 1831 and returned to live there after killing a man in California who had stolen his wife.

During that transitional period of about thirty years, Fort Hall (now Pocatello, Idaho), 200 miles northwest, was the nearest trading post, with the exception of Fort Bridger, which only operated between 1843 and 1853. The Oregon emigration and the California gold rush brought thousands of covered wagons through South Pass, a hundred miles north, but had no noticeable effect on the handful of trappers isolated in Brown's Hole.

Then, suddenly, in 1868, word came that a transcontinental railroad was being built across the desert almost at its front door, through a newer pass discovered by Jim Bridger. This startling information did not worry old residents, for between their hidden valley and the railroad lay 65 miles of mountainous country through which only those familiar with Indian trails could penetrate. There was little danger, they thought, that their sheltered retreat would be disturbed by the passing of the iron horse.

Arrival of the railroad, however, changed the social aspect of Brown's Hole almost overnight. From a peaceful community of Indians, trappers, and halfbreeds, it became an outlaw rendezvous without rival in the West. Hundreds of fictional yarns have been written around Robbers' Roosts located in any convenient spot; but the real story of Brown's Hole— the original outlaw hideout—has never previously been told. It was such a perfect hideout and its secrets were so well kept that few except the outlaws themselves knew of its existence.

To set the stage for the entrance of Butch Cassidy it will be necessary to set down some of the Hole's history between the arrival of the railroad at Rock Springs, Wyoming, and the coming of Cassidy's Wild Bunch. For most of that early record we are indebted to William G. Tittsworth's little-known volume *Outskirt Episodes*. To his history has been added information gathered from newspaper files and old residents of the country.

Steel rails connecting the Atlantic with the Pacific had been laid but a few months when Major John Wesley Powell arrived at Green River, Wyoming, with boats and men to begin his historic voyage through the canyons of the Green and Colorado rivers. On that first expedition, made in 1869, Powell passed through Brown's Hole but gave it scant space in his journal other than to record his relief on entering its thirty-five miles of quiet water. At that time he officially changed the name to Brown's Park. In spite of this writer's admiration for the one-armed major, whose voyages made history, the original name will be used in this story as being more descriptive as well as having the authority of forty-five years' previous use.

On his second expedition in 1871 Major Powell found that white settlers had already penetrated to the isolated valley with herds of cattle. He was able to obtain a few supplies and send out mail with the Harrell brothers, who were, so far as recorded history shows, its first stockmen, employing a dozen Mexicans.

Shortly after the Civil War enormous herds of Texas cattle driven north to stock the immense ranges of Wyoming, Montana, and Nevada began to arrive in Wyoming over the old Cherokee Trail which passed near Rock Springs. Occasionally a herd was delayed and forced to winter in Wyoming. Brown's Hole was ideal for that purpose and was so used whenever the owners could procure a competent man to guide them through the narrow mountain defiles.

Placer gold had been discovered in South Pass as early as 1862. South Pass City and Atlantic City were already flourishing gold camps when the railroad came to Green River, and had attracted the usual run of riffraff, gamblers, holdup men, and horse thieves. Previous to arrival of the Texas herds, horses were the only form of property in the country worth stealing, and all pre-railroad outlaws were horse thieves. The arrival of immense herds of cattle, however, changed all that; thereafter Brown's Hole became principal headquarters for the more profitable cattle-rustling business.

First rustlers in Brown's Hole were Texas cowboys who had been discharged when it was found necessary to winter in the vicinity of Rock Springs, a new coal-mining town on the railroad directly north of the Hole. Those cowhands, disgruntled at the treatment they had received, took advantage of the distress of such herds as got into trouble crossing the Red Desert or were delayed by winter storms. While offering to assist in rounding up strayed stock, they usually succeeded in running a few hundred head into Brown's Hole, where they were safe from discovery and could easily be marketed after fattening on the rich pasturage along the river.

Beginning in 1869, the history of Brown's Hole centers upon a peculiar character—a Negro of many aliases but best known as Isom Dart. Isom had been born a slave in the Ozarks and named Ned Huddleston. At fifteen he ran away to join the Confederate army in the capacity of helper to a Mexican cook. Deserting the army, he went to Mexico for a time but left between two days after killing a Mexican priest. He then went to Texas and worked on the Goodnight ranch, becoming an expert in the use of a rope, branding iron, and six-shooter. When boys at the ranch jokingly told him a brother of the dead priest was looking for him, the young Negro left Texas on the lope. Landing in Wyoming, he got a job as second cook for a railroad-construction camp at Carmichael Cut between Green River and Rock Springs.

Chang Lee, chief cook, ran a gambling house and sold whiskey as a sideline. Finding the Negro adept in any kind of shady game, the Chinaman made him a partner in his layout. He soon earned the name of Quick Shot. One night the Irishmen, believing they were being cheated, staged a riot, and as a result Chang Lee and Quick Shot left between suns, on a raft, headed down the Green River. Both carried considerable sums of money. In course of time the Negro drifted back to South Pass City, sporting a large roll of bills, and it was naturally surmised he had killed the Chinaman.

Jesse Ewing was as tough a character as one could have found anywhere in the West. Prior to the South Pass gold rush he had been station keeper for the Overland Stage line, having charge of some of the most dangerous posts on that route. He had fought holdups, Indians, and grizzly bears; one of the bears had clawed his face so badly he was known as the ugliest man in South Pass, a place boasting its share of ugliness. He disdained a six-gun, depending on his unusual ability with a knife. In close quarters cold steel was a better persuader than powder and lead. Men who knew his reputation were careful to let him strictly alone.

Ewing was the first man to prospect mountains around Brown's Hole for minerals. As early as 1867 he found copper ore in one of the canyons that entered the Hole from the north, built a cabin there, and did some preliminary work. Prospects for a mine appeared to be good, so he returned to South Pass to obtain supplies and find capital to help him develop his property. When the Negro, Quick Shot, showed up with his big roll, Ewing induced him to buy a half interest, and together they returned to the prospect in what is still called Jesse Ewing Canyon. From their cabin they could look directly down into Brown's Hole.

Work in the tunnel progressed slowly, because the Negro was not an experienced miner. When his money was gone, Ewing drove his colored partner off the premises with a knife.

An expedition of government geologists had been sent into the Flaming Gorge country that year, guided by Johnny Pare and "Petrified" Johnson. Fleeing from Jesse Ewing's knife, Quick Shot stumbled into the geologists' camp and was engaged as cook. Within a few weeks another party of prospectors passed that way searching for diamonds, and the

Negro joined them. The diamond hunters, under Col. Eels, had been taken in by what is known to historians as "The Great Diamond Hoax" and were headed for the mountain lying between Brown's Hole and the Uintah Basin, ever since known as Diamond Mountain. A few genuine diamonds, previously planted by a clever prospector, were found and the expedition returned jubilantly to San Francisco where, through no intentional dishonesty on their part, one of the greatest swindles in American history was perpetrated.

Jesse Ewing had no part in the diamond hoax. At the time he was busy working his copper prospect, assisted by a new partner, an old man named Coulter. After a few weeks Coulter became sick and returned to Green River. On his next trip to town, Ewing, to force out his new partner, accused the old man of trying to kill him and took a shot at Coulter. He was arrested and thrown in jail. Quick Shot showed up in town at the same time, was charged with the murder of Chang Lee, and was thrown in the same cell with Ewing.

Ewing had already earned his reputation as a bad customer. The Negro was also considered a tough egg. Bets were laid by railroaders as to which would come out of the cell alive, it being a foregone conclusion that one would be killed. Imagine the jailer's astonishment when he looked in the cell next morning, to find the Negro on his hands and knees, his broad back being used by the white man as a breakfast table. Ewing had beaten the tough black into submission with his own boots.

Chang Lee showed up a few days later and Quick Shot was discharged. Coulter, knowing that Ewing would attempt to kill him at the first opportunity, thought it best to beat the miner at his own game by going to the jail and taking a shot at his former partner through the bars. For this attempt Coulter was arrested and sentenced to three years' imprisonment, while Ewing, the aggressor, was freed. Such was justice in Green River, Wyoming, in 1871.

To obtain cash for further prospecting, Ewing took a contract to cut ties for the railroad with another new partner. After the ties were cut he tried his old trick. His partner, however, showed fight; so he killed the man as he was crossing the Green River on the ice, slashed his body to ribbons, and left it for the river to dispose of in the spring. The ice was stained with blood for half a mile downstream.

In the meantime Quick Shot left Green River with two or three other men looking for stolen horses. In a few days they fell in with a party of trappers preparing to make winter camp near the upper end of Flaming Gorge, where old Jim Baker once had his tepee. Caught in a heavy fall of snow, they all went into camp together.

In Brown's Hole lived a Ute Indian known as Pony Beater, with his squaw, Tickup, a Shoshone captive, and her small daughter, whose father had been a white man. Pony Beater was also a wife beater, and the squaw with her daughter soon showed up at the trappers' camp, bruised, hungry, and footsore, headed for the Washakie reservation where her relatives lived. The runaways were fed by the trappers and their Indian wives, remaining in camp several days.

Then began one of the strangest episodes in the history of Brown's Hole. The Negro, Quick Shot, formed a strong attachment for the little halfbreed Indian girl, took the mother into his tepee as housekeeper, and appointed himself guardian of mother and daughter. Pony Beater arrived in a few days and took his squaw by force; but she was back again in a short time, having killed her Ute husband with a butcher knife. She and the girl then left for the reservation on horses supplied by Quick Shot.

The free and easy trapper life cured the black man of any further desire to cook for a gang of Irish railroaders. In the spring he joined up with three professional horse thieves, Tip A. Galt, the "Sagebrush King of Bitter Creek," J. L. Pease, and a Mexican known as Teresa. Being an expert in running a "hair brand," Quick Shot was a valuable addition to the gang.

After working with the thieves for a time, the Negro felt impelled to visit his protégés on the reservation, with the idea of inducing them to come away with him. He was accompanied by his new friends; and to make the trip pay expenses they loaded their horses with cheap whiskey to be bootlegged to the Indians.

At the Shoshone camp on Ross Fork, near Fort Hall, Galt and his partners began dispensing the snakebite, ably assisted by Jack Bennett, a notorious character who made that occupation his principal business.

Since returning to the reservation the squaw had taken to herself a "fancy buck." The camp was scattered over a considerable area, and by the time the Negro had located her, she was gloriously drunk. In the big brawl which followed, Tickup shot her "fancy buck" and was once more a widow.

When the Indian agent came out to stop the commotion, the horse thieves beat a hasty retreat; and to make their trip doubly profitable, they stole all the Shoshone horses. With proceeds of this deal they returned to upper Brown's Hole and made camp at Dutch Spring.

Since arrival of the railroad many cattle ranches had been started near Rock Springs. Cattle could be disposed of more easily and with greater profit than horses; so Galt turned his attention to rustling. His operations were so successful that cattlemen decided to eradicate his gang. A trap was laid into which they fell that next summer, and the entire gang was wiped out with the exception of the Negro, who was shot in the hip and left for dead.

Horseless and without food, Quick Shot crawled into an aspen grove, where he was found several days later by William G. Tittsworth, a white man of his own age who had played with him as a boy on his father's farm in the Ozarks.

Tittsworth recognized his former playmate and nursed him back to health. The black boy had apparently fallen into bad company, but the white man believed he could be induced to make a new start in another part of the country. When he was able to travel, Tittsworth gave him a horse and started him toward White Pine, Nevada, at that time a roaring mining camp.

The Negro had some money of his own and had succeeded in retrieving the money carried by his dead companions, so when he left for Nevada he was in possession of plenty of funds. His first concern, after saving his own hide, was for the welfare of Mincy, the little halfbreed Indian girl. He learned that she and her mother were being used as come-ons by Jack Bennett in his bootlegging activities. Not daring to go back to the reservation, he hired Jim King to kidnap them from the clutches of Bennett and furnished money to send them to Oklahoma, where the girl was put in school. After an unsuccessful attempt to learn the mining business, Quick Shot followed his protégés to Oklahoma, bought a cotton plantation in partnership with Clouse Casebeer, and changed his name to Isom Dart, by which he was always thereafter known.

Little Mincy soon began to blossom into early womanhood. In course of time a dashing young man drove into town behind a pair of high-stepping horses and the girl immediately fell in love with him. His name was Matt Rash. The horses and rig had just been stolen.

Tickup, Mincy's mother, was stricken with smallpox about that time and soon died, leaving her daughter alone in the world—except for her black friend, Isom Dart. Learning that the law was close on his trail, Matt Rash induced the girl to leave with him for her old home on the reservation. They disappeared together one day. Weeks later Matt Rash turned up in Brown's Hole, safest hideout in the West. The halfbreed girl was never seen again.

On his plantation Isom Dart heard rumors that Mincy had been abandoned on the desert to suffer a lingering death. To ascertain the facts he sold his place and with his partner started for Brown's Hole. When he arrived, Rash told such a plausible story that the Negro decided not to kill him, at least for the present.

Once he was again in his old haunts, it was easy for Isom Dart to drop back into his old habits. Cattle were being shipped and driven into Wyoming by thousands; the ranges were rapidly being stocked, leaving the almost impenetrable Brown's Hole a backwash in the current of events. When not otherwise occupied, Isom sometimes worked for Virginia-born Mrs. Bassett as cook.

Brown's Hole—
Outlaw Period

Freighting across the plains with ox teams had ended with arrival of the iron horse, and Ashael C. Beckwith climbed down from his wagon to found an immense cattle empire extending all the way from the Bear River in western Wyoming to the Red Desert east of Rock Springs. When the golden spike was driven, Pat Whalen and Pat Barrett dropped their picks and soon became owners of immense herds. A dozen others whose names have been indelibly stamped on Wyoming history had done likewise—all in an incredibly short space of time.

With large owners hogging all the range, there was no room for small ranchers with a few hundred head of cows. The homesteader or "nester" was unwelcome and, if he did not heed the voice of warning, was run out by force. If he attempted resistance his body might be found later in some dry gulch, food for ravens. "Dry gulching" was a favorite method of disposing of troublesome nesters.

Finding himself pushed off the range—government land intended for the benefit of all citizens—the homesteader or small rancher felt justified in rounding up cattle belonging to big operators. With so many thousands of cattle roaming the country there were always some that managed to escape roundups and carried no brand. These mavericks, according to the law of the range, belonged to the man who first put his mark on them. From branding mavericks to branding young calves or altering existing marks was an easy step. Because of its isolation it was an easy matter to drive whole herds into Brown's Hole, brand the calves, then drive the cows back to their own range.

Isom Dart was an expert with a rope and branding iron and the hot wire used in running "hair brands," which looked genuine until the hair grew out again. When he decided to become a rustler on his own account he adopted the "wagon wheel" brand, with which he was able to cover almost any other mark on a critter's hide. It soon became a sort of universal rustler's brand, and any animal carrying the wagon wheel could reasonably be presumed to have been stolen.

Isom Dart's ranch was located at Summit Springs, on Cold Springs Mountain. On a ledge above the spring he built a cabin commanding a narrow trail leading down into the valley. In his rustling activities he was joined by Con Dresher and Matt Rash, the young man he had threatened to kill. Old-timers agree there was bad blood between Isom and Matt; they quarreled frequently, yet it is a certainty they were associated in the rustling business. When he first came to Wyoming, Matt Rash worked for the Middlesex Cattle Company. Later he worked for Tim Kinney. When Kinney fired him he stole seven hundred head of Kinney's cattle, driving them to Brown's Hole, where the Circle K brand was easily transformed into a wagon wheel.

When Isom Dart returned to Brown's Hole trailing Matt Rash, the place had already become headquarters for a number of wild characters, most of whom had good reason to hide out. Jack Bennett had come west after spending two years in an Arkansas pen. He first operated as bootlegger to the Indians, assisted by a certain "Madame Forrestall." Later he located at Fossil, Wyoming, where he lived with a young woman from Ogden, Utah. Tiring of his drunken orgies, the girl accepted attentions from a young fellow named Louis Ebert. When Bennett found them together on June 8, 1889, he killed Ebert with a knife, leaving for the Hole on short notice. His partner, William Pigeon, was a man of about the same type.

In the meantime a few permanent settlers had drifted to Brown's Hole. Among the first was Valentine Hoy, whose biography is given in later pages, with his two brothers, Jesse S. and Harry. The Hoys planned an exclusive occupation of the Hole for the purpose of building up a small cattle empire of their own, as Beckwith, Quinn, Whalen, Swan, Barrett, Sparks, and others had done in the upper country. When Tittsworth brought in a small herd of cattle one winter, he was run out. Other men, however, were not so easily frightened. Among them were Tom Davenport, Herbert Bassett, and Charley Crouse. The Hoy ranch was located on the Green River near Lodore Canyon. Bassett lived at the foot of Cold Springs Mountain on the north side of the valley. Crouse settled at the mouth of Beaver Creek, larger of the two streams. Davenport located at the head of Willow Creek.

The Law family from Cache Valley, Utah, came in about 1878. William G. Tittsworth married Jean Law and attempted to settle in the Hole, but he found the environment a little too tough for one of his peaceful temperament. Charley Crouse, a two-fisted, hard-drinking fighter from the hills of South Carolina, married Mary Law, who eventually worried herself into a early grave. Crouse, who had no education, built the only schoolhouse in Brown's Hole and hired Pete Dillman from Vernal as teacher. He might have saved that expense; children born in the Hole were as wild as Indians and refused to attend classes.

Tom Davenport, a Welsh miner formerly employed in the coal mines at Rock Springs, located on Willow Creek in 1879.

About 1852 Sam Bassett, an army scout, visited Brown's Hole. When his brother, Herbert, wanted to go west he recommended the place as an excellent ranch site. Herbert came to Evanston in the early '70s, worked for a time as bookkeeper for A. C. Beckwith & Co., then went to the Hole to start his ranch. He was an easy-going, jovial person; his wife was from an aristocratic Virginia family. Two of his daughters, Josie and Ann, grew up to be the best cowhands in that wild section, the latter becoming famous later as "Queen Ann."

Albert Williams, a Negro, whose brown skin was spotted with black freckles, came to the Hole with Davenport. The "Speckled Nigger," as he was known, outlived all his contemporaries and was the last survivor of the old Brown's Hole pioneers. From old "Speck," three weeks before his death in 1934, this writer obtained a great many facts concerning those who passed through the Hole during his lifetime, and although he could neither read nor write, his story was found to be amazingly accurate when checked against available records.

Jesse Ewing, who continued to prospect in Ewing and Red canyons, found life somewhat empty and decided to "go outside" for a wife. He returned to the Hole accompanied by a "coupon woman" known as Madame Forrestall, who had formerly bootlegged liquor to the Indians in Brush Creek Canyon with Jack Bennett and Tom Crowley. One whose face has been clawed by a bear is not in a position to be too fastidious. The couple lived in one of Ewing's cabins on the Green River near the mouth of Red Creek opposite a ferry operated by the Speckled Nigger. All went along smoothly until a young and handsome outlaw named Duncan drifted to the Hole after a shooting affair in Rock Springs and made arrangements to board at Ewing's cabin. While Jesse prospected, Duncan loafed at the cabin.

One morning Ewing left, supposedly for the day, but

slipped back to watch developments from the vantage of a ledge of rock just below. When he thought the moment for action had arrived he reached for his knife, always worn in a scabbard over his shirt pocket, and started around the point of rocks. Duncan, suspecting just such a move, was watching through a crack in the chinking. As Ewing's head appeared, Duncan fired with an old-fashioned, heavy-caliber rifle, striking the old prospector in the neck and literally shooting his head off.

Duncan and the woman immediately packed their belongings on Ewing's horses. Before leaving, the killer strolled down to the ferry, crossed over to John Jarvie's store, and told the storekeeper Ewing was sick and wanted to see him. The couple then disappeared and were never seen again. Jarvie found the prospector's decapitated body and with the assistance of Speck and others buried it near the cabin. It is not recorded that there were any mourners, and it is extremely doubtful if Isom Dart, Ewing's former partner, laid any flowers on the grave. Three of Jesse Ewing's old cabins still stand in the canyon bearing his name, and prospectors still search for the "lost Ewing mine."

Tom Davenport, who soon acquired a large number of cattle, employed several cowboys. One was called Buckskin Ed because he always wore buckskin pants that were stiff and bent at the knees, giving him the appearance of a man ready to jump. Ed packed a pair of long-barreled, wicked-looking six-guns. He had come to Brown's Hole after assaulting a 16-year-old girl at Hyattsville, Wyoming, on January 1, 1896. His real name was Edwin Howell. On a trip to Green River, Davenport took Buckskin Ed and the Speckled Nigger to help load a shipment of cattle. After being paid off, Buckskin entered the nearest gambling joint, where he was quickly cleaned out. Borrowing eight dollars from Speck, he went back to try his luck again, with the same result. He was badly in need of clothes, so before he left town he went into a store run by a Jewish merchant and ordered a complete new outfit. When it was wrapped he grabbed the package and started for the door.

"Hey!" yelled the proprietor. "You didn't pay me for them clothes."

"Write it on the ice," returned the cowboy as he stepped into the street, "and if it don't melt off I'll pay you sometime maybe."

But the man was unwilling to sell his goods on those terms. Grabbing a shotgun, he started down the street after the cowboy, but couldn't fire without hitting innocent bystanders. On the edge of town where the crowd thinned out, the merchant let him have it. Most of the charge missed, but the scattering shot which stung Buckskin's legs caused him to drop the bundle and increase his speed toward Brown's Hole, with the two long-barreled six-shooters banging against his legs. Speck, who was a witness, repeated the story on his return, and the expression "write it on the ice" became a byword in Brown's Hole.

Bob Hunter was another member of the colony of thieves in the Hole. Hunter, said old Speck, was just a "natch'l bo'n thief." He would steal anything, whether it had any value or not. When nothing better appeared, Hunter would hang up his own hat and steal it from himself just to keep in practice —according to Speck. The unwritten law of Brown's Hole forbade stealing from residents; but Hunter could not resist temptation and one day stole a saddle blanket from the Hoy place. Valentine Hoy followed and, to teach him a lesson in manners, shot him in the mouth, knocking out most of his teeth and splitting his upper lip. Kind-hearted Mrs. Davenport patched him up, but his lip never healed properly, causing an impediment in his speech. He was always afterward known as "Snifflin' Hunter." He was too big a thief to live in Brown's Hole, so the rustlers eventually ran him out.

After Speck Williams had been in the Hole some years he

decided to try ranching for himself and rented a place in partnership with Greenhall, a cockney blacksmith from Rock
Springs. Greenhall made all branding irons used by the rustlers,
including the famous wagon-wheel brand. To brand cattle, in
the cockney's idiom, was to "put the 'ook on," an expression
still surviving there.

In a community where men far outnumbered women, the
Bassett girls were naturally very popular. Joe Davenport, son
of Tom, laid claim to Josie's affections, a claim disputed by
Jim McKnight. Both young men were products of the West
in its wildest and woolliest form and threatened to kill each
other on sight. A day came when their paths crossed. Both
were riding and both drew their guns. As they passed they
glared at each other with death-dealing looks, but neither
fired. Two irresistible forces had met—but no one was injured. Some time later Jim McKnight made good his claim to
Josie Bassett; but the hard-riding, straight-shooting cowgirl
was not content to play the part of a meek housewife. In
course of time she quarreled with her husband, ordered him
out of the house, and emphasized her remarks by shooting
McKnight, who departed suddenly with a leaden souvenir.
Afterward Josie had several husbands, but her affairs of the
heart always seemed to go sour.

Matt Warner was already located on Diamond Mountain,
just south of the Hole. During his absence the place was often
occupied by Butch Cassidy and his new partner, Elza Lay.
Matt and some of the boys had already robbed a Jewish
peddler and distributed his wagonload of goods among their
friends. A similar holdup was pulled in about the same place
at a later date. The *Green River Star* had some comments to
make in its issue of August 26, 1895:

The old outlaw gang which has made life miserable for years
for the settlers in that section where the states of Wyoming,
Colorado, and the territory of Utah meet, are reported to be

quite active this season. Members of this gang are accused of being responsible for the recent holdup of Mr. Andursky, the jeweler of Rock Springs, and their other depredations are numbered by the hundreds. The authorities of the three commonwealths should combine in putting a stop to the work of this remaining gang of Jack Shepards. Matt Warner is said to be the leader of this body of outlaws.

As years passed, Brown's Hole settled into its own routine. Early settlers with good locations constantly added to their herds, marketing their steers in Rock Springs. The outlaws came to town in detachments large enough to prevent any argument over ownership. Altered brands were not evidence in court unless the animal was killed and the original scar examined from inside the hide. Everyone knew that most cattle shipped from Brown's Hole were stolen, but rustlers spent their money freely and no attempt was made to investigate the source of the profits.

Nearly all the wild characters of Wyoming and Utah drifted in and out of the Hole at various times, but the place was carefully avoided by officers of the law. Only three trails entered the sheltered valley, two from the north and one from the south, all difficult, easily ambushed, and known only to those who found it necessary to travel them.

Although the Hole fell within the boundaries of three states, no county officer ever went there to assess or collect taxes. Such an effort would have been useless, even if a man had been found brave enough to undertake the job. Within an hour all livestock could have been driven from Utah into Wyoming, from Wyoming into Colorado, and back again into Utah. None of the three states ever spent any tax money for schools, roads, or bridges, and the residents were perfectly satisfied with their status as a forgotten community. They were a law unto themselves. A post office was maintained in Dr. Parson's store in the Utah end of the valley, where mail was brought in from Vernal during the winter and from

Green River in summer, but this mail service was their only direct connection with the outside world and their only concession to government.

Children grew into young men and women without benefit of education, except what little they may have had forced upon them in Charley Crouse's schoolhouse. Young men naturally became expert rustlers.

Supplies were obtained principally from Rock Springs or Green River, Wyoming; but at times, especially in winter, some of the boys used to visit Vernal, Utah, fifty miles over Diamond Mountain. Such trips to the Mormon settlement were usually celebrated by shooting up the town. The outlaws sometimes paid for their purchases but when short of cash took what they wanted, leaving an itemized list with a promise to pay at some future date. Such goods were "sold on account"—not stolen.

The Uintah Basin and surrounding country was being gradually occupied by cattlemen, mostly small ranchers hostile toward the big cattle barons and sympathetic toward rustlers, when not actually rustlers themselves. Even those who were strictly honest minded their own business and looked the other way when rustlers passed with stolen stock. Homesteaders or nesters constituted a voting majority and usually elected sheriffs who were not too zealous in examining brands.

The first known instance of an officer of the law entering Brown's Hole occurred when one of the cattlemen swore out a warrant for the arrest of Isom Dart. Rock Springs officers did not relish the assignment, so the sheriff deputized Jim Philbrick, a tough hombre who was himself wanted in three states. Details of this arrest are not known, but Philbrick got his man and started back to town in a buckboard, over trails which had rarely seen the passage of a wheeled vehicle. It was a two-day trip, necessitating one night camp, but the Negro made no attempt to escape. On the second day, at a particularly narrow place in the road, the buckboard slipped over the bank and dashed down a steep incline to the bottom. Officer, prisoner, horses, and buckboard were piled in a heap, with Jim Philbrick underneath, badly injured. One might have expected the prisoner to abandon his captor and make his escape. Instead, the Negro lifted off the buckboard, bandaged Philbrick's wounds, caught the frightened horses, patched up the torn harness and drove the officer into town, then surrendered himself to the sheriff.

From his hospital cot Philbrick cursed the sheriff when he learned Isom Dart was being held in jail. According to his code the Negro's act merited freedom from whatever charge had been brought against him. He swore that if he lived he would do everything possible to bring about Dart's release. When the trial came up several weeks later the deputy was recovered sufficiently to testify on behalf of the man he had arrested, who was promptly freed by the jury.

No other officer, so far as the records show, ever entered Brown's Hole until John T. Pope was elected sheriff of Uintah County, Utah.

Until the summer of 1896, outlaws in Brown's Hole had been horse thieves and cattle rustlers almost exclusively, with a sprinkling of men wanted by the law for other crimes. But with the arrival of Butch Cassidy after his release from the Wyoming pen it was to enter upon a new era. Cassidy had received a full pardon from Governor Richards and might have made a clean start; but his mind had been made up long before to make a name for himself as an outlaw.

The debacle at Delta, Colorado, in 1893 had completely broken up the McCarty gang. Tom was still haunting the sagebrush trying to get a shot at Simpson, the man who had eliminated half the gang, but he never fulfilled his threat and finally dropped out of sight. Matt Warner had been reconciled with his wife and moved back to his ranch on Diamond Mountain. Cassidy decided it was time to organize his own gang and begin the larger operations he had planned. From the time of his release he looked upon horse stealing as "petty larceny."

Cassidy's first step was to choose his associates and train them for the business he had in mind. There was plenty of material in Brown's Hole, but ordinary rustlers didn't have enough imagination to go after big money, nor guts enough to follow a daring leader. To obtain money in the higher brackets required something besides "badness."

The man he finally chose for his closest associate and partner was Elza Lay. Born Ellsworth Lay, in Boston, this handsome, pleasant young man had been well educated, but otherwise we know nothing of his early history until he came to Denver. In that city he obtained a job driving a horse car. One day, when a drunk tried to molest a woman on the car, Lay threw him off onto the pavement with considerable force. Believing the man was dead, he abandoned his car and fled to the mountains, eventually finding his way to Brown's Hole, where he worked for some of the ranchers. On Diamond Mountain he met Matt Warner and later Butch Cassidy.

At that time there was a strip of land just south of Fort Duchesne in the Uintah Basin which by some surveyor's error was not on any official map. The Strip, as it became known, was soon occupied by saloons and gambling joints for the benefit of soldiers at Fort Duchesne. It had no law whatever and became the wildest spot since Deadwood. Elza Lay, with Pat Johnson, ran a saloon there for a time. Later he started counterfeiting silver dollars, which were passed by another saloonkeeper, Henry Lee. A family named Davis had a ranch on Diamond Mountain, and Lay married Maude Davis, one of the girls. They had two daughters. Several outlaws used the "double roof" of Davis's place for a hideout when necessary.

Since Lay was the one who suggested robbing the Jewish merchant around 1884, he was already well known in those parts before Cassidy arrived.

Bob Meeks, of Huntington, Utah, a friend of Lay's, was also selected as a member of the Cassidy gang, together with three or four other young fellows who wanted some excitement.

A proper hideout was the next essential, although as a matter of fact men were safe enough anywhere in the valley, being welcomed at any cabin in the Hole. Cassidy was good company in any gathering, bubbling over with dry humor, while Lay was tall, dark, and handsome. But to play their part in accepted style they must have a secret hideout. For this purpose they selected a rocky point high above Charley Crouse's cabin on the face of Diamond Mountain, now known as Cassidy Point. On a sandstone ledge they built a small cabin protected on three sides by the cliff, easily defended in case of attack. Supplies, packed in from Rock Springs, included plenty of whiskey and numerous decks of cards with which to kill time during those months when mountain passes were full of snow. Mrs. Crouse, then living south of the river at the foot of the trail to Cassidy Point, kept the boys supplied with home-baked delicacies and was liberally rewarded for her efforts.

The young fellows occupying the "roost" were as lively a set of young roosters as one might meet anywhere in the intermountain country. They attended all dances in the valley and by practical joking and daredevil stunts soon earned the name of "The Wild Bunch." The group's personnel changed from time to time as various members dropped out or were eliminated by the law, but Cassidy's leadership was never challenged.

That leadership was well merited. Cassidy had set out to become a famous outlaw, had served his apprenticeship, and was determined to let nothing stand in the way of his ambition. He was always a canny drinker, never imbibing more than he could handle; but, more important, he never let women interfere with his work. When in funds he always dressed neatly and for that reason was sometimes called a "lady's man"; but the phrase in his case meant only that he was popular with women—not that he was a woman chaser. Josie Bassett rated a considerable portion of Cassidy's time when he was in the Hole, but when Josie thought she was ready to settle down she picked Jim McKnight, the young rustler who spent most of his time in the vicinity of Herb Bassett's ranch.

When Butch Cassidy returned to Brown's Hole in the winter of 1896, he was broke and probably rustled cattle to pay expenses until his plans were matured. But the snow was not yet out of the mountains before an incident occurred which gave him an excuse to begin his larger operations at once.

Montpelier
Bank Robbery

Rᴀʏ Sɪᴍᴘꜱᴏɴ had shot the heart out of the McCarty gang after the bank holdup of September 7, 1893. Matt Warner had patched up affairs with his wife, had returned to his ranch on Diamond Mountain, and was in a fair way toward becoming a solid citizen. For three years his tracks were not seen on the Outlaw Trail.

Some time after Rosa had joined her husband on Diamond Mountain she suffered a distressing accident. Several stories are told to explain it. According to one, Rosa was sitting in a chair with her feet on a box when Matt playfully dropped down in her lap, breaking one of her knees. Another report is that Matt was trying to break a wild horse, lost his temper, and beat it unmercifully. When his wife objected he lashed her to the frightened animal and turned it loose. A third, reported by the nurse who later attended Rosa, states that Rosa's injury was due to a kick administered by her husband. According to Queen Ann, she was watering her cows from a hole chopped in the ice during one of Matt's long absences when she fell and broke her leg. Matt himself told me all such stories were false. At any rate, Mrs. Warner developed a cancer on one of her legs and had to have it amputated in the military hospital at Fort Duchesne. The operating surgeon denied such stories at that time, which proves they were in circulation as early as 1895. From that time on, Matt is said to have treated his wife with the greatest consideration.

At the head of Brush Creek, near Vernal, Utah, a rich copper deposit was being worked by Dr. J. K. W. Bracken at a good profit, the ore being hauled over the Uintah Mountains by ox team to Carter, Wyoming, for shipment. In Dry Fork, west of Brush Creek, some sheepherder found a green stain on the rocks which he believed was another rich deposit of copper.

E. B. Coleman, then living in Salt Lake City, heard of the reported discovery and determined to file on the prospect. Coleman was a tall, thin man of fifty-two from Davenport, Iowa, who had prospected all over the West. He claimed to have been the original discoverer of the Homestake mine in the Black Hills, fountainhead of the Hearst millions, and had also been among the first at Alder Gulch in Montana. On his Dry Fork expedition he was accompanied by another miner, Robert Swift. They secured a pack outfit in Vernal and began combing the hills. At last they located the sheepherder who had seen the outcrop, learned its general location, and started out to stake claims.

Three other prospectors from Vernal, David Milton, Adoniram W. Staunton (known as Dick), and his brother, Isaac Staunton, learning that Coleman and Swift were on their way to locate some rich claims, began to follow them, intending to make locations in the immediate vicinity. Coleman tried to shake them off his trail by traveling through extremely rough country, but every night when he made camp the other three would pitch camp close by. Day after day the same performance was repeated until Coleman got tired of it.

Coleman and Swift at last reached Taylor's Draw in Dry Fork, within a few miles of the prospect. That night Milton and the Staunton brothers came up and camped fifty feet from Coleman's tent. Coleman ordered them off, but they refused to move. Considerable argument ensued. Milton finally made a proposition that if Coleman would pay him $1,000 he would go back to Vernal and remain ten days. The latter said he couldn't raise that much money, but would give him $500, to which Milton agreed. Coleman then returned to Vernal, leaving Swift in camp.

Coleman attempted to borrow $500 in Vernal on his note but only succeeded in raising $100. In a saloon that evening he met Matt Warner and William Wall, a gambler, both of whom had just returned from a prospecting trip to Gosling Mountain with Sheriff John T. Pope. Pope was still in the mountains. Discussing his dilemma with Warner, Coleman decided that rather than buy off the three men he would pay Warner and Wall to frighten them off. A contract was entered into whereby the latter were to accompany Coleman back to Dry Fork, frighten off the three trailers and receive $500 for their "protection." All three started for Dry Fork next evening, timing their arrival at camp by sunrise.

Just as day broke on May 7, 1896, Ike Staunton arose, stepped out of his tent and began building a fire. Hearing horses approaching and suspecting trouble, he grabbed his rifle and started shooting, killing Matt's horse. He then raced for a nearby group of aspen trees.

Matt fell to the ground cursing. "Take your medicine, you dirty sons of bitches," he yelled as he began pouring a volley of lead into the tent. Wall had dismounted and was also pumping lead.

One of the first shots into the tent fatally wounded David Milton, who was still lying in bed. Dick (A. W.) Staunton rushed outside long enough to receive a leaden messenger, then fell back inside. Two of the three were definitely out of the fight, and the other badly wounded, having been hit in the neck and thigh.

From his place behind a good-sized aspen tree, Ike Staunton began shooting at Warner, who immediately took refuge behind another tree thirty yards away. Wall also took cover and both began firing at Ike. They were armed with .44 repeating rifles, while Staunton's rifle was a .45-110 single shot.

The tree behind which Matt had taken refuge was thirteen inches in diameter. Matt was a stocky man and had to stand sideways to keep from being hit, in which position it was awkward for him to shoot. Although Staunton had only a single-shot gun, he was a good marksman and held his own against the two hired outlaws, directing his particular attention to Warner. Seeing he could not make a direct hit, he began firing at a spot about the size of a dollar on Warner's tree, with the idea of boring a hole through it with bullets. The green aspen wood was soft and each heavy bullet went deeper. At last the hole was almost through. From his side of the tree Matt saw the white bark begin to bulge as bullets struck and realized the next shot or two would come through, yet he could not step away without being drilled. It was a ticklish moment and one he never forgot. Just at that moment, one of Wall's bullets struck Staunton across the bridge of the nose, filling his eyes with blood and knocking him senseless. The fight was over.

When the firing ceased, Robert Swift came up from his own tent fifty feet away. Under the excitement of the moment Warner fired at him.

"For God's sake don't shoot!" he yelled.

"Get your hands up, then," replied Warner.

"I've got 'em up as high as they'll go. Don't shoot me, I'm Coleman's partner." Warner was still suspicious. Coleman, at the first shot, had disappeared behind a ridge and was nowhere to be seen.

"Tear down them tents," commanded Warner, "so we can see if there's anyone else hiding in 'em." Swift complied.

The falling canvas revealed Milton and Dick Staunton lying

mortally wounded. One bullet had entered Milton's shoulder and ranged down along the spine. Dick Staunton was shot in two or three places and both were bleeding profusely.

"My God!" exclaimed Matt when he saw them. "If I'd known it was you fellows I wouldn't have shot."

"It ain't your fault," replied Milton, "and I don't hold it against you, Matt. It's that Coleman. He's at the bottom of the whole trouble. He went to Vernal for the money, and look what he brought back! Give me a gun, some of you fellows, and I'll kill the son of a bitch yet before I die."

Milton and Dick Staunton were still alive, though in poor condition. Ike Staunton had stopped three bullets and was temporarily unconscious. Matt immediately took charge of the situation. He stripped off Milton's clothes and tried to bandage the wounds. Then he attended to Dick, and lastly to Ike Staunton. He put Wall on a horse and sent him galloping toward Vernal to bring a doctor and a wagon to carry the wounded men back to town.

William Wall, outlaw and gambler, made a dust for Vernal. Arriving in town he met Marcellus Pope, 22-year-old brother of Sheriff John T. Pope, acting sheriff during his brother's absence.

"What's the excitement?" Marcellus asked.

"Three men shot in Dry Fork!" he yelled as he rode down the street. "Tell you about it later."

Wall rushed to Dr. Lindsay's office. "Three men shot in Dry Fork," he gasped. "Go back with me right away."

"Can't do it," replied Lindsay. "Get Dr. Rose."

Wall rushed to Rose's office. "Can't go," said Rose, "I'm sick myself."

"I'll give you twenty dollars if you'll go up there," begged Wall.

"Sorry," said Rose. "See if you can get Dr. Hollingsworth."

Wall rushed to Hollingsworth's office, only to be again refused. Evidently doctors didn't relish the idea of getting mixed up in a gunfight. At last he hunted up Deputy Pope.

"You're the sheriff while your brother's away; get a wagon and go up Dry Fork after Milton and the Staunton brothers. They've been shot."

"Haven't got a wagon," said young Pope.

"Well, I'll hire one then," shouted Wall. "Get ready and go back with me. There's been a fight and those three fellows are badly hurt. We've got to get them to town; the doctors won't go back with me."

Wall, the gambler, one of the men who had done the shooting, then paid ten dollars for the use of a team and wagon and started back with Marcellus Pope to look after the injured. They reached Taylor's Draw after several hours, where they found Matt Warner bathing the wounds of the injured. Wall had brought several bottles of whiskey along to revive their spirits.

Warner and Wall then loaded their victims into the wagon, which had been half filled with hay, and drove carefully back to Vernal. Swift stayed at the camp. Coleman came back to town next day. Dick Staunton died that night, followed in the morning by David Milton. Ike Staunton, who fought the duel with Warner, was not expected to live but did recover eventually after losing his leg.

Citizens of Vernal were incensed at the killings, as both dead men were well known. There was talk of lynching, so Warner, Wall, and Coleman insisted on being locked up for their own safety. In a day or two Sheriff John Pope came down from Gosling Mountain and took charge of affairs. By that time a vigilance committee had been formed. The evening after Pope's arrival a mob advanced on the log jail, demanding the prisoners. Milton had done considerable talking before he died and the mob was more anxious to get their hands on Coleman than on the actual killers.

Heavy logs had been hauled some time before for an addition to the jail. Pope arranged them into a breastwork, defended by himself, his four brothers, and his eighty-year-old father. There was considerable parleying between the defenders and the mob, but Pope had the last word.

"You didn't want these men bad enough to go after them while they were armed. Now that they're harmless you are mighty brave. You had your chance; now they're in my custody and I'm not going to turn them over to anyone but the court."

There was no further trouble from the vigilance committee.

Three weeks after the tragedy of Dry Fork, Butch Cassidy rode into Vernal, tied his horse outside the jail, and asked if he might see Matt Warner.

"Sure," replied Sheriff Pope, "but you'll have to take off your decorations."

"O. K., sheriff," smilingly replied Cassidy as he hung his belt on the saddle. "I forgot. It's been a long time since I went anywhere without 'em." While Pope listened, Cassidy visited with Matt.

"I'll send Douglas Preston over from Rock Springs right away," Cassidy promised. "He's the best lawyer in Wyoming; if he can't get you off nobody can. How are you fixed for money?"

"Busted as usual," replied Matt. "Could you raise enough to get me out of this scrape?"

"Haven't got a dime right now," admitted Cassidy; "it's only a short time since I got out of the pen, you know. But I can damn soon get some, so don't worry. I'll be back in a few days with my pockets full of gold."

He strapped on his guns, vaulted into the saddle and loped back to Brown's Hole. Gathering the Wild Bunch he explained that as a former member of the gang Matt rated assistance; it was up to them to see that he got it while it would do some good.

The quickest way to raise funds was to rob a bank. During the next few weeks Cassidy investigated a number of possibilities. He had given his word not to pull any rough stuff in Wyoming and intended to keep that promise—at least for a while. He did not want to run the risk of pulling another job in Colorado. Utah was his native state and he disliked taking chances of being recognized. That left Idaho as the next best bet. The victim finally selected was the bank at Montpelier. It was well isolated, carried considerable cash, and the surrounding country made a getaway easy.

From Brown's Hole, Butch Cassidy, Elza Lay, and Bob Meeks rode to Cokeville, Wyoming, just over the line from Idaho and directly east of Bear Lake on the old Oregon Trail. As a blind they all went to work on a ranch eight miles north of Cokeville, operated by Mrs. P. Emelle, wife of a Montpelier jeweler. Mrs. Emelle says they were the best workers she ever had, but always went heavily armed and made several mysterious trips during their stay at the ranch. Just before the holdup they drew their pay and left. Next day they were seen in town by Mr. Emelle, who wondered why they had quit their jobs.

On August 13, 1896, the three outlaws tied their horses to a hitch rack in front of a saloon near the Montpelier bank and went in for a drink. They attracted no unusual attention, as there were always riders entering or leaving town. Cassidy strolled past the bank, noted the position of the cashiers, laid his plans, and instructed his two partners.

Just before closing time Cashier Gray came out of the bank and stopped on the sidewalk to talk to an acquaintance. There was no time to lose, so Cassidy and Lay, with guns concealed under their coats, walked up to the two men, ordered them to keep quiet, and led them back into the building.

A. N. Mackintosh, paying teller, Cashier Gray, and a girl stenographer were then lined up with their faces to the wall and kept in that position by Lay, while Cassidy scooped all the cash in sight into a gunny sack. From his position near a side window Mackintosh observed a man across the street holding three horses. He seemed nervous. Mackintosh suspected him to be one of the robbers and carefully noted his appearance. With $6,165 in greenbacks and $1,000 in gold and silver, the three robbers rode away swiftly.

As soon as they were out of sight the cry of "Robbers!" was raised. There were plenty of horses tied along the street and plenty of cowboys to ride them, but considerable time elapsed before a posse took up the pursuit. A relay of fresh horses had been posted a few miles from town and the robbers were soon far in the lead. Sheriff Davis and Mike Malone followed the trail several days. They sent back word on the sixteenth that the bandits were only twelve hours ahead, sleeping days and traveling nights. It was a wide-open country and a plain trail, they said. After that no further report was received from the sheriff. He returned some days later without any prisoners. Cassidy, Lay, and Meeks were safe in Brown's Hole.

In the meantime Warner, Wall, and Coleman had a preliminary trial before Judge Hart in Vernal. They were represented by D. N. Straup, of the firm of Powers, Straup & Lipman, and Judge Thurman of Thurman & Wedgewood, both of whom later became justices of the supreme court of Utah. Counsel asked for a change of venue because of the threat of lynching, which was granted. Trial was slated to be held in Ogden, Utah, and the sheriff was ordered to deliver his prisoners to the Weber County jail.

Sheriff Pope had a tough assignment. To deliver his prisoners safely he had to run the gauntlet of both the vigilance committee and Warner's friends from Brown's Hole, who sent word they would take him from the sheriff somewhere along the road. To prevent such a delivery Governor Thomas told Pope to deputize a hundred men if necessary; Colonel

Randlett, commander of Fort Duchesne, also offered to furnish a company of troops.

Pope declined both offers. He had a trick up his sleeve which he thought would work. In previous years he had prospected along the entire foot of the Uintah range and crossed it in several places. He knew an old military road leading directly over the range northwest of Fort Duchesne, which had been abandoned many years. Starting with his three prisoners and five deputies in the middle of the night, he was high in the mountains on the forgotten trail before daybreak, completely outwitting Matt's friends.

For that trick, and because Pope kept him handcuffed during the entire ride, Matt took an extreme dislike to the sheriff and carried his grudge to the grave.

Heber Wright, sheriff of Weber County, relieved Pope of responsibility when the men reached the Ogden jail. Wright's brother was jailer. He remembers that Warner and Wall were model prisoners and gave no trouble whatever.

A few days after their arrival Douglas A. Preston, of Rock Springs and Evanston, came to Ogden to assist in their defense. They then had an array of the best legal talent in the intermountain country. Preston brought with him his advance fee of $3,000 and enough more to furnish Warner and Wall with whatever luxuries they desired while awaiting trial. Warner bought a complete new outfit of clothes, including the best Stetson hat obtainable in Ogden. Preston left word with the jailer to get them anything they wanted. . . . Butch Cassidy had made good his promise.

The case against the two men who had done the actual shooting looked bad. They had acted as hired killers. Preston wasn't sure he could get them off. It seemed to Cassidy the safest plan would be to go to Ogden with a few of the boys and take them from the Weber County sheriff. Following that plan, he rode down Weber Canyon and made camp in the willows along the river seven miles from town. He then sent Warner a note by Robert Swift, Coleman's partner. Chief of Police Davenport got wind of the message, searched the messenger and found the following note:

Dear Matt: The boys are here. If you say the word we'll come and take you out.

Davenport told Swift to deliver the note without letting Matt know it had been read and to bring back his reply. Under the chief's eye he did so. The answer said:

Dear Butch: Don't do it. The boys here have been mighty good to us, and I wouldn't want them to get hurt. Preston says they can't convict us. If they do, we'll be out in a couple of years. Don't take the chance. Thanks anyway.

Matt's reply satisfied the officers; it also revealed the suspected presence of Cassidy in the vicinity. One more note came from Butch. It read:

Dear Matt: If they keep you more than two years we'll come and take the place apart sure as hell. Good luck.

The trial began before Judge Rolapp on September 8, 1896, and lasted until the sixteenth. Telegrams were introduced to show that Coleman had offered the two outlaws $500 "to protect his interest" in Dry Fork. There was some conflict as to who fired the first shot. Even Ike Staunton, the survivor, couldn't be sure. He admitted shooting Matt's horse; Matt swore he didn't start shooting until after the animal fell dead. Hating Coleman, but grateful for Warner's kindly ministrations after the shooting, Staunton proved a valuable witness —for the defense. The prosecution charged him with having "diarrhea of the jawbone," but Warner said he told the exact truth, and if he, Matt, ever came into any money he would like to set Staunton up in business. Old Christian Christiansen was also a witness as to his son's character, but his testimony in broken English didn't do the defense much good.

It was proved the two killers had received a hundred dollars from Coleman. Both men had paid their bill at the saloon before leaving for Dry Fork, and Matt had given his wife twenty-one dollars, certain proof to the jury that he was suddenly flush.

The verdict was five years in the pen for Warner and Wall. Coleman was acquitted—in the opinion of this writer a rank miscarriage of justice not without precedent.

Coleman and his comely wife left immediately and were never seen in Utah again. William Wall was then twenty-nine and admitted he had met Cassidy and Warner while working as a packer in the mines at Telluride, Colorado. Matt Warner was thirty-two; his wife and daughter were then living in Salt Lake City.

Just as he was leaving the jail, on September 21, 1896, to be taken to the penitentiary, Warner slapped his new Stetson hat on jailer Wright's head.

"Keep that as a souvenir," he said. "I don't want them sons of bitches down there to get it."

The amputation of Rosa's leg had not halted her cancer. A few months after Matt's conviction she gave birth to a son, then died. Her husband attended the funeral in handcuffs. The child, a boy, lived and was given to Frank Taylor of Salina. He died before reaching maturity.

The two outlaws served three and a half years and were released on January 21, 1900.

On the second day of the trial the *Herald* in Salt Lake City printed a front-page story to the effect that Douglas A. Preston, who was known to be Cassidy's attorney, had received his fee from the proceeds of the Montpelier bank holdup. It stated that Cassidy and Lay were then camped at the mouth of Weber Canyon with the intention of rescuing their friends and had consulted Attorney Powers in Salt Lake City. This bit of news aroused the ire of Preston, who made a statement to Ogden reporters next day.

I was employed last July, before the Montpelier robbery, and was paid at that time, but not by Wall. . . . All this rot about receiving any money from the gang that robbed the Montpelier bank, after that robbery, is absolutely and unqualifiedly false. The statement that Cassidy and his gang are near Ogden or that he was engaged in the Montpelier robbery is also false. Cassidy is at this time in the town of Vernal and has been there for some time past. They say there is a reward of $2,000 for the capture of Cassidy. If any party will deposit $2,000 in any bank in Ogden or elsewhere, I will guarantee to deliver Cassidy to any part of the West within 48 hours.

Sheriff Heber Wright, of Ogden, also stated that no notes had passed between Cassidy and Warner and that Robert Swift had been in Dry Fork since the shooting.

There had always been considerable jealousy between Salt Lake and Ogden. The smaller town embraced every opportunity to put one over on the capital city. Recriminations passed between journals of the two towns for several days. The *Herald* was threatened with libel suits by all the defense attorneys—a formidable array. But it did not retract its statements and the libel suits were never brought, for the reason that the statements were true.

Jailer Wright and Chief of Police Davenport, both still living in 1935, told this writer of seeing the notes and allowing them to be passed. Sheriff Pope of Vernal remembered distinctly the promise Butch made to Warner in the Vernal jail. Preston was known to be Cassidy's attorney in Lander, and his statement exhibited intimate knowledge of the outlaw leader's movements.

To prove the case further, two salesmen, Joe Decker and W. C. A. Smoot, met Butch Cassidy and Bob Meeks in Loa, during the trial, and returned with an interview which was published in the *Salt Lake Tribune*. Cassidy and Meeks, they said, were staying at the same hotel in Loa. They asked about the progress of the trial. The salesmen had late newspapers which they showed the two outlaws in a barn that day. Cassidy read the "fake" story printed in the *Herald* and declared that it had been obtained from Mrs. Warner, whom he described as a loose woman who wished to see Matt go to the pen so she could carry on affairs with other men. He said she had written him, promising him "anything he wanted" from either herself or her sister, if he would come to see her. He believed it was a trap. He admitted writing the notes to Warner and gave Matt's reply. He said he would not attempt to take the two men by force but would rescue them "if money could do it." He and Meeks were posing as cattle buyers. They both exhibited large rolls of money and said they were buying cattle to take back to Vernal. They were in no way disguised and were stopping at hotels along the route. Cassidy was described as being 5 feet 8 inches in height, weighing exactly 155 pounds, with light-brown hair showing a "cowlick" in front. Meeks was about the same height and weight. They appeared to be about 25 years old.

Warner admitted on the stand that his mother-in-law, Mrs. Rumel, and he were not friends, and attributed the stories to her. She and Rosa's sister, Sadie, had given the newspapers similar stories once before, while Matt was in the pen at Ellensburg. Cassidy stated during the interview that Sheriff Pope of Vernal took his orders from the tough element around Vernal and let them "dictate what's what." Pope's history, however, as outlined in later pages, seems to disprove that statement, in spite of the fact that he was Matt Warner's partner in a mining prospect at the time of the killings in Dry Gulch.

After his release from the pen on January 21, 1900, Matt Warner returned to his old haunts near Lavan, Utah. As he rode into Nephi one day he was seen by Andrew Hendrickson, the boy he had nearly killed with a rock many years before. Hendrickson's father had been a member of the famous Mormon Battalion which marched from Leavenworth

to Los Angeles in 1846-1847. When he saw his old enemy—
Matt Warner the outlaw—riding up the street, he rushed into
the house, grabbed the old Battalion rifle, rested the muzzle on
a fence post, took careful aim, and pulled the trigger. The
bullet cut part of the brim from Matt's hat.

Warner continued on into town, swore out a warrant, and
had Hendrickson arrested. At the trial Hendrickson was
prosecuted by W. C. A. Bryan (living in 1948, in Nephi),
and escaped being sent to the pen only because the defense
insisted he was crazy. He was sent to the asylum in Provo
for two years. A few years later, during a Pioneer Day parade
in Nephi, the victim of Matt's rock saw one of the marchers
wearing his father's old uniform. Again he grabbed the old
muzzle loader. That time he blew the man's head off and was
again sent to the asylum, where he died.

The green stain on the rocks of Dry Fork Canyon was later
found to contain no copper whatever, and the claim on which
the two men had been killed was abandoned. The spot is still
known locally as the "scrapping grounds." The tree behind
which Warner stood was cut down and the section containing
the hole bored by Ike Staunton's rifle removed as a souvenir.
The balance of the tree trunk lies there yet, badly decayed.

William Wall afterward ran a hotel in Rock River, Wyoming, and died in San Diego in 1932.

Meeker
Bank Robbery

AFTER the Montpelier rob-
bery, Cassidy returned to Brown's Hole, where he told and
retold the story of that raid. It had been an easy job, with
almost no danger attached. The three robbers had made a
clean getaway and were in no danger of being followed to
their hideout. Their identity was still a mystery. Officers laid
the job on Tom McCarty, who was then in Robbers' Roost.

Cassidy's story of his exploit, told with great gusto around
campfires and firesides in the Hole, aroused the imaginations
of some of the younger boys to such a pitch that they finally
decided to organize a gang of their own, a "Junior Wild
Bunch." Using Cassidy's methods, they could see no reason
why they should not be equally successful. After proving
their mettle they would be eligible to join the older organization. Every young fellow in Brown's Hole yearned to become
a member of the Wild Bunch.

The Junior Wild Bunch, organized in the fall of 1896,
consisted of George Harris, George Bain, Joe Rolls, and
young Shirley, all between eighteen and twenty years old.

George Bain, nineteen years old, seems to have been the leader, by virtue of the fact he was a nephew of Joe Tolliver, toughest man in the Hole. His stepfather's name was Law, and he was sometimes known as George Law. Joe Rolls already had a reputation as the poorest horse thief in Brown's Hole. According to Sheriff Pope, he used to wear out his stolen animals moving them from one place to another.

The first victim selected by the Junior Wild Bunch was the Bank of Meeker, in Colorado. Meeker was seventy-five miles directly east of the Hole, on the White River, ninety miles from Rifle, nearest telegraph office. The boys had been there many times and knew the country. It looked like an easy, safe job.

The quartet arrived in the vicinity of Meeker on the morning of October 13, 1896. Imitating Cassidy, they placed a relay of fresh horses in a hidden spot a few miles from town, leaving Joe Rolls in charge. The other three rode in to get the cash.

The Bank of Meeker was a small institution operated in connection with a general store. A door connected the bank with the store. A cashier was the only bank employee, but the teller's window was in full view of all the clerks in the mercantile department.

Two of the boys entered the store and held up the clerks, while a third went to the teller's window and ordered the cashier to "stick 'em up!" To emphasize the order and to show the cashier what a really bad man he was, the boy fired his six-shooter. The cashier, somewhat dazed by this unusual procedure, was slow in getting his hands up, so the robber fired again. He then grabbed all money in sight, dumped it in a gunny sack, and called to his friends. The three rounded up the employees of the institution and marched them out the front door into the street, while they made their own exit from the back door.

The two shots in the bank had almost instantly attracted

the attention of the whole town. When the boys emerged from the back door with their loot, the building was completely surrounded by citizens armed with six-shooters, shotguns, and rifles. They were much more courageous and determined than most volunteer posses and immediately opened fire as the robbers came out.

Finding themselves hemmed in on all sides, the boys put up a desperate battle lasting several minutes. About a hundred shots were fired. W. H. Clark, Victor Dickerman, C. A. Booth, and W. P. Herrick were struck by bullets, but none seriously injured. Odds were against the robbers, however. All three were shot down; Shirley and Bain were killed instantly, but Harris lived two hours.

When his friends failed to return on schedule, Joe Rolls got panicky, jumped his horse and started for Brown's Hole, leaving the three relay horses tied to a fallen tree. When found, a week later, they were almost dead from thirst and had eaten the bark off the dead tree as far as they could reach.

Rolls returned to the Hole, where he broke the bad news to relatives of the would-be robbers. The bodies were left on exhibition in Meeker for a day or two and were photographed. One of those photographs still hangs in the lobby of a hotel there, a warning to any other outlaws who might pass that way.

That was the end of the Junior Wild Bunch. They had plenty of reckless nerve, as evidenced by their fight against overwhelming odds; but they lacked a leader with brains who could keep cool in an emergency. By unnecessarily firing his guns in the bank, one of the robbers had given the signal for formation of a citizen's posse which cut off all avenues of escape. Except for that act of nervousness or foolish bravado they might have succeeded and earned their right to join Cassidy's Wild Bunch.

After Joe Rolls returned with news of the disaster, the Wild Bunch sent word to Craig that they were coming to

"smoke up" the town in revenge for the deaths of the three
boys. Citizens of both Meeker and Craig loaded their rifles,
set them in handy corners and sent word they were ready
to receive all comers; but the raid never materialized. The
citizens of western Colorado were too quick on the trigger.

Hole-in-the-Wall

WHILE General Custer's command was being wiped out on the Little Big Horn in 1876, General Crook was camped on Little Goose Creek in the Big Horn Mountains. Crook had been chasing Sioux Indians all over Wyoming, guided by Frank Grouard, his chief scout. Grouard, whose father was a Mormon missionary and whose mother was a South Sea Island native convert, had been captured by the Sioux when a boy. On account of his dark skin his captors believed he was part Indian and he was adopted by Sitting Bull. He had hunted over every inch of the Powder River country and often camped in the hideout now known as Hole-in-the-Wall.

The modern highway running north from Casper to Sheridan crosses the Powder River at the little town of Kaycee, named after the old K-C ranch, forty-six miles south of Buffalo. Hole-in-the-Wall is thirty miles west of Kaycee. To reach the old hideout one follows the Powder River about twenty miles, passing through a canyon of black rock. The road then leaves the river through a side canyon, where the

107

formation changes suddenly to a brilliant red sandstone. Turning a bend at the abandoned settlement of Barnum, it passes
through a narrow opening cut through the Red Wall by
erosion. This Hole-in-the-Wall is just wide enough to allow
passage of a wagon or car and could easily have been defended
by two riflemen against a small army. But no such occasion
ever occurred, all fiction writers to the contrary. The reputation of the outlaws was a better defense than the Red Wall,
and for many years no law officer ever dared penetrate their
hideout.

The place selected by the outlaws as headquarters was
located in a small valley several miles south of the entrance
at Barnum. Near this Outlaw Ranch, as the location is still
known, was a narrow V-shaped opening in the wall, just
wide enough to admit a horse and rider. It may be that this
was the original Hole-in-the-Wall, but the one near Barnum
is more spectacular and has become famous in fiction. The
Red Wall was in fact penetrated in several places by creeks
tributary to Buffalo Creek, plus the wide gap where Buffalo
Creek cut through to join the Powder River. Behind the Red
Wall, which extended many miles north and south, was a
large, beautiful, grassy valley furnishing marvelous grazing to
great herds of cattle, and a perfect wintering ground. While
the west side of this valley was protected after a fashion by
the Red Wall, the east and south sides and part of the north
consisted of open rolling hills extending for many miles. The
outlaws had a trail running through this open country to
Casper, and it was well known to all law officers, who were
careful not to use it.

Outlaw headquarters consisted of half a dozen one-room
log cabins located reasonably close together. They called this
Hole-in-the-Wall ranch, but it is better known as the Outlaw
Ranch. Nothing remains today to indicate the location of this
famous hideout except the foundation of one cabin hidden in
the sagebrush.

After the Sioux Indians had been quieted, white settlers began drifting into the Big Horn country, one of the finest cattle ranges outdoors. Roving bands of renegade Indians occasionally attacked the ranches, stole a few horses, and rode on. The danger most feared by settlers was from white outlaws who had discovered Hole-in-the-Wall and made it their headquarters.

Deadwood, South Dakota, directly to the east, was on the boom during the late '70s, a magnet attracting the country's worst characters. When things got too hot in Deadwood, the bandits rode west toward the Big Horns and camped along the Powder River, a fine game country. When they craved a change from a meat diet they raided scattered ranches for flour, coffee, and sugar.

The James brothers, Jesse and Frank, were among the first to use Hole-in-the-Wall as a hideout. They were seen there as early as 1877, after leaving Deadwood on the lope. Others of the same stamp, but less well known, who made their headquarters behind the Red Wall were Big Nose George, Persimmon Bill, Teton Jackson, Dutch Henry, Black Hank, Bill Zimmerman, Tom Reese, Jerry Overholt, Jack Campbell, Herman Leslie, Bill Evans, Cully, Phoenix, Odell, Madison, and McGloskey. Some were obscure, while others left a wide reputation.

One of these characters, Big Nose George, has become somewhat of a legend in Wyoming. He had made a business of robbing travelers on the old Oregon Trail, operating along the Sweetwater River. When stagecoaches ceased their runs he turned to the more profitable work of robbing trains, gaining a reputation for cold-blooded brutality. Eugene McAuliffe, in *Early Coal Mining in the West*, gives an authentic account of his spectacular end.

Big Nose George and a partner had robbed a train in Wyoming, late in 1878. Two deputy sheriffs, W. Vincent and Tom Widdowfield, followed their trail and were examining a recently abandoned campfire on Rattlesnake Creek, near Elk Mountain, when both were shot from ambush. Some time later the partner was captured and was put on a train for Rawlins by Sheriff James Rankin. When it stopped at the town of Carbon, citizens took the prisoner and quickly hanged him from a telegraph pole. He was buried next day, January 24, 1879.

Big Nose George was not captured until July, 1880, in eastern Montana. He was tried in Rawlins and sentenced to be hanged on April 3, 1882. A week before that date he had overpowered Sheriff Rankin and tried to break jail. Mrs. Rankin, hearing a commotion, quickly locked the outside door and fired a revolver in the air. A crowd gathered almost immediately. Taking Big Nose out to the street, they forced him to climb a ladder set against a tall lamppost, put a rope around his neck, and told him to jump. He did, but the rope broke. The citizens shot him as he lay on the sidewalk.

A young doctor in Rawlins, J. E. Osborne, recently arrived from the East, later exhumed the body of Big Nose "for medical purposes." First he made a cast of the face, then skinned the body and had a cowboy vest and pair of moccasins made from the tough outlaw's hide. The vest has disappeared, but the cast and moccasins still are on display in the Rawlins National Bank. The doctor became governor of Wyoming in 1893 and later assistant secretary of state under President Wilson in 1913. He died in 1943 at the age of eighty-nine.

Persimmon Bill was a wild character from Tennessee who operated around Sidney, Nebraska, and later at Rock Springs. His activities have been recorded by Robert B. David in *Malcolm Campbell, Sheriff*. Teton Jackson later organized the Jackson Hole gang of horse thieves and held that stronghold against all comers for many years. His history is related in the same volume, and the extermination of the gang is described in Stone's *Uinta County, Its Place in History*. Jackson was jealous of his little kingdom and did not welcome outlaws from other sections. Hole-in-the-Wall has frequently been confused with Jackson's Hole by fiction writers and armchair historians, although there was little communication between the two places.

Dutch Henry, who hailed originally from Dodge City, later became an associate of Ben Tasker, of Centerville, Utah, most successful early-day outlaw of southern Utah. Tasker eventually murdered his partner in the vicinity of Desert Springs, on the Old Spanish Trail to California, and burned the body. One of a pair of derringers always carried by Dutch Henry was found in the ashes and came into the possession of the late Don Maguire, of Ogden, Utah. According to former Sheriff George Searle of Vernal, William Wall, who was with Matt Warner at the fight on Dry Fork, was with Tasker on another occasion when he made a Frenchman dig his own grave and shot him into it.

Other early denizens of Hole-in-the-Wall mentioned by Frank Grouard, the scout, passed on their devious ways without leaving much in the way of recorded history. Grouard was engaged several years in running them out of the country, but it was too big a job for any one man; as fast as they were driven out others took their places. Hole-in-the-Wall soon became known as the best and safest hideout in Wyoming and was used by a larger number of rustlers and outlaws than any other station on the Outlaw Trail, with the exception of Brown's Hole. The name "Hole-in-the-Wall" first appeared in print after robbery of the bank at Belle Fourche, South Dakota. It appealed to writers of fiction and has since been used as the locale for thousands of imaginary yarns, while Brown's Hole, earliest and most important of western outlaw headquarters, remained unknown.

Hole-in-the-Wall was only one hard day's ride from Casper and the Overland Trail, and it soon became headquarters for an organized gang of horse thieves operating from Minnesota to Oregon. Stolen horses, passed from one station to another, were wintered behind the Red Wall and sold in the spring. Like outlaws at all other stations on the Outlaw Trail, the earliest comers were horse thieves.

The Powder River country east of the Hole was such a fine cattle range that it was rapidly settled by stockmen, who brought in immense herds of Texas cattle. Beef prices were good and cattle rustling soon became the principal business of the Hole-in-the-Wall gang. They stole cattle in wholesale lots, wintered them behind the Red Wall, and sold them in the spring at some convenient railroad point, usually Casper. In those days possession indicated ownership and no questions were asked.

By 1885, hundreds of thousands of Texas cattle had been brought in over the old Cherokee Trail to stock the vast Wyoming ranges. The business was controlled by a handful of cattlemen, employing hundreds of cowboys. As herds scattered to every corner of the plains and mountains, it became increasingly difficult to gather all the calves each year. In course of time thousands of unbranded cattle, mavericks, were feeding on the open range. Little attention was given them in the beginning, but as they increased in numbers stockmen began gathering them in, paying the cowboy five dollars a head.

Some cowhands concluded they might as well gather mavericks for themselves instead of the boss. They began on a small scale, working on their own time during the off season, while holding their regular jobs. When they had accumulated fair-sized herds, they started small ranches of their own, working for the big cowmen off and on to earn a little cash. Thus there came to be two classes of cattle rustlers—those who "worked and rustled on the side" and those who "rustled and worked on the side"—a distinction without a difference.

The big cattle barons could not see any logic in that procedure. They had grabbed the entire range, parceling it out among themselves, but were intolerant of anyone else who tried to do the same thing. In 1884 they signed a petition, circulated by Horace Plunkett, to boycott any cowboy found collecting mavericks on his own account. As a result, discharged cowboys spent their entire time gathering unbranded cattle, which proved more profitable than working for wages. It was an easy step from gathering mavericks to gathering branded stock. Old brands were worked over, and rustlers' herds increased by leaps and bounds.

Then came the disastrous winter of 1886-1887, when an unusual snowfall and low temperatures prevented cattle from obtaining the sun-cured natural hay on the range. When spring came, the big cattle barons found themselves practically wiped out, able to save only about ten per cent of their herds. Naturally, they counted carefully every surviving animal, and any new losses were quickly noted. Hundreds of cowboys, thrown out of work, began rustling to keep from starving, more than doubling the previous number of thieves.

Within a year or two, rustlers had become so numerous that they controlled northern Wyoming, including the counties of Johnson, Natrona, and Converse, with headquarters at Hole-in-the-Wall. They fell into a loose organization known as the "Red Sash Gang," under the leadership of Nathan Champion, a big, fearless Texan. Champion's operating headquarters was at the K-C ranch, on the Powder River, thirty miles east of the Hole and seventy miles south of Buffalo.

By 1892 all three counties were under the absolute control of the Champion gang, and herds of the big cattlemen steadily diminished. The sheriff of Johnson County, W. G. (Red) Angus, was a member of the gang, as well as three of the county commissioners. Charles H. Burritt, attorney for the rustlers, was mayor of Buffalo. They could obtain unlimited credit from Robert Foote, the town's leading merchant. Of 180 arrests made in Johnson County for rustling, there had been but one conviction.

In those days the Board of Livestock Commissioners of Wyoming fixed the dates of various roundups. To get the jump on legitimate owners, rustlers of Johnson County in the spring of 1892 organized an "association" of their own, fixing the date for their roundup a month earlier than usual, gathering in all unbranded calves regardless of ownership.

Faced with such conditions and with no redress in court, big cattlemen of the three counties met to devise some method of combating rustlers. All other remedies having failed, it was decided to invade Hole-in-the-Wall and Johnson County with a small picked army of fighters, who would eliminate, one by one, the seventy men on their black list and put fear into the hearts of all others. Organizers of this movement consisted of twenty-five prominent stockmen, who put up $1,000 each to finance the invasion. Not wishing to subject their own cowboys to possible reprisals, they hired twenty-five gunmen from the Rio Grande to assist in the extermination.

This expedition of fifty-five men, led by Major Frank E. Walcott, a Kentuckian, set out from Denver, April 5, 1892, on a special train loaded with equipment, horses, provisions, ammunition, and three supply wagons. It was planned to make a swift, secret movement northward from Casper, surprising the rustlers in their hideout and checking them off as they swept through the country.

But the Invasion, as this expedition is known, was ill-fated from the first. Starting too early in the season, these invaders were overtaken by April blizzards which threw them off schedule and caused the Texans great suffering. Before they reached their objective the secret leaked out and all of Johnson County turned out to meet them, armed for war. They reached the K-C ranch, where they checked off Nate Champion and his partner, Nick Ray, after a spectacular twenty-four-hour battle, but that was the extent of their offensive. Riding northward toward Buffalo, they were compelled to fort up at the T-A ranch, where they were besieged by four hundred rustlers recruited by the sheriff of Johnson County.

The invaders fought bravely during the four-day battle

that followed. At the end of that time all their supplies and ammunition were exhausted. Just as they were about to make a wild dash for freedom, expecting to die fighting, they were rescued and arrested by a company of United States cavalry from Fort McKinney, near Buffalo. Under military guard the invaders were transferred to Cheyenne, where, after lengthy legal proceedings, the charge of insurrection and murder under which they had been held was dismissed. They were defended by Willis Vandevanter, later U. S. Supreme Court justice.

This Invasion, most spectacular episode in the history of Wyoming since the Custer affair, resulted in complete failure. The rustlers had tried their strength and proved themselves masters of the situation in northern Wyoming. The vigilante invaders had eliminated only two men from their list of seventy and had been placed under arrest themselves. Leaders of the "defenders" were Sheriff Angus, Arapaho Brown, an old Indian fighter, and the Reverend Bader, a publicity-loving Methodist preacher. Through crafty propaganda, public sentiment had been molded in favor of the cattle thieves, who posed as small cattlemen persecuted by big cattle barons. When the facts became better known, sentiment turned the other way, and for their own good the rustlers did not reelect Sheriff Angus. His successor, Al Sproul, did his best to enforce the law, but his efforts were futile, since no convictions could be had in Johnson County.

As an illustration of the attitude of Johnson County people, here is an interesting quotation from Matt Warner, who made a raid with Butch Cassidy near Belle Fourche at this time:

This move to exterminate cattle rustlers and put an end to cattle rustling seemed to us like the final blow to the Old West. We listened to Butch Cassidy's eloquent call to action, grabbed our Winchesters, and rode out to defend and preserve the Old West. Our peculiar way of defending the Old West was to get a good tough outfit of horses together and plenty of artillery, make a fast dash up into the Belle Fourche or Johnson County country, take a big herd of cattle right from under the noses of the cattle kings, and show 'em they couldn't get away with their game of murdering and exterminating rustlers. . . . "If we let 'em get away with what they've started," said Butch, "this here won't be a free country any longer."

After the death of Nate Champion, leadership of the Hole-in-the-Wall gang fell to George Curry, a rancher formerly from Chadron, Nebraska, who had taken up rustling as a profession. Curry's principal associates were the Logan brothers.

Henry, Johnny, Lonny, and Harvey Logan were born in Rowan County, Kentucky, but raised by an aunt, Mrs. Lee, in Dobson, Missouri. From one grandmother, a Cherokee squaw, they had inherited their dark complexions and black hair. Henry, the oldest, was never an outlaw, so far as is known, and died a natural death at Steamboat Springs, Nevada. Johnny, Lonny, and Harvey, with their cousin, Bob Lee, had drifted to Johnson County, Wyoming, some time previous to the Invasion. They joined Curry even before the death of Nate Champion and were known as the Roberts brothers. A year or two before the Invasion they moved a large herd of stock to Montana and went into business as honest ranchers, five miles from the little mining town of Landusky in the Little Rockies. In Montana they were known as the Curry brothers. Their brand was 4 T.

After the Invasion a large number of rustlers from Hole-in-the-Wall went to Montana to await developments. Between native cowboys and Wyoming bad men, Landusky was as wild a spot as could have been found anywhere in Montana in 1894. It was solemnly asserted a man could catch a pint of bullets by swinging a tin cup around his head in the middle of Main street on any Saturday night.

Pike Landusky, founder of the little village, was a fighting Missourian who had licked every man in that section of the West. It was said he had killed several Indians and one or two

white men with his bare fists. With a face scarred by many
battles, he was as ugly as he was hard. After the town was
located he married a widow with four grown daughters.

On his arrival in Landusky, Lonny Logan—known as
Lonny Curry—began paying attention to Elfie, one of Landusky's stepdaughters. In course of time and without benefit
of clergy, Elfie became the mother of a son whom she named
Lonny Curry Junior. Pike Landusky objected to this loose
state of affairs, and because of his objection an increasing enmity grew up between Landusky and the Logan (Curry)
brothers. This slumbering feud was brought to a head when
Lonny and Harvey were arrested for cattle stealing. While
awaiting trial they were left in the charge of Landusky, who
took the opportunity to heap them with abuse. He also testified
against them at the trial, but in spite of the evidence they were
released.

Christmas of 1894 saw the new mining camp booming. Full
of civic pride, residents planned a monster celebration. Personal animosities were temporarily forgotten; Johnny Logan
donated the use of his big new barn, and Lonny fiddled for
the dance. There was plenty of liquor for everyone—too
much for some. Several men continued the celebration for a
day or two, among them Pike Landusky and the Logan
brothers. They were still drunk on December 27 when trouble
started.

"Jew Jake," a one-legged man from Great Falls, had just
opened a combination clothing store and saloon. On that
afternoon, as Pike Landusky was standing at the bar in the
front part of the building, Lonny and Harvey Logan and Jim
Thornhill entered. As they passed the bar, Harvey Logan
struck Landusky on the jaw, knocking him to the floor.
Lonny and Thornhill then drew their guns to prevent interference while Harvey proceeded to whip the champion of
Montana. Landusky had a gun, but disdained to use it. However, besides being fifty years old, he was handicapped by a

heavy overcoat, and the younger man, although lighter in weight, had all the advantage from the start. In a few minutes he had beaten Landusky into an unrecognizable hulk and had him calling for help. Still Logan continued to hammer his face. Finally, with a last spurt of energy the older man raised himself and reached in the pocket of his overcoat for his gun. In an instant he had Harvey covered. He pulled the trigger but the gun wouldn't work; it was a new type, and he was unfamiliar with its safety mechanism. When Harvey saw that the gun was useless, he pulled his own six-shooter and shot Pike Landusky dead.

Echoes of that shot were still reverberating when Jew Jake, one-legged proprietor of the place, beating all his two-legged customers, came out the back door with his hands in the air and fell flat on his face. John B. Ritch, who told the story of this fight in the *Great Falls Tribune* of January 20, 1935, was an eyewitness of Jake's hurried exit, and thought the Jew was the one who had been shot.

Lonny and Harvey, with their partisan, Jim Thornhill, immediately left town in a buckboard driven by Johnny Logan. In spite of his reputation as a fighter, Pike Landusky had many friends. Harvey Logan had started the fight and would have small chance in court. So, to avoid further trouble, the three Logan brothers hit the trail back to Hole-in-the-Wall.

George Curry used his ranch in Johnson County as a blind for rustling activities. Lonny Logan also started a ranch in the near vicinity. With Curry as leader, the Logans—using the alias of Roberts—began again where they had left off. Besides rustling cattle, they began a series of holdups, robbing stages, sheep camps, post offices, and stores.

On one of their raids the Logan brothers returned to Montana to get revenge on W. H. (Jim) Winters, the man who had them arrested in Landusky. On January 16, 1896, they approached the Winters ranch with the intention of killing their old enemy. Winters, however, had been warned and was ready for them. When they got within close range he let fly with a shotgun loaded with scrap iron. Johnny Logan fell dead. The other two galloped back to Hole-in-the-Wall.

In 1897 Sheriff Al Sproul appointed William Deane as deputy. Deane, according to Shorty Wheelwright, "had always wanted to be an officer," and decided to make a reputation for himself by arresting, single-handed, the entire Curry gang at the K-C ranch, Nate Champion's old headquarters on the Powder River.

It was April 13, 1897, when Deane rode up to the ranch. From what little is known of the circumstances, it appears he saw but one man when he attempted the arrest. At his shout "Hands up!" three others jumped him. Seeing he was trapped, he turned his horse to escape, but was brought down by the fire from four guns. The killers then roped his body and dragged it through the sagebrush until it was unrecognizable. No attempt was ever made to arrest the killers, although it was well known that Flat Nose George Curry and the Logan brothers had done the job.

Like most small towns, Buffalo had two newspapers. The *Voice* had been started to compete with the older, more conservative *Bulletin*. Its editor apparently tried to curry favor with the outlaws, knowing they were in control of Buffalo. After the killing of Deane he commented:

There is neither sense nor justice in waking the slumbering feud of '92, in discussing the violent death of William Deane. The Invasion, its causes and results have reduced Johnson county from a flourishing community to one where the great majority of the inhabitants are barely making a living. Its memories do more than any other thing to retard the lift into greater prosperity, the impulse upward which the natural advantages of the country and the character of the large majority of its citizens would seem to assure.

The Latrona *Tribune* also made a brief note:

The K-C ranch in Johnson county is becoming famous. During the Invasion of 1892 two men—Nick Ray and Nate Champion—lost their lives at this ranch and Jack Flagg ran the gauntlet and saved his scalp by a hair's breadth at the same time. The last act in this interesting drama was enacted on the 13th inst., when Deputy Sheriff William Deane of Buffalo, was shot near the same spot. At last accounts the murderers had not been apprehended.

A week after the Logan brothers killed Deane, Butch Cassidy held up the paymaster at Castle Gate and escaped with $8,800. The story of that exploit, a spectacular piece of banditry, was played up in all newspapers, and appealed to Curry and the Logan boys as a masterful bit of work. If a Mormon cowboy could make such a reputation for himself, there was no reason why they could not do likewise. Accordingly, they began making plans for a bank robbery—and chose for their first victim the bank at Belle Fourche, South Dakota, some distance east of Hole-in-the-Wall. A dispatch from Deadwood, dated June 28, 1897, describes the action:

This morning shortly after 9 o'clock, six men rode into the town of Belle Fourche on horseback. They rode up to the side entrance of the Butte County bank, dismounted and entered the bank. The officers of the bank and customers were covered with revolvers and ordered "hands up." At first Arthur Marble, assistant cashier, snapped his revolver in the face of one of the robbers. The weapon failed to explode and was thrown aside, and Mr. Marble obeyed the order of "hands up." The gang then cleaned out the money in sight.

One robber rushed out of the bank by the front door and the balance by the side, with revolvers in each hand, and began a fusillade in all directions, and coolly tightened the cinches on his saddle and mounted and rode off.

One robber failed to mount. His horse shied and he was not able to catch up with the others, and his horse followed. He made frantic efforts to secure a mount, but failed, and in the excitement he rushed around the crowd and tried to cut a mule out of harness. Just then he was recognized as one of the robbers by Rev. E. E. Clough, who was in the bank during the holdup. He was then captured. He gave his name as Tom O'Day. He had in his possession $392.

The other robbers started off across the prairie and by that time all the people of the town who had a gun took after them and every horse in town was put into service and the chase commenced. At 12:30 o'clock word came to town that all five were corraled at the Clay ranch, about 12 miles from town. Another large party, fully armed, immediately left in wagons. Over a hundred shots were fired and no one was hit, although Mr. Day, a hardware merchant, caught a stray bullet which cut off part of his ear. Mr. Miller, who was in front of the pursuers, had his horse killed by the people who were in the rear.

Deputy Sheriff Dan Arnold brought his prisoner to Deadwood for safe keeping, as the Butte jail burned last week.

O'Day had the appearance of a laboring man and was a stranger in this section. Mr. Marble, the banker, says the entire gang were amateurs at the business. The loss of the bank, which is owned jointly by Clay, Robinson & Co., commission dealers, is not stated, but was the entire amount on the counter for the day's business.

Many years later Mr. Marble said all that the robbers took was $72.00 which had just been deposited by a customer.

Tom O'Day, the robber whose horse ran away and left him, was an old-timer behind the Red Wall, well but not favorably known to cattlemen. In April, 1897, he had held up Bader's ranch and moved northwest to the Lost Cabin country, seventy-nine miles from the Hole, a hideout used occasionally by outlaws who needed a rest cure. The cabin at Bader's had been occupied at the time by several men, among them ex-Marshal Bell, of Casper, who attempted to dive through a small window but forgot that age had widened his figure beyond the capacity of the opening.

Sheriff Sproul of Johnson County visited O'Day in his cell at Deadwood, after the Belle Fourche robbery. On his return he announced that the story of Cashier Arthur Marble snapping a gun in the faces of the robbers was highly exaggerated; that no shots had been fired in the bank, and that if the cashier had been a taller man his hands would have been still higher in the air.

The bank immediately wired a description of the robbers to sheriffs in surrounding counties, stating they were members of the Curry gang and were probably heading back toward Hole-in-the-Wall. They offered a reward of $100 each, later increasing it to $2,500 for the entire gang.

There are two accounts of how the gang was captured, but the one which seems most reliable is from the *Times* of Billings, Montana. Since there had been so little profit in the Belle Fourche holdup, the robbers decided to rob a bank in Red Lodge. But they were recognized in that vicinity and made tracks for the Yellowstone River. A posse, led by stock detective W. D. Smith of Miles City, followed and caught up with the outlaws twenty miles from Lavina, in Fergus County.

When Walter Putney (who still lived at Pinedale, Wyoming, in 1948) was discovered on a ridge, the posse closed in and caught Harvey Logan unsaddling his horse. Logan ducked behind the horse, resting a rifle over his saddle, but a bullet from Deputy Dunn caught him in the wrist. He then mounted and started to ride away, but another bullet killed his horse. When it fell he began running.

In the meantime other members of the posse had captured the rest of the gang, including Flat Nose George. Then they all followed Logan, who was hiding behind a sand dune. Finding himself outnumbered, he finally came out with his hands up. The gang members were all lodged in the Deadwood jail, and President Marble of the Belle Fourche bank paid the promised reward.

In the meantime, a group of cattlemen and cowboys determined to go into Hole-in-the-Wall to round up cattle belonging to them. This expedition was headed by Joe LaFors, stock inspector, and Bob Devine, foreman of the C-Y ranch (owned by J. M. Carey, later United States senator from Wyoming and father of the Carey Act). Representatives of the Keystone and Pugsley outfits were also present, making a force of about twenty men. To notify the rustlers of what was about to take place—a very unusual procedure—Devine published a letter in the Casper *Tribune*, dated July 19, in which he stated that he was entering Hole-in-the-Wall as a working man in charge of a roundup and was not looking for a fight, although if the outlaws wanted a fight they would be accommodated. To Devine's warning, the outlaws replied as follows, according to A. J. Mokler:

Bob Devine you think you have played hell you have just begun you will get your dose there is men enuff up here yet to kill you. we are going to get you or lose 12 more men you must stay out of this country if you want to live we are not going to take any chances any more but will get you any way we can we want one hair apiece out of that damned old chin of yours you have give us the worst of it all the way through and you must stay out or die. you had better keep your damned outfit out if you want to keep them. don't stick that damned old gray head of yours in this country again if you don't want it shot off we are the 12 men appointed a purpose to get you if you don't stay out of here. Revenge Gang.

In answer to this threat Devine and his men rode directly to Hole-in-the-Wall ranch, rustler headquarters. The gang were informed of their movements and went out to meet them. The two forces met in a narrow canyon about a mile from headquarters, on July 23. According to an eyewitness, they passed each other almost at arm's length, both sides riding slowly with rifles in their hands, pointed down, waiting for someone to make the first move. Al Smith and his brother Bob, and Bob Taylor, who had left a murder charge behind him in Missouri, were the only rustlers in sight. When they had ridden some distance past the cowmen, Bob Smith got off his horse. Devine interpreted it as a hostile move and, dismounting, took a shot at Bob from behind his horse. Or it may be that Smith shot first—depending on who tells the story. At any rate a shot was fired and then the battle began. Several of the hired cowboys legged it for cover, leaving Devine, his son Lee, and LaFors to fight it out. About a hundred shots were fired. The air was thick with powder smoke and dust. When finally the atmosphere cleared, Devine and his son Lee were injured, and Bob Smith was dying. Al Smith had disappeared up the canyon. Bob Taylor stood with his hands in the air. He could have escaped, he said afterwards, but remained to assist his friend Bob Smith.

Two or three men then rode up from the direction of the outlaw ranch and offered to look after Smith. According to Taylor, Devine objected to giving him even a drink of water. He wanted to disarm Smith's friends, but they refused to give up their guns. They put Bob on a horse, but he was too far gone to ride, so they carried him back to the cabins and laid him on the grass. Shorty Wheelwright then came up and did what he could, but in a few minutes Bob was dead.

Bob Taylor was taken to Casper, then sent back to Buffalo. He was freed in a few days, as the sheriff of Johnson County said there was no use wasting money on a trial when everyone knew the rustler could not be convicted. Devine surrendered to the sheriff in Casper, but was also released without trial.

This fight and the death of Bob Smith were not reported in the Buffalo *Bulletin* for more than two weeks. Under the news item was printed this significant paragraph:

Finally, we beg it as a favor, do not believe that the *Bulletin* is "adjusted" to any situation except the obligation laid on every newspaper to tell the truth.

The editor of the *Bulletin* was in a difficult situation during those hectic days. Buffalo was the commercial center for the

Hole-in-the-Wall country. All rustlers visited it from time to time and bought supplies from its merchants. They subscribed to both its newspapers. Buffalo merchants depended on the rustler trade and would not support with their advertising any newspaper which openly opposed the outlaws. The boys from behind the Red Wall came in town frequently to celebrate and it would have been an easy matter for them to shoot up the newspaper office.

After Bob Devine's expedition returned, bringing a large number of stolen cattle, Sheriff Al Sproul of Buffalo decided to enter Hole-in-the-Wall on a similar errand. He started from Casper on July 30, accompanied by Sheriff Patten of Natrona County, a number of the same cowboys who had been with Devine, and the sheriff of Butte County, South Dakota. The latter was in hopes of meeting George Curry and the gang who had broken jail.

When this posse reached the Hole, two days later, they found notices posted along the trail warning them to stay out. Every rustler in the Hole was watching the officers, but they kept well out of rifle range. Cowboys with the expedition rounded up 550 head of stolen stock and drove them back to Casper without interference. Sheriff Sproul saw a large band of rustlers in the distance on one occasion, and at another time he surprised a second group, who disputed his path; he allowed them to pass on after "giving them a good talking to." He found that brands on many cattle in the valley had been "run over," the original mark of ownership being obliterated, and the officers made quite a strong statement to the effect that a stop should be put to such work. The Belle Fourche robbers were not seen during the expedition for two reasons: the officers did not look for them; and they had already left for Montana and the Canadian line.

Some of the Wyoming newspapers were quite caustic in their remarks after this famous roundup. The Douglas *News* said:

The attitude of a number of Johnson county people in upholding the Hole-in-the-Wall thieves is not likely to increase the number of advocates favoring a state appropriation of money to pay for the Invasion trial expenses. A county that persistently tolerates a gang of outlaws in its midst; that even refuses or neglects to protect property owners, will receive no support from the law abiding citizens of the rest of the state. If the Hole-in-the-Wall gang had been in any other county of the state the whole outfit would have been in the penitentiary years ago for the full limit of the law.

This statement gives a hint of certain conditions existing, more fully explained by another editorial in the Basin City *Herald:*

Should O'Day's companions in the Belle Fourche robbery be arrested or killed by the posses in pursuit, it will go far toward breaking up the gang which has defied the authorities for so long with such strange impunity. But the death or capture of these men will not be a full satisfaction of justice. The moneyed scoundrels who aid and abet them, who take their stolen stock, who make their stealing possible and profitable, are far more guilty than O'Day or the rest of the gang. When the dragnet of justice is hauled in, if these pseudo respectables who have played the role of fences are not caught in the meshes, it will be a gross miscarriage of justice. If it be true that the receiver is worse than the thief, then there are some respectable—in appearance at least—members of society who should sport the striped jacket before O'Day or his brethren.

This editorial was a brave effort for a struggling newspaper editor of that period and carries a far deeper significance than appears on the surface. It is a well-known but quietly whispered fact among old-timers of the Powder River country that certain supposedly respectable men financed the wholesale shipments of stolen cattle from Hole-in-the-Wall. It is equally well known that certain officers of the law were protecting and aiding the outlaws, warning them of approaching danger. One of the principal receivers of stolen cattle, it is said, became a well-known banker in Casper. Certain bankers also invented a new racket which was worked in connivance with the Hole-in-the-Wall gang. They would announce the shipment of money on a certain day, by stage. The stage would be held up. They would then collect from the stage or express company for losses of money which in reality had never been sent.

On September 9 the *Wyoming Derrick*, edited by W. H. Korns, announced that the Hole-in-the-Wall gang had ridden in a body to Cooperville on the preceding Friday to hold a shooting match with the sheep shearers and dippers assembled there. The story reads like a society item; the sheepmen won all the money, but refreshments were served and "a good time was had by all." Under such conditions there is little wonder that the sheriff of Butte County never saw anything of the Belle Fourche bank robbers at Hole-in-the-Wall ranch.

On November 4 the Belle Fourche robbers escaped from Deadwood jail after overpowering the jailer and abusing his wife. This time the officers sent for bloodhounds and started for Hole-in-the-Wall. Bill Stubbs, a typical Texas cowboy still living in the Hole in 1937, was driving a freight outfit at the time. Arriving at a camp where a number of men were gathered, he was asked if he had seen anything of Curry, the bank robber.

"Yes," drawled Stubbs, "I seen him a few miles back. He stole the bloodhounds and now he's trailin' the sheriff with 'em."

This bit of humor reached Casper, where it was printed as fact. Substance was lent to the joke because the sheriff had lost one of his hounds in the dense brush on the mountain.

After this escape the Belle Fourche robbers again headed for Montana, stealing horses and whatever supplies they needed. Winter was upon them; they wanted to stock up with sufficient supplies to last until spring. At Gillette, Wyo-

ming, they stole thirty head of horses. Another fifteen head
were taken from the Northern Cattle Company near Perry.
Deputy Sheriff Ricks, of Butte County, South Dakota, followed the trail for fifteen days and finally located the thieves
in the Bearpaw Mountains. His posse was ambushed, but after
a lively battle succeeded in capturing all the accumulated supplies. The robbers then took to the Badlands on foot.

Between then and December 1 the gang held up two post
offices. Augmented by a government detective, the posse kept
hot on the trail; the outlaws, fearing the rigors of a Montana
winter, decided to head back to Hole-in-the-Wall. On December 15 the officers again met the Curry gang, this time in their
own hideout on the bottoms of Buffalo Creek at Hole-in-the-
Wall ranch. It was cold weather and the outlaws were all
gathered at headquarters, their six cabins containing probably
thirty or forty men. The posse began firing into the cabins
from the top of surrounding bluffs, but their bullets had little
effect, as the log structures had been built for just such an
emergency. A hot fight ensued, the officers finding themselves
targets for every rifle in the outlaw camp. They were greatly
outnumbered, besides being poorly protected. When two of
their number had been seriously wounded, they called the
battle a draw and retired with their casualties to Casper. Only
one outlaw was injured, and the officers never got close
enough to identify any of the Curry gang.

No further effort was ever made to run down the Belle
Fourche bank robbers. They had proved the impregnability
of their fortress, and from that time on it was used as headquarters for many bank- and train-robbing expeditions.

Because of their success in this instance, George Curry and
the two surviving Logan brothers, Lonny and Harvey, became famous in Wyoming and were shortly admitted as bona-
fide members of the Wild Bunch under the leadership of
Butch Cassidy, who was already well known in that section
and had used the hideout before his arrest in 1894.

Shorty Wheelwright, ninety-year-old Indian scout and one of the first squatters in the Hole, took up a placer mining claim "on the mountain" above the valley soon after finishing his service with General Crook. It was this writer's good fortune to be guided to Hole-in-the-Wall ranch by Shorty himself. The old scout's memory was stored with interesting incidents of outlaw days and with names of those who had passed through the Hole from time to time on various errands, but he could remember no definite dates. Although he was never a rustler, he lived on friendly terms with the outlaws and never betrayed their confidence.

Shorty remembered George Cassidy (as Butch was there known) with affection. The leader of the Wild Bunch cultivated the old man's friendship and was generous with money when he had it. In turn, Shorty sometimes stole blankets and grub for his friend when Butch found himself hard pressed. That was previous to 1894.

Cassidy had served his apprenticeship with the McCarty gang. As leader of his own gang he had successfully robbed the Montpelier bank and had more recently become famous through his spectacular Castle Gate robbery, as will be detailed later.

Several unusual events, it will be recalled, had taken place at Hole-in-the-Wall during the summer of 1897. Deputy Sheriff William Deane had been killed by Curry and the Logan brothers at K-C ranch; Joe LaFors had made a raid into the hideout resulting in the death of Bob Smith; Sheriff Sproul had searched the valley for stolen cattle; the Belle Fourche bank had been robbed and the Curry gang had battled with a South Dakota posse at Hole-in-the-Wall ranch. These incidents, taken as a whole, made old-time rustlers a little jittery, so they finally decided to travel for their health until things quieted down. On August 19, 1897, seventy-five members of the Hole-in-the-Wall gang, led by George Curry, rode out of the Hole headed for Butch Cassidy's headquarters at Powder Springs. They passed through Meyersville, robbing sheep camps as they went, and crossed the Lander stage road at Lost Soldier Pass.

Powder Springs, situated in Powder Wash, a tributary of the Little Snake River in Moffatt County, Colorado, had been originally located by old Dick Benda (or Bender), who may have been one of the murderous Benders who operated near Cherryvale, Kansas, in the 1870s. The place was rustler head-quarters for several years and had sheltered such outlaws as Harry Tracy, Dave Lant, and Pat Johnson. Benda died at Baggs, Wyoming, during Cassidy's famous celebration there in July, 1897, leaving Cassidy leader of the combined Wild Bunch and Powder Springs outlaws. In the latter part of August, George Curry arrived with his seventy-five recruits from Hole-in-the-Wall, making Powder Springs the outlaw capital of the entire West.

Powder Springs at once became prominent in current news, and the gang began to make such a reputation for themselves that the Buffalo *Bulletin* took particular pains to inform the public as to the difference between Powder Springs and Pow-der River. It felt grieved to learn that depredations of the Powder Springs gang were being laid to the Powder River gang from Hole-in-the-Wall, forgetting that seventy-five of Powder River's choicest outlaws had just moved to Powder Springs. It described the two places in detail, but claimed that the Powder Springs outfit was vastly more desperate than their own outlaws had ever been. "We protest," said the ed-itor, "against the carelessness which would create or encourage unjust prejudice against this part of the state and needlessly injure its good name." He pointed out that there were other places in Wyoming almost equally as lawless as Johnson County, although he did not specify their location.

With his Wild Bunch as a nucleus, Butch Cassidy formed a new organization and planned to enter a new field. This group was to be known as the Train Robbers' Syndicate.

Almost every express car on the Union Pacific carried large amounts in currency, and the looting of those shipments promised to be much more profitable than anything previously undertaken.

News of the new syndicate leaked to the outside and finally came to the attention of Union Pacific officials. They immediately sent one of their best detectives, Charles Siringo, to investigate. This operative disguised himself as a cowpuncher, posed as an outlaw, and actually joined the Wild Bunch, learning their plans and obtaining a copy of their secret code. Through the use of that code he broke up plans of their first train robbery and gave the syndicate a year's setback. Thereafter they used messengers only and never put anything in writing.

The inner circle of this syndicate was composed of members of the Wild Bunch, and new recruits were selected from the Powder Springs and Hole-in-the-Wall gangs. Cassidy's chief lieutenant was still Elza Lay. New members were George Curry, Lonny and Harvey Logan, and Harry Longabaugh. Curry had some experience as a leader and was able to control his two quarter-breed henchmen to a certain extent. Harvey Logan was a fearless killer, valuable in a fight, but too reckless unless carefully handled.

Harry Longabaugh, a newcomer, hailed from Sundance, Wyoming, and went under the name of the "Sundance Kid." Little is known of his early history. In 1887, when he was seventeen, he applied for a job on the Suffolk ranch in Wyoming, located on the Cheyenne River at the mouth of Lodgepole Creek. Posing as a horse wrangler, he said he was from Colorado. During his first week he whipped three old hands and threatened to kill the cook. After that, they let him alone. One day, when he returned to the ranch house, he was arrested by a sheriff for robbing an old man of $80 in Lusk, Wyoming. He made his escape the following night. No other record of his activities appears until after he became a member of the

Wild Bunch. In disposition he was similar to Cassidy—pleasant, friendly, and cool in any emergency. The two men quickly formed an attachment which ended only when they died together in their last stand.

Castle Gate
Payroll Robbery

WHEN the Denver & Rio Grande Railroad built its line through Price Canyon, construction crews, blasting the cliffs, exposed large veins of coal. Within a short time many valuable coal properties were developed. The largest coal camp in 1897 was at Castle Gate, just below the magnificent rock formation from which it takes its name. Hundreds of men were employed in the mines, and the payroll, brought from Salt Lake City every two weeks, was large.

Price, county seat of Carbon County, was the railway supply point for Fort Duchesne, Vernal, and Uintah Basin. It was frequently visited by many Brown's Hole outlaws as well as those who sometimes holed up in Robbers' Roost, south of Greenriver, Utah. The outlaws had been unusually active in 1896, and it was suspected they would sooner or later attempt to rob the mine payroll. For that reason, men were paid on irregular days, arrival of the paymaster being announced by a certain blast of the mine whistle.

Butch Cassidy was known in Castle Gate chiefly by reputation. He had been in Colorado and Wyoming several years and had never operated in Utah, a fact that was to his advantage in planning the Castle Gate holdup. For his assistants on this occasion he again chose Elza Lay and Bob Meeks, lately from Huntington, thirty miles west of Price. Both were familiar with every inch of the country.

For making his getaway, Cassidy would need the best horse he could find. Such an animal, a magnificent gray, was owned by Joe Meeks, Bob's cousin, at Huntington, and was cheerfully loaned for the job.

In Austria, twenty years before, a young man by the name of Neibauer had been a messmate of Archduke Rudolph during his period of compulsory military service. Becoming enamored of a woman, the prince committed suicide in 1889. To prevent this fact from becoming known, the prince's messmates were accused of murder and executed, with the exception of Neibauer, who escaped to America. After working in the mines at Bingham Canyon, Utah, several years, he contracted rheumatism and was forced to quit. He located on a little ranch near Price, where he became acquainted with some of the outlaws. One day Cassidy came to Neibauer's cabin, leading Meeks' beautiful gray horse.

"Keep this horse for me," said Cassidy, "until I call for him. Feed him well and keep him up in the corral." Neibauer agreed. In about a week Cassidy called for the horse. Next day the Austrian left for Colorado to take treatments for his rheumatism at the hot springs near Grand Junction.

Two days later a man who appeared to be an ordinary cowpuncher rode into Castle Gate on a big gray horse, tied the animal to a hitching post, and entered a thirst emporium. Bellying up to the bar he ordered a shot of Old Crow and questioned the bartender about chances of finding work on a ranch. The barkeep replied that things were rather dull, but if he'd hang around something might turn up.

A little after noon the train from Salt Lake whistled for

Castle Gate, and the cowpuncher said he guessed he'd ride down to the depot. At the station he drew his spirited horse up short near the puffing engine. Unfamiliar with trains, the animal reared and plunged, to the amusement of onlookers, but the cowboy kept his seat. After a while he rode back to the saloon, where he spent the balance of the afternoon. Toward evening he bought two bottles of Old Crow and rode out of town.

Next day the cowboy returned, spending most of his time at the saloon. Whenever a train pulled in he rode to meet it, training his horse to stand quietly beside the engine.

No one knew the exact day on which the payroll would arrive, and for that reason Butch Cassidy met every train that week. He soon became a familiar figure around town. To depot loafers he was just another crazy cowboy in from the desert to have a good time. By the following Tuesday his money was exhausted, so he hit the bartender for credit on four bottles of Old Crow.

On Wednesday, April 21, 1897, at 12:40 P.M., the Rio Grande train from Salt Lake pulled in and Cassidy rode to meet it as usual. Passengers got off and went about their business. Mail and express were loaded onto trucks and hauled into the baggage room. E. L. Carpenter, paymaster, then entered the express office, accompanied by two men, Phelps and Lewis. When they came out, each was carrying a heavy bag of money—the semimonthly payroll for the Pleasant Valley Coal Company. Phelps walked ahead with $700 in gold, Carpenter came next with $8,000, and Lewis followed with $100 in silver.

The company office was over a store, seventy-five yards from the station and entered by an outside stairway. At the foot of the stairs two men were loafing. Just as Phelps started to go up, Butch Cassidy stuck a gun in his ribs and told him to hand over his bag. He started to push past, but was knocked out with a blow on the head from Elza Lay's six-shooter.

Realizing it was a holdup, Carpenter handed over his $8,000 without argument. Lewis, bringing up the rear, dropped his $100 in silver and dived into the open door of the store.

Frank Caffey, an old-time mining man living as recently as 1938 in Salt Lake City, was leaning against the counter just inside the door reading a newspaper when Lewis dived in. Curious to know what the excitement was all about, Caffey stepped to the door and onto the plank platform running across the front. Lay, who was watching for possible interference, had been keeping a sharp eye on the store. When Caffey stepped out, Lay whirled, drew a bead on his rather broad belt line, and yelled: "Get back in there, you son of a bitch, or I'll fill your belly full of hot lead!" Caffey says that polished six-shooter shining in the sun looked as big as a cannon, and he lost no time in obeying orders.

Cassidy and Lay leisurely gathered up their loot and prepared to leave Castle Gate. Lay, with $700 in gold, $100 in silver, and a small bag of checks, was first underway. He had ridden only a short distance when he either dropped or discarded the bag of silver. Cassidy, with his heavy bag of $8,000 in gold, had considerable difficulty in mounting the gray, which was suspicious of the unusual object and shied two or three times. Cassidy finally succeeded in getting into the saddle and followed Lay. Two or three other riders then fell in behind and all left town in a cloud of dust.

During the holdup, both station and store were crowded with men, yet no one had made a move to stop the proceedings. When it was all over, one of the store clerks grabbed a rusty rifle and attempted to shoot after the robbers, but the weapon wouldn't fire. Another man took a shot at them, already half a mile away, with a shotgun. The outlaws fired a few warning shots in the air and rode south toward Helper. After the dust had settled, Caffey drove down the road in his buggy and picked up the silver dropped by Lay.

Officers of the law had been conspicuous by their absence

during the holdup. When Carpenter tried to call the sheriff in Price, he found the wires cut. When news finally reached him, Sheriff Donant ran around in circles, lost several hours, and when he at last got underway, started off in the wrong direction.

Cassidy and his pals rode south to Spring Canyon, coming in from the east. Riding up the creek, they circled the town of Price then struck the highway leading to Cleveland, where they again cut the wires. Word had already passed, but citizens of Cleveland made no attempt to stop them. Arriving at Peterson Spring at the foot of Cedar Mountain, ten miles from Cleveland, they picked up a relay of fresh horses and rode on to Buckhorn Flat. They reached the San Rafael River at 7:00 P.M., where they probably camped for the night, knowing they had crossed the deadline.

Back in Castle Gate, a switch engine had been requisitioned. Loaded with men, it puffed down the track in the direction the robbers had taken but never caught sight of them. One man, David Kramer, fell off and was injured. Word was telephoned to Castle Dale, Huntington, and Cleveland, and posses were sent out from the first two towns. The anxiety of those men to capture the robbers may be guessed from the fact that Joe Meeks, owner of the big gray which Cassidy rode, was leader of the Huntington posse. He rode down Buckhorn Wash in the dark, received a shot in the leg from the Castle Dale posse—and galloped back home. He later received thirty dollars for use of his horse and the saloon-keeper got ten dollars for the four bottles of Old Crow Cassidy bought on credit.

Harry Ogden, who met Butch Cassidy in Robbers' Roost, says the money taken in the Castle Gate robbery was carried to the Roost in relays, through Black Dragon Canyon; that two men who were to take it from the San Rafael into the Roost on the last lap of the run decided to double-cross the others and keep it all for themselves; that they turned off the

trail near the Flat Tops and headed in the direction of Hanksville; that some other riders who had come out to meet them
saw the move, suspected treachery, and rode after the two
carrying the money. A running gun battle over a distance
of twenty miles ensued. One of the traitors' horses was shot
and the two men tried to ride double on the other animal.
When they saw they couldn't get away, they buried the loot
and put up a flat rock for a marker. Harry Ogden later saw
the marker and searched for the supposedly buried money,
but without success. The story of this running fight is vouched
for by an old man in Greenriver, Utah, who ought to know.
But if any money was buried, it did not remain underground
very long, as Butch and his gang had plenty of cash during
their stay in the Roost.

The attitude of all Utah officers toward the Robbers' Roost
gang was fittingly expressed by the *Tribune* correspondent,
who reported:

There are some who are acquainted with the country and
with the Robbers' Roost gang's manner of procedure, who freely
assert that if they are the ones who planned the robbery of
yesterday, the coal company may as well give up any attempt
to capture the holdups or regain the cash. The robbers are too
well organized and the country so unsettled and so little known
that a sheriff's posse would fare badly should it attempt to dislodge the desperadoes.

The nearest route to the Roost from Castle Gate was the
one Cassidy had taken—south to the vicinity of Price, west
to Cleveland, then down Buckhorn Wash to the San Rafael
and across fifty or sixty miles of sandy desert to the hideout.
Relays of horses had been provided, and in their getaway
Cassidy and Lay were guarded at important points by other
members of the gang, who kept out of sight. After the loot
was safe the gang apparently split, to confuse any possible
pursuit. At any rate there are stories of outlaws being seen at

various places on their return from the Castle Gate robbery. On the following night eight horses were taken from the corral at the Bracken & Lee ranch in Nine Mile Canyon, eight hard-ridden animals being left in their place. Late in the afternoon of the next day a rider on an exhausted horse held up Mr. Cashell, Indian agent on the White Rocks reservation, exchanged mounts and rode on toward Brown's Hole. About a month later Cashell's horse was returned in the night with a tobacco can tied to the saddle containing five twenty-dollar gold pieces.

There is undisputed evidence that Elza Lay and one of the gang named Fowler rode to the Roost by way of Torrey and Hanksville. At Torrey, eighty miles east of Richfield, they stopped to attend a dance. Albert Morrill, about twelve years old, observed the men hiding some bags of money in a haystack after their arrival late in the afternoon. Elza Lay, a favorite with the girls, danced while Fowler held the horses and kept guard outside. From Torrey they rode on to Hanksville, where they stayed for two or three days. Since Hanksville was one of the Roost's supply stations, they felt perfectly at home and left their money bags lying in plain sight at their camp on the edge of town. Court Stewart, then living in Hanksville, remembered the incident distinctly. News of the Castle Gate holdup did not arrive until several days later.

It was definitely known within a few days that Butch Cassidy had planned and executed this robbery. It was the most spectacular job ever pulled off in Utah up to that time, or since, and did more to make Butch Cassidy famous in outlaw circles than any other single exploit. Previously he had worked principally with the McCartys. As yet, it was not definitely proved he had led the Montpelier bank robbery. But after this last affair he was the undisputed king of all bandits then on the Outlaw Trail.

Robbers' Roost, most isolated hideout in the West, had been entered only once by any representative of the law. For that reason Cassidy chose it as his hiding place until the excitement died down.

That the reader may be able to appreciate its advantages, he should now be made acquainted with Robbers' Roost.

Robbers' Roost

Robbers' Roost, most southerly of the three principal stations on the Outlaw Trail, lies in the extreme eastern end of Wayne County in southeastern Utah, two hundred miles by airline and three hundred miles by highway south of Brown's Hole.

Except for its proximity to the Green River, which protects it on the east, it is the exact opposite of the Hole. Instead of being a "hole," protected on all sides by mountains, it is an elevated plateau lying on the summit of the San Rafael Swell. It has no timber except an occasional grove of mountain cedars, and no vegetation other than stunted sagebrush and scattered tufts of sand grass. Except for three or four small springs, it is absolutely arid. While Brown's Hole had once been a hunter's paradise, the Roost country was almost totally lacking in any sort of game. It was difficult of approach and more dangerous to enter than any other section of the state.

After entering Lodore Canyon and cutting its way through the Uintah range, the Green River flows through the eastern end of Uintah Basin. Leaving the Basin, it again enters another long series of deep canyons, suddenly emerging from the Book Cliffs at Greenriver, Utah, a town which should not be confused with Green River, Wyoming. Both towns were sources of supply for outlaws, and both were approximately the same distance from a hideout.

Traversing a few miles of open country, the river again enters a canyon, which extends all the way to Needles, California. The section known as Cataract Canyon, one of the worst stretches of fast water on the river, lies directly east of the Roost, the speed of the current being due to its rapid descent down the southern slope of the San Rafael Swell.

Forty or fifty miles south of Robbers' Roost and on the same side of the Green River rise five black peaks of the Henry Mountains, an isolated group of laccoliths discovered by Major Powell in 1869 and the last group of mountains to be put on the map of the United States. Rising to a great height straight out of a flat desert, their tops gather enough moisture to support a considerable growth of timber and grass on their lower slopes. The Orange Cliffs, eastern exposure of the Roost country along the Green River, were also first seen and named by Major Powell.

There are only three trails into the Roost: one from Greenriver, one from Hanksville, and one from Dandy Crossing. The Greenriver trail runs almost due south twenty miles to the San Rafael, a tributary of the Green, then forty-five miles up a gradual, sandy ascent to the summit of Sam's Mesa. In those last forty-five miles—over the original trail—water was found only at one place, called the Tanks, a crevice in sandstone rocks impossible to find unless one knew just where to look. After crossing the San Rafael, guiding landmarks were three flat-topped buttes on the summit of the mesa northwest of the Roost.

The trail from Hanksville was only forty miles long, but more difficult. The Dirty Devil River, which irrigates a few fertile acres at the settlement, passes into a deep canyon bisecting the desert between Hanksville and the river. It can be crossed in only one place, over an extremely difficult trail. Dry lateral canyons leading into the Dirty Devil make the journey from Hanksville to the Roost rough and dangerous.

The trail leading from the Roost into Colorado was as picturesque as it was difficult. It led south toward the Henry Mountains, across Dirty Devil Canyon and forty miles of dry, sandy desert, then down the bottom of Trachyte Canyon for another thirty miles to Dandy Crossing of the Colorado. Opposite the mouth of Trachyte, White Canyon comes in from the east, the junction of these two streams forming a ford in the Colorado passable at low water. Passing upward and eastward through White Canyon, this trail enters what is now Natural Bridges National Monument, runs down the eastern slope to Blanding, and thence east to Mancos, Colorado.

The Sevier River valley, lying between parallel north-and-south ranges of the Wasatch Mountains, was settled by Mormon pioneers as early as 1852. The trail from the Sevier valley to Robbers' Roost runs east from Richfield, over a high divide, then strikes the upper Dirty Devil River in a valley between Fish Lake plateau and Boulder Mountain. A red rock formation known as Wayne Wonderland begins at Bicknell. Two miles east of Fruita is a side canyon called Grand Wash, in which the outlaws built a dugout cabin for overnight stops. In Capitol Reef National Monument the trail runs through an extremely narrow canyon called Capitol Gorge, with walls a thousand feet high. One enters with caution if storm clouds are in sight, because of the danger of meeting a solid wall of water from which there is no escape.

Emerging from the eastern opening of this gorge, the trail drops down to Notom ranch on Pleasant Creek, a tributary of the Dirty Devil flowing along the magnificent Water Pocket Fold. At Pleasant Creek the country changes abruptly to gray badlands of eroded shale, splotched here and there with all of nature's colors except yellow. The trail across that dreary but picturesque waste is dangerous at any season: in summer because of the complete absence of water, and in winter because of sticky mud in which a horse can scarcely travel. It is almost bare of vegetation.

This badland formation extends all the way to Hanksville, the last settlement, situated on the Dirty Devil River fifty-five miles west of the Colorado River and thirty miles northwest of the Henry Mountains. Beyond Hanksville the formation changes to red sandstone, which continues to the Colorado. Between the Henrys and the Roost this desert is cut by deep, dry canyons, and the only water fit to drink is at Poison Springs in Poison Springs Wash. Waters of the Dirty Devil are scarcely fit for human consumption, especially in summer, when the stream is stagnant.

The view from the summit of the Roost country is either sublime or depressing, depending upon the amount of water in one's canteen and one's knowledge of waterholes. From Roost Spring you may look forty, fifty, or sixty miles south to the Henry Mountains, etched sharply against a flat, gray background. To the east, half hidden by red cliffs on the east side of Cataract Canyon, may be seen peaks of the LaSal Mountains. Sixty-five miles north, the Book Cliffs lie level against the skyline. Forty miles west rises the jagged outline of the fantastically colored Water Pocket Fold. From where you stand the country slopes gradually away in every direction, apparently smooth, but actually criss-crossed with deep, dry ravines and covered with red sand. Everything within vision is known as the Roost country.

The first white men to explore the Hanksville section were four Mormons who had been accused of the murder of Dr. Robinson, of Salt Lake City, a Gentile physician who had come to Utah with Colonel Patrick E. Connor's California Volunteers in 1860. Those four, advised by Brigham Young to lie low for a time, first saw the bottom lands along the Dirty Devil on which the town of Hanksville was later built.

During polygamy prosecutions in the 1880's a number of Mormons who had collected more wives than the law allowed sought a place of sanctuary where they could live according to the dictates of Joseph Smith, their prophet. Eph Hanks, a pioneer of 1847 and member of the band of religious outlaws known as "Danites" or "Destroying Angels," possessed several wives. Being under suspicion on account of several mysterious disappearances in the vicinity of Salt Lake City, he decided to move to some isolated section unvisited by Gentile officers. His choice was Pleasant Creek, three miles south of Capitol Gorge. His cousin, Ebenezer Hanks, continued on east to the Dirty Devil bottoms where, with several polygamous families, he founded the settlement of Hanksville. No safer spot could have been found. It was and still is the last settlement in that direction—the last place where a blade of grass can be irrigated.

In those days the Dirty Devil was a meandering stream, lined with willows. Since then, because of the straightening of the channel and overgrazing of surrounding country, it has become a roaring torrent in flood time and has cut a channel half a mile wide and fifty feet deep, fully living up to its name. Land formerly cultivated by Ebenezer Hanks has long since been washed down to the Gulf of California.

Between the Dirty Devil and the Henrys this desert, in early days, supported a stand of wild grass which made excellent winter stock feed. Two large cattle ranches were established east of Hanksville—Starr's ranch in the Henrys and Granite ranch at the northern foot of Mount Hillier.

The first outlaws to use Robbers' Roost as a hideout were horse thieves; but that business was soon abandoned for the more profitable occupation of cattle rustling, after the railroad came to Greenriver. Cattle were gathered in the Sevier River valley, driven to the Henry Mountains, wintered near the Roost, and sold in the spring. Rustlers knew every foot of country and had no difficulty in eluding pursuit.

Utah was settled almost exclusively by converts to the Mormon faith recruited mostly from England and the Scandinavian countries. Available agricultural land had been parceled out by Brigham Young in small lots to families of converts as fast as they arrived in Zion. Within a few years all irrigable acres had been occupied.

Cattle did well on the desert ranges, although it required from thirty to sixty acres for each animal. In pioneer times only enough sheep were raised to provide wool for family weaving. Late-comers to Utah were compelled to go into the cattle business, and for that reason hundreds of small ranches were established. There were no great cattle empires such as were founded during the same period in Arizona and Wyoming.

In Wyoming, whole herds were run off by rustlers without the owners' being aware of their losses until roundup time. In Utah, however, a different system was necessary. Rustlers were well organized, having representatives in every community, most of them operating small, isolated ranches. When a herd of stolen cattle was to be assembled, word was sent to outlying agents of the gang, each of whom would pick up a few head and start them moving toward the rendezvous. A second man would pick up the strays left on his land by the first, add a few more to the bunch and move them on to the third station, and so on. Each man was absent from home only a day or two. None of them had *stolen* any stock; they had merely moved a few head of strays off their own range. These small bands were finally assembled in some isolated place, such as Robbers' Roost, held for a safe period of time, then sold either at Greenriver or some point in Colorado. The only man who ran any risk whatever was the one who sold the cattle. Profits were split all the way down the line. This system was so foolproof and so profitable that almost every other small rancher in southern Utah was a rustler on the side.

Those who sold the cattle and took the greatest risk made

their headquarters in Robbers' Roost. It was a No Man's Land. No sheriffs ever went there looking for rustlers, and because of its safety as a hideout it rapidly grew in population and reputation.

Robbers' Roost history does not run so far back as that of Brown's Hole. It was first used as an outlaw hideout around 1883. Among those who drifted in about that time or shortly afterward were Al Akers, Kid Jackson, "Blue John," "Silver Tip," Jack Moore, Jack Cottrell, Monte Butler, "Gunplay" Maxwell, Joe Walker, the McCarty brothers, Pete Neilson, Charley and Rains Lee, George Curry, and Tom Dilley, as well as others of lesser importance.

Roost Canyon runs north for many miles from its mouth on the Dirty Devil. Its walls are sheer, and there is no entrance or exit except through its mouth. On the ledges above its "blind" end is a more open extension of the same canyon. In those upper reaches above the main canyon, leading down from the San Rafael Swell were several secluded sandstone caves or shelters used by the outlaws as headquarters for several years. Water was obtained from small springs flowing from a stratum of white sandstone just below the caves. The entrance to one large cave was partly walled up for protection in case of attack.

In summer the caves were comfortable enough; but in winter they were rather drafty. So the man known as Blue John built a cabin further north at a good spring. It was always known as Blue John's cabin and the spring is still known as Blue John Spring. There being no other timber in the vicinity, this cabin was constructed of small logs of mountain cedar, noted for their twisted shapes. It was probably the only cabin in the state built of such material, and its construction required considerable art as well as an unlimited amount of patience. But the logs of the structure were no more crooked than the men who occupied it.

Jack Moore (whose real name was Jackson) had been so

popular in Texas that upon leaving he was followed by a
sheriff's posse urging him to remain. He came to the Roost
accompanied by his "wife" Ella, who seems to have been a
guiding influence among the rustlers.

Jack and Ella Moore made their headquarters most of the
time with J. B. Buhr at Granite ranch, twenty-five miles
southeast of Hanksville. Buhr, an Englishman, had come west
for his health, being a sufferer from chronic asthma. On account of his affliction he was known among the Roosters as
"Wheezin' Buhr." Ella Moore nursed him through his bad
spells, and in return she and Jack were welcome to the comparative luxury of the substantial ranch house Buhr had built.
J. B. Buhr was the original of the Englishman in Zane Grey's
story *Robbers' Roost*, and the only character in that bale of
cheap fiction with any semblance of reality. So far as records
show, he was never a rustler, although he was sometimes accused of being the "king bee" in the Roost, since Roosters
were always welcome at Granite ranch. Trachyte from the
Henry Mountains superficially resembling granite gave rise
to the ranch's name.

Jack Cottrell, also from Texas—by way of southern Utah
—was one of the most successful cattle thieves in the Roost.
His headquarters were on Bull Creek, east of Buhr's place.
Cottrell was unmarried. Having shown too friendly an interest in Ella Moore, he and Jack had become enemies.

In 1889 W. C. Snow and his brother Sam, from Lehi, heard
of the good range in the Roost country and decided to take in
a band of sheep, the first seen in those parts. They worked
their way in by slow stages and were in that section a month
or two before being discovered. Then one day Jack Cottrell
rode into their camp.

"This is a cattle country," he told the Snows. "We don't
aim to have no sheep in here. You get out, and get quick, or
by God I'll kill the damn sheep and you too." The threat was

backed up by an ugly .45 Colt. The sheepmen promised to leave as soon as possible, but were out of grub and asked for time enough to replenish supplies. The incident ended by Cottrell inviting them to his cabin for dinner.

W. C. Snow left Sam with the sheep and started to Hanksville. From Granite ranch he rode in a buckboard with Jack Moore. On the desert they met Cottrell, who had sworn to kill Moore on sight. The latter drove off the road, grabbed his rifle and waited for the other man to make a hostile move. Cottrell kept his rifle trained in the direction of the buckboard, but rode on. Snow believed it was the nearest he ever came to being shot as an innocent bystander.

Charley Rains (his real name was Rains Lee) was a son of John Doyle Lee, executed in 1877 for participation in the Mountain Meadows Massacre of 1857. Rains' two brothers, Charley and Walt, sons of Sarah Caroline Williams, one of John D. Lee's seventeen wives, lived at Torrey, 57 miles west of Hanksville. A young Mexican named Ed Chaves had been herding sheep in Colorado one season and was returning, by way of Dandy Crossing, to visit his brother Joe at Monroe, Utah. Coming up Trachyte Canyon, he met Rains, who insisted he stop overnight for a game of cards. The boy refused, knowing the outlaw intended to cheat him out of his wages. His refusal angered Lee, who then held him up at the point of a gun. The boy offered a ten-dollar bill, claiming it was all he had. Rains then shot him in the face, took the balance of his money, his horse and outfit, and left him for dead.

The bullet had passed through the boy's mouth, breaking the jaw bone and tearing away part of his chin and most of his teeth. Some hours later he recovered consciousness. He was still sixty miles from Hanksville, without horse, grub, or canteen.

With almost superhuman effort the young Mexican started walking toward the settlement. He was weak from loss of

blood, dizzy with pain, and suffered untold agonies from thirst
as he dragged himself across the last forty miles of dry desert
in the blazing sun. Two days and one night later he stumbled
into Charley Gibbons' store and fell on the floor in a faint.
Gibbons patched him up as best he could, nursed him for
several days, then sent him to Monroe in the care of Jerry
Jackson. Blood poisoning soon set in and he died from his
wound.

After the funeral, Joe Chaves came to Hanksville looking
for Rains. He spent two or three days assembling an outfit,
borrowing a rifle from Eugene Sanford, grub from Charley
Gibbons, and a horse from Lorin Taylor. He was gone thirty
days but failed to find his man. News had drifted into the
Roost that "a large force of Mexicans" was assembling to
clean the place out; Charley Rains disappeared in a cloud
of dust and was never seen again in those parts. Joe Chaves
later told Jerry Jackson the score was finally settled in a
saloon in Arizona.

In 1894 the population of the Roost was increased by the
arrival of Moen Kofford and Jim Mickell, two sheepherders
who had killed Sheriff Burns of Carbon County; a wife murderer from Colorado; and Tom McCarty. Joe Walker, whose
history will constitute another chapter, arrived in 1895, after
having "captured the town of Price." C. L. Maxwell, alias
John Carter, also arrived about the same time.

The Starr family had started a large ranch on the opposite
side of Mount Hillier from Buhr's ranch, where they ran several thousand head of cattle. They were from the Sevier River
valley. Alfred Starr was a medium-sized, quiet, inoffensive
man who minded his own affairs; his wife was a big, aggressive
woman who wore the pants. As long as they welcomed
Roosters to their home they prospered. But one day Maxwell,
the rustler, and some of his friends fleeing from the law helped
themselves to some of Starr's choice saddle horses. For this
breach of hospitality Mrs. Starr made up the family's mind

to run Maxwell out of the country and sent him word to that effect.

To show their contempt for Mrs. Starr's edict, the rustlers kidnaped her husband one fall and kept him prisoner most of the winter in a cave along the Colorado River, guarded by a Negro. In the spring they sent him home with the message that the Starrs must leave the country within twenty-four hours. Mrs. Starr declared neither hell, high water, nor Maxwell could move her from the Henrys. The rustlers then began to move in on the Starr cattle, driving them across the river at Dandy Crossing in herds of five hundred head. Within a few months there wasn't a Starr brand left in the mountains. The family was compelled to move to Springville, where they started again from scratch.

On one of his trips to Colorado with a herd of Starr cattle, Jack Cottrell was accompanied by a partner named Tomlinson. After disposing of the herd in Durango, the two men started back. In due time Cottrell arrived in the Roost alone, explaining to Mrs. Tomlinson that they had both been attacked by a gang of robbers and in protecting their treasure her husband had been killed. He consoled the widow with such success that in a short time she became known as Mrs. Cottrell. Old-timers believe he killed Tomlinson for his money and the woman.

This woman was the mother of two children, the oldest a girl about thirteen years old. In a year or two a warrant was sworn out at Loa, the county seat, charging Jack Cottrell with being the cause of the girl's pregnancy. John Hancock, twenty-two-year-old sheriff of Wayne County, was asked to serve the warrant; but such crimes were so common in Utah in those days that Hancock doubted if a conviction could be had. Rather than put the county to the expense of a trial, with chances of acquittal, he decided on another course of action. He sent word by one of the Roosters, probably Pete Neilson, that he had a warrant for Cottrell. When Jack heard the news he saddled his fastest horse and left the country between days. On his deathbed he confessed to killing Tomlinson and throwing his body into the Colorado River.

With the arrival of Butch Cassidy and his friends after the Castle Gate holdup in April, 1897, Robbers' Roost reached the climax of its fame as an outlaw hideout. By his spectacular coup, Cassidy had become king of the Roosters, an aristocrat among common cattle rustlers. His saddlebags were bulging with gold and he could afford to put on airs. Instead of holing up in the well-known outlaw caves or at Blue John's cabin, he brought in tents and made a deluxe camp in Horseshoe Canyon, twelve miles east of the older headquarters and nearer the narrow trail leading down "under the rim" of the Orange Cliffs.

Cassidy's camp was supplied with every cowboy luxury in the way of eats and drinks. It even boasted the society of three women. One was Ella Butler; the other two were Millie Nelson and a girl named Maggie Blackburn, both from Loa.

Cassidy never approved of having women in camp, but in this case they proved very useful. While the dogs of the law were still barking over the Castle Gate holdup, two of the women were sent out for supplies. They first appeared in Greenriver, where they bought, among other necessities, eight hundred rounds of ammunition. Again, in August, they appeared in Price and bought all the ammunition in town. On these trips they were accompanied by some hangers-on from Cassidy's camp, who kept out of sight while the women went shopping. These large purchases of ammunition served two purposes: they helped the boys kill time in target practice, and they served as a warning to all officers that they had best keep away from the vicinity of Robbers' Roost.

Cassidy and his friends spent their time in eating, drinking, target practice, horse racing, and gambling, principally the last. Everyone was welcome at camp. Tom Nichols, a saloon-keeper from Price, who had hired Blue John to look after some of his cattle on the San Rafael, attended one of those all-night poker sessions. Maxwell, the rustler, was also present. Toward morning Butch found himself cleaned out.

"Keep 'er going, boys," he said as he left the tent. "I'll be back with my pockets full of gold." He was gone about an hour. When he returned he had plenty of golden eagles and the game went merrily on.

A year later, after Maxwell had been sent to the pen for bank robbery, he sent for Nichols.

"You remember that night when Butch went broke and came back with a hatful of gold?"

"Sure," said Nichols. "What of it?"

"Cassidy had a cache out there in Horseshoe Canyon where he buried the money he got in the Castle Gate holdup. He only spent a little of it; the rest is still buried and I know exactly where it is. If you'll go out there and dig it up, we'll split. Here's a map showing the exact location of the cache. You know the country and you could find it easily."

Nichols agreed to try. He rode to the Roost, located the spot indicated on Maxwell's map, and spent considerable time digging, but found nothing. Believing he had mistaken the landmarks, he returned for further instructions.

"You were right close to it," explained Maxwell, "but you picked the wrong cedar for a marker. You should have gone down the canyon a few rods further."

With his new instructions Nichols went back a second time, spending a month in prospecting every likely-looking place in Horseshoe Canyon, but he never found Butch Cassidy's cache. Maxwell had been drawing on his imagination in the possible hope that Nichols might find something and divide with him. Cassidy was too smart to leave anything of value buried in Robbers' Roost.

During his stay in the Roost, Butch Cassidy himself sometimes came to Hanksville with some of his friends for supplies and news. On one such trip he stayed overnight and slept un-

der the immense cottonwood trees which stood in front of
Charley Gibbons' old store. At the head of his bed he laid a
new Winchester rifle.

"Let me borrow that rifle tonight?" asked Gibbons.
"There's a damn coyote been hanging around here lately; I
see him every morning about daylight. I believe I could get
him with that gun."

"Sure," replied Cassidy, "you can borrow it; but wait till
morning. Come and get it when the coyote shows up."

At daybreak the coyote started his salutation to the dawn.
Gibbons slipped out, picked up Cassidy's rifle, got a bead on
the critter and fired. The coyote turned a somersault and lay
still.

"You're not such a bad shot yourself," grinned Cassidy
when Gibbons came back dragging the animal by the tail.
His mind had been put at rest as to Gibbons' purpose in wanting to borrow the rifle. As a matter of fact, Butch had worked
for Gibbons as a cowhand after Mike Cassidy left the Henry
Mountains and the two were good friends, even though Butch
had turned outlaw.

Gibbons sold thousands of dollars' worth of supplies to
the outlaws at the Roost over a period of many years. They
always paid cash and he never had any difficulties with them.

George T. Watkins, of El Paso, while prowling in odd
corners of the West in 1933, recorded the following story,
told him by Mr. Weber, oldest resident of Hanksville:

"Frank," Cassidy told Weber, "I'm not as bad as I've been
painted. I done a poor feller and his wife a good turn this trip.
As I was cutting across the hills I came to a run-down-look-
ing outfit, but I stopped to see if I could get something to eat.
There was an old man and an old woman there. They had
tried to make a home, but old age hit quicker'n they imagined,
and the fact is they were just about to be run off the place by
a feller who had a note again' 'em. I asked 'em who this gent

was and they said they looked to see him show up any minute. 'Which way will he come in?' I asks, and the old woman pointed at an old trail. I made the old lady take five hundred dollars, the amount due, and I told her to give it to the feller. I said goodbye and left. I hid out along the trail, and along comes a feller on a horse. He has on black clothes and I had a hunch this was the collector, so I watched him and he went to the old log cabin and the old lady let him in. Maybe five minutes later he come out. When he came up the trail I stopped him, took the five hundred—and here I am!"

Before the summer of 1897 was over, every sheriff in Utah knew that Butch Cassidy and his gang were hiding in Robbers' Roost, but no effort was made to go in after them. Some of the smaller Utah newspapers commented on this situation. The *Utonian*, of Beaver, had a couple of especially pertinent paragraphs. It said, in April, 1897:

Something must be done to break up the gang of robbers and murderers now ensconced in the San Rafael mountains, and the state will have to do it . . . For many years it has been known that if a desperado reached the mountain fastnesses in that region he had entered the "City of Refuge." No officers have ever gone there, for the reason that for a small company of officers to do so would simply be to go into a trap where death would be as certain and swift as if they plunged into the mouth of a volcano. Officers have followed desperate fugitives to the canyons which are the gateways to the Robbers' Roost, as that country has lately been called, and found that when they arrived there all they could do was to become targets for the rifles of the outlaws . . .

Carbon county has a board of commissioners who must be in with the gang of cutthroats and thieves that infest the mountains of that section of the country. Last week they refused to allow a bill of Sheriff Donant for actual supplies furnished in pursuit of the notorious Walker and his thieving crowd who sent a rifle ball through the thigh of Sheriff Tuttle of Emery county while pursuing them, and which may yet cost him his life. With such encouragement an officer is a fool to attempt the capture of such criminals.

The *Utonian*'s editor was more than half correct when he said that county commissioners were in league with the outlaws. Carbon County was full of cattle rustlers who had friends or relatives among county officials. No officers ever entered the Roost, and those who rode in that direction, to save their face always rode white horses! They could be seen at a long distance, and the outlaws would have time to escape.

Influenced perhaps by Cassidy's presence in the Roost, cattle rustling reached a new high that summer. The Ireland Cattle company, one of the heaviest losers, finally organized and financed an expedition of eight men with the announced intention of cleaning out all cattle thieves. The posse was headed by Joe Bush, a deputy United States marshal from Salt Lake City, formerly an officer in the wild mining camp of Silver Reef. They outfitted at Torrey, then pushed on to Hanksville. From the latter settlement they rode bravely into the Roost country, taking the main road—the only wagon road—to J. B. Buhr's Granite ranch at the foot of the Henrys, thirty or forty miles from outlaw headquarters.

The prime object of this manhunt was the capture of Blue John, the cockeyed rustler who had built a cabin at Blue John Spring. At the moment, John was working for Buhr and was known to be at Granite ranch. In Hanksville, Bush deputized Jack Cottrell, who volunteered his services to divert suspicion from himself and to get even with his enemies, Jack Moore and Blue John.

The posse camped on the desert that night. Before daybreak on the morning of June 16, 1897, they moved on and surrounded Granite ranch. Just at sunrise Blue John stepped outside to answer the call of nature and was instantly covered by Cottrell. He snapped his gun in Cottrell's face, but it missed fire, and he was quickly disarmed by other members of the posse.

The big manhunt was over! A gesture had been made and the posse returned to Loa with their prisoner, who was turned over to Sheriff George Chappell of Wayne County. Cottrell, who made the arrest, remained at his place on Bull Creek, but sent the following note to Chappell:

Hanksville, Utah, June 16, 1897

To the Sheriff of Wayne County, Loa, Utah:

Dear Sir:—This is a bad man. Better send him to Salt Lake or Provo for safekeeping. He is the one that informs the entire Roost gang by carrying mail and other information. He has lots of backing on his line and may get away from you or be taken from you. Better make sure and put him in a good place.

JOHN COTTRELL,
Deputy Sheriff of Wayne County

At his trial in Loa, Blue John swore he was merely a cowhand for J. B. Buhr and that he had "ridden all over the Roost country without seeing any such outlaws as are supposed to infest that region." He stated—truthfully—that he did not know Cottrell was an officer, and in pulling a gun he had done so to defend himself. The jury quickly acquitted him of the charge of resisting an officer and he returned to his former occupation in the Roost. He was never tried on the horse-stealing charge.

The Beaver *Utonian*'s editor was strictly correct in saying that an officer was a fool to risk his life trying to run down outlaws who could never be convicted.

Court records describe Blue John, whose real name was John Griffith, as a man thirty-five years old, with sandy hair. His left eye was blue, his right was brown and cocked, giving him a perpetual squint. He was dressed in disreputable clothes, always wore his shirt open all the way down the front, and spoke with a cockney accent. It was thought he acquired the nickname because of his one blue eye.

Silver Tip, Blue John's partner, whose real name was James F. Howells, was about forty-five years old. Born in Texas, he had moved to Tennessee, then to Missouri, and finally to Utah. He had brown eyes, gray hair, black mustache and black beard. The tip of his beard had turned gray, hence his nickname.

This peculiar pair, who seem to have been the original discoverers of Robbers' Roost, were horse thieves and all-around bad eggs. They never rustled cattle in wholesale numbers, like some later denizens of the Roost, yet they were always in trouble. They had once worked for the Carlisle outfit, near Monticello, owned by an English syndicate, the largest cattle ranch in Utah. To prevent thieving, the Englishmen hired the toughest bunch of cowpunchers they could find. Carlisle hands frequently smoked up the towns of Monticello, Blanding, and Moab. On one such occasion Blue John and Silver Tip had some trouble with the sheriff of Moab and decided to lay low for a while. That is how they happened to go to Robbers' Roost.

The Wild Bunch
Celebrates

Butch Cassidy and his friends
went into the Roost in April, immediately after the Castle Gate holdup. It was a lonely place at best: hot and dry, a long ride from the nearest saloon. Three women who accompanied the outlaws were not able to relieve the monotony of camp to any noticeable extent; three months of almost continuous gambling began to pall; men began to get restless; the law had apparently given up any idea of pursuit; so the Wild Bunch decided to "go to town."

Camp was quickly broken and the long-riders joyfully forked their mounts for a new expedition. They reached Greenriver after dark on the first day; on the second they climbed the steep trail over Book Cliffs near Thompson to the head of Hill Creek; in three days they were at the ford of the Green River near Ouray, in Uintah Basin; on the fourth day they passed through Vernal and camped on Brush Creek; and on the evening of the fifth day they rode down Crouse Canyon into Brown's Hole.

Only a small part of the Castle Gate loot had been spent,

159

and their pockets were burning. There were no saloons in the Hole—unless John Jarvie's store might have been in that category. Rock Springs was too "civilized" to be safe, as a sudden flood of golden eagles would excite suspicion. The best places to celebrate, they decided, were Dixon and Baggs, two little cowtowns northeast of the Hole, in Carbon County, just over the line in Wyoming. Dixon was the home of Jim Baker, celebrated mountaineer and trapper.

So Butch Cassidy, accompanied by his personal retinue of eight long-riders and a number of friends from the Hole and the Roost, set out for Dixon and Baggs to put on a real old-time celebration and spend the Castle Gate payroll. They rode into Dixon first, whooping and yelling, shot up the town "in approved border-ruffian style," as the Rawlins paper reported, then rode on to Baggs to finish the celebration. The date was July 29, 1897.

News of the approaching tornado had reached Baggs, and when the Wild Bunch appeared on the horizon the local constable took one look and suddenly remembered he had important business elsewhere. With nothing to dampen their exuberant spirits, they proceeded to shoot up the little settlement. Punctuating their requests for "snake-eye," they shot twenty-five holes in the bar of the saloon and then, to show there were no hard feelings, gave the saloonkeeper a dollar for each hole to compensate him for damages. They drank the health of E. L. Carpenter and paid for the drinks with gold which had but recently belonged to the Pleasant Valley Coal company.

Butch Cassidy, the "lady's man," always liked to dress up when he took his relaxation, so he called on the local store-keeper and bought the best outfit in stock, from patent-leather shoes to derby hat. His eight associates who had shared in the loot followed his example. Then they returned to continue the festivities. Between rounds of drinks they related stories of their exploits, with particular emphasis on the last one, interspersed with plenty of bragging about big jobs planned for the future. It was a big, jolly get-together meeting for all the outlaws of Brown's Hole and surrounding country.

Some outsiders or would-be outlaws soon found themselves short of funds and unable to hold their own with the Wild Bunch. One in particular, known as "Tarheel," wishing to make an impression on Cassidy, rode out on July 30 to a sheep camp, shot the Mexican herder, robbed him of $480, and returned to Baggs, where he bought drinks for the crowd.

Cassidy himself drank sparingly, but he was always the life of the party. Some of the other boys had no brakes and imbibed too much for their own good. There were several fights; Jack Moore, from the Roost, got a bullet in the hip, but miraculously no one was killed. Cattlemen approaching town for supplies heard the celebration a mile away and prudently turned back.

There was one sad note in this joyous affair. Old man Bender, chief of the Powder Springs gang, was brought into Baggs suffering from a bad case of pneumonia. When he suddenly grew worse, one of the boys who went under the name of Johnson was delegated to nurse the old man; another was sent to Rock Springs for a doctor, but although he offered $2,000 in gold, he could get no physician to accompany him back to Baggs. So old man Bender died and was buried with proper ceremony.

When everyone had acquired a proper headache, the Wild Bunch rode on to Brown's Hole and the constable came in from the sagebrush to survey the wreckage. Baggs was shot full of holes, but the Bunch had left behind a good slice of Castle Gate gold. The saloonkeeper made enough to open the finest bar in Rawlins.

This celebration at Dixon and Baggs is still vividly remembered by old-timers around Brown's Hole. When Cassidy rode away, his reputation as a successful outlaw leader was secure. Wyoming newspapers, for the first time, recorded the passing of "Cassidy's gang."

One face was missing at the gathering in Baggs. About a week after the Castle Gate robbery Bob Meeks rode into Fort Bridger, where he was well known, wearing an expensive Mexican riding outfit and sporting a fine silver-mounted bridle and Mexican saddle. Men who knew him only as a loafer suspected he had never earned such an outfit herding cows.

Charley Guild's place of business was a combination post office, store, and saloon. During the next two weeks Bob Meeks spent most of his time with one foot on the brass rail and seemed to have plenty of money.

At 9 P.M. on the evening of June 15, 1897, when there was no one in the store except himself and the proprietor, Meeks stepped out the front door for a few minutes. Almost immediately two masked men entered, held up Guild, and robbed the post office of $123. The business only required a few minutes. As soon as the robbers disappeared, Bob Meeks came back.

"Damn you, Bob," said Guild, "I believe you had a hand in that business."

"What business?" asked Bob innocently. "Whatja mean?"

"You know damn well what I mean. You planned that job and you stepped out to give those fellows the signal. Get your hands up pronto," Guild commanded as he covered Meeks, "and keep 'em there. Don't make a false move or I'll plug you."

Protestingly Meeks obeyed. But Guild didn't know what to do with his captive. He was alone in the store and there was no telephone. He hoped someone would drop in to help him tie up Meeks; but no one seemed to be thirsty at that time of night. An hour passed. It was long after closing time. At last Mrs. Guild, becoming worried, came to the store to see what was keeping her husband. Glancing through a window she observed the situation and ran to a neighbor's for help. Meeks was then securely tied and a rider dispatched to Evanston to notify Sheriff John Ward.

Guild had been suspicious for some time that Meeks had had a hand in the Montpelier bank robbery, but made no effort to verify his suspicions until after his own store had been robbed by Meeks' friends. The two actual robbers, arrested shortly afterward in Vernal by government officers, proved to be John Henry, alias Dick Thompson, and Charles Stevens, alias Waterhole Charley, both from Brown's Hole.

Sheriff Ward arrived in Bridger next day, put Meeks under formal arrest, and started back to Evanston. It was rumored that Butch Cassidy had been seen in the vicinity within a day or two, and Guild warned Ward to be on his guard in case a rescue was attempted. The sheriff, however, reached Evanston safely with his prisoner, without seeing any suspicious characters. The outlaws weren't playing tag with John Ward.

Bob Calverly, Ward's chief deputy, who had arrested Butch at Afton in 1894, had a hunch when he saw Meeks. Following that hunch, he sent for paying teller Mackintosh, of the Montpelier bank. When Mackintosh arrived, Calverly led him to Meeks' cell.

"That's him!" shouted the banker. "That's the man who held the horses while the other two robbed the bank. I watched him through the window while I had my face to the wall. That's positively the right man."

On that evidence Meeks was sent to Idaho. At his trial on September 3, 1897, Mackintosh again identified him as one of the robbers. Although the outlaw was defended by two good lawyers, he was able to produce only two alibi witnesses, Henry and Ike Lee, both of whom were discredited by their own testimony. As a result, Meeks was sentenced to serve thirty-two years in the pen, the maximum under Idaho law.

Life in the pen, however, did not agree with the long-rider who had ridden beside Butch Cassidy on the Outlaw Trail. During long, tedious days of hiding after the Montpelier and Castle Gate robberies, the Wild Bunch had often discussed methods of escape in case of capture. Meeks soon put into operation the one which seemed most likely of success. Each day he ate a small piece of soap. In a short time he appeared to have every symptom of tuberculosis; he coughed, spat up mucus, lost weight, and ran a temperature. On doctor's orders he was transferred to the prison hospital. After quitting the soap diet he rapidly improved.

A scaffold having been erected against the hospital wall to facilitate some repairs, Meeks determined to make his escape by jumping two full stories to the ground. The earth proved much harder than he anticipated; one leg was broken near the hip and the flesh so badly lacerated that the leg had to be amputated.

Believing that a one-legged bandit was no bandit at all, officials released Meeks after his discharge from the hospital. He returned to his old haunts near Fort Bridger, but never again rode with the Wild Bunch.

Practically everyone in Rock Springs knew that Butch Cassidy made his headquarters in Brown's Hole, but no officer felt the urge to go in after him. They figured some day he would come to town for a little excitement and could easily be picked up without their making a long and dangerous trip through the mountains.

The day came when news reached David G. Thomas, a young officer, that Cassidy was staging a spree in one of the saloons. Thinking to put one over on older minions of the law and claim the large reward being offered, the young deputy armed himself, entered the saloon, and spotted his intended victim. In the hilarious crowd he was unnoticed as he carefully maneuvered his way to a position directly behind his man. Then, thrusting his gun in the outlaw's ribs, he shouted, "Stick 'em up!"

Cassidy was taken completely by surprise. Thomas looked

determined and seemed to have the weight of argument on his side.

"Looks like you've got me this time," smiled the outlaw. "I ought to be arrested for being so careless. Well, I guess that calls for a drink all around. You don't mind, Sheriff, if we have just one more before I go to jail? It'll probably be a long time before I get another."

"I guess one more won't do any harm," agreed Thomas, trying to be a good sport.

"Belly up to the bar!" shouted Cassidy. "The drinks are on me!"

The bartender filled the glasses. "Here's how!" said the prisoner, and every man lifted his glass, including the young deputy. Just at that moment Cassidy pulled his own gun, catching his captor off guard, disarmed him, and backed out into the night.

"Charge that one to the sheriff!" he called as he vaulted into the saddle.

David G. Thomas later became a prominent and respected member of the bar in Rock Springs, and a judge. He died in 1935.

A short time after the incident above, a Catholic priest of Kemmerer, Wyoming, was called to visit a sick man on a ranch ten miles from town. It was a cold night and he wore a heavy overcoat that concealed his clerical habit. Not being familiar with the country, he lost his way and was riding aimlessly in the dark when he dimly saw three horsemen approaching. Outlaws had been reported in the vicinity of Kemmerer, and the priest felt sure he was about to be robbed.

As the first horseman approached he called to the priest to halt and throw up his hands. Not being an expert rider, he held up one hand but kept a grasp on the reins with the other.

"Get 'em both up, quick!" said the leader. The cleric complied.

"Get off your horse," came the command. Then the other two riders approached and went through the victim's pockets looking for weapons. In doing so they unbuttoned his overcoat, exposing the black garb of a man of the church.

"Are you a minister?" asked the leader.

"Yes. I am a Catholic priest on an errand of mercy."

"Pardon me, Reverend," said the outlaw politely, "I had no idea who you were. We were expecting to meet the sheriff and thought you might be him. Where were you going?" The priest explained.

"Well, Reverend, you're off the road two or three miles. We're riding that way and we will set you right." Accompanied by the three outlaws, the cleric soon arrived at his destination.

"We'll be leaving you now," said the leader. "I'm Butch Cassidy. If you meet the sheriff on your way back, tell him not to bother looking for us. And here is something you might be able to use for charity," he added as he handed the priest a fat roll of bills."

"I'm sorry, Mr. Cassidy, but I couldn't accept that kind of money. However, I'm greatly obliged to you for your courtesy."

"Well, so-long, then; we must be traveling. I'm glad you weren't the sheriff."

"So am I!" replied the priest fervently.

Joe Bush had gone into Robbers' Roost after Silver Tip and Blue John during the time Cassidy was hiding in Horseshoe Canyon. He had proved the place was not impregnable, yet no attempt was ever made to arrest Cassidy. The outlaw was seen in Salt Lake at various times and passed through other Utah towns where he was well known. He stayed for weeks at a time with friends in Vernal. Yet no Utah officer (with one exception) ever attempted his arrest. None could be found who wanted the job of putting irons on the leader of the Wild Bunch, in spite of the well-known fact that he had never killed a man during his career as an outlaw.

Old-timers in Salt Lake City tell of the time Cassidy came in to attend the funeral of a relative. He was dressed in the best of clothes and passed openly up and down the streets. The officers all knew there was a price on his head, but they let him strictly alone.

While he was in the city in 1900 to interview Orlando W. Powers, the lawyer, he hung out at the old Casino saloon. Newspaper boys, getting wind of his visit, put up a job on a green cub reporter. The boy was anxious for an important assignment, so they sent him to the Casino with instructions to get an interview with Mr. Cassidy, whose name meant nothing to the kid. Entering the saloon with all the confidence of youth, he asked the bartender where he could find Mr. Cassidy.

"Right over there," said the bartender, pointing. The cub walked over to Cassidy, who was sitting in a corner with his eye on the door.

"Are you Mr. Cassidy?" the kid asked.

"Some people call me that. Why?"

"I'm from the *Tribune*," the cub replied, proudly. "The editor sent me down here to ask you what you are doing in town and where you are going."

"You go back, son, and tell the editor to come and see me himself if he wants to know where I'm going. And hereafter," he added with a grin, "don't go around asking for Butch Cassidy. I wouldn't want you to get hurt!"

One day Cassidy and his Wild Bunch rode up to an isolated shack on the desert and asked if they could get dinner. The lone occupant of the cabin was an old woman. The boys were hungry, but possibilities for a good dinner seemed dubious. There was nothing on the place but a couple of cows and a few fat hens. The old lady, frightened out of her wits, promised to cook something and retired inside the cabin. As she was poking up the fire she heard pistol shots in the yard. Looking out, she saw Butch Cassidy shooting the heads off her hens.

"Good Lord!" she yelled as she rushed to save her pets. "Can't you find nothing better to practice on than an old woman's chickens? Them hens is all I got to live on. You ought to be ashamed of yourself!"

"We wanted a chicken dinner," laughed Cassidy, "and we've got money to pay for it. Here, will this pay you for your precious hens?" He rolled into her wrinkled palm a golden eagle for every chicken he had shot.

Tears came to the old woman's eyes as she counted the coins. It was more money than she had ever seen. The boys had their chicken dinner; and it goes without saying that any posse which might have passed that way later would never have learned from her which way the outlaws were traveling.

Harry Ogden, a fourteen-year-old boy, came to Escalante, Utah, in 1895 and got a job riding for a cattle outfit. He saved his money and bought a good horse and a sixty-dollar saddle. One day in 1898, after the Castle Gate robbery, he was riding alone north of the Henry Mountains in a section bordering Robbers' Roost. Suddenly an outlaw rode up on a worn horse, forcibly took Ogden's fresh animal and fine saddle, gave the boy a kick in the pants and rode away, leaving him afoot in the desert.

About three weeks later, three men rode up to Ogden. One was Butch Cassidy and one of the others was the outlaw who had taken his horse. Butch asked the boy if he had been robbed of a horse. He replied that he had and identified the horse ridden by the third man as his own. Butch immediately ordered the man to dismount, turned the horse over to Ogden, then told the outlaw to start walking toward a distant gap in the hills and keep on going. Said Cassidy, "We don't have any room in this country for a man who will mistreat a young boy."

On another occasion some months later, Ogden had made camp on the bank of a small creek and was frying some trout for supper when Cassidy stepped around the corner of a large boulder and greeted him with "By God, hello!" Butch asked if he could get something to eat, and Ogden invited him to help himself. He caught some more trout and fried them in bacon fat, throwing the rinds into the fire. "Don't do that," said Cassidy, "we may need all you've got." In a few minutes Elza Lay came up and was fed, and when both had eaten, Cassidy disappeared and in his place another man came in. This last man was short, dark, and hard looking, impressing Ogden as a born killer. The man ate silently, then disappeared in the dark. Ogden never saw him again; but he believes he was Harvey Logan, the most dangerous man who ever associated with Cassidy.

Joe Walker

Joe Walker, a Texas cow-puncher, arrived in Price, Utah, some time in 1891. He rode the range for a while, meeting many members of the gang which later made its headquarters in Robbers' Roost. He once worked for the Day brothers in their sawmill at Huntington. But Joe didn't like any work that couldn't be performed from the deck of a horse, so he was soon back among the cowboys. In a short time he made a reputation for himself drinking and fighting.

On one of his drunken rampages in 1895 Joe Walker, with a half-witted cowpuncher, had attempted to "capture the town of Price" but found he had taken on too large an assignment. Not long afterward he tried to kill a man named Milburn in a saloon. When the sheriff sought to arrest him for attempted murder, he forked his mustang and rode hell-bent for the Henry Mountains, hiding for some time in Cass Hite's cabin at the mouth of Trachyte Creek on the Colorado River. From Hite's place he went to the Roost, where he was made welcome.

From that time on, Walker made a specialty of stealing horses from the vicinity of Price, and particularly from the Whitmore ranch. The story is told that Walker had married one of the Whitmore girls against the objections of her brothers, and the latter had done everything they could to make life miserable for him. In any case he had a grudge against the Whitmores, who were breeders of fine horseflesh. In March, 1897, he stole three fine horses from their ranch, located near the head of Nine Mile Canyon.

The Whitmore brothers decided to put a stop to his activities. They swore out a warrant for his arrest and offered to assist the sheriff in running him down. The posse which left Price consisted of Sheriff Ebenezer Tuttle, J. M. Whitmore, M. C. Wilson, J. M. Thomas, and C. L. Maxwell. The last named, whose history will be detailed in another chapter, was himself a well-known rustler operating in the Nine Mile country. He knew every foot of the Roost and acted as guide for the posse because he hated Walker, who had been trespassing on his preserves.

Walker's trail led from Price to Cleveland, then down Buckhorn Wash to the San Rafael River, on the edge of the Roost country. As a usual thing the law stopped at Cleveland. On this occasion, however, Sheriff Tuttle violated custom by riding down the wash. Buckhorn Wash, a picturesque, highly colored, narrow canyon, is a dry tributary of the San Rafael. Fresh sign at Buckhorn Flats assured the sheriff his quarry was not far ahead, so he pushed on to the San Rafael.

Walker, who did not expect to be followed beyond Cleveland, was camped at the mouth of a small blind canyon at Mexican Bend. The posse, suddenly turning a point of rocks about noon, found him cooking dinner. There was no time to get to his horse, so he grabbed his rifle and ran up the blind canyon, where he hid behind some large boulders. He was known to be a dead shot, so the posse was careful not to approach within range of his hiding place. They were in no particular hurry, as they had him cornered in a place from which there was apparently no escape. Sheriff Tuttle called on him to surrender, but received no reply.

The sheriff and his men discussed the situation for three or four hours, without arriving at any solution. It was impossible to get behind the outlaw, due to perpendicular walls of rock. He was perfectly protected behind a group of large sandstone blocks. He had not fired a shot all afternoon. At last, tired of inactivity, Tuttle decided on a frontal charge, right up the open draw. Thomas and Wilson were left with the horses. Tuttle took the center, with Maxwell and Whitmore at some distance on each side. Their objective was a group of boulders behind which they would be somewhat protected from Walker's bullets if he started shooting.

The three men had almost reached the boulders when Walker cut loose at a distance of 150 feet. His first shot was aimed at Maxwell, whom he considered a traitor. The bullet struck the barrel of Maxwell's rifle and glanced off. Maxwell dived behind a rock and was out of the fight, claiming afterward his rifle had been ruined by the shot. Whitmore also found protection, being near the edge of the draw. But Tuttle, walking up the middle, was entirely unprotected and a perfect target. Walker's next shot struck the sheriff in the thigh, breaking the bone and knocking Tuttle to the ground. That ended the battle of Mexican Bend. It was 4:00 o'clock of March 26, 1897.

The shooting of Tuttle completely unnerved the posse. Wilson and Thomas were afraid to enter the draw to attend the injured man, and both Whitmore and Maxwell were afraid to leave it for fear of being shot. So things remained in status quo until long after dark, when Whitmore and Maxwell carefully made their way back to their horses. No more had been seen or heard of Walker, but rather than chance another volley, they allowed Tuttle to lie on the ground all night without attention.

Late next morning four men again approached the draw. Tuttle was motionless, apparently dead. Walker was nowhere in sight. It was suggested that perhaps they could rescue the sheriff, if he were still alive, under a flag of truce, but no one had any white cloth. One of the men finally took off his red flannel undershirt and waved it, but received no response. Carefully they edged their way into the draw, and finally reached Tuttle, who was in very bad shape. Walker had escaped in the night.

Wilson then rode to Cleveland and telephoned for Dr. Winters at Orangeville. He spread the news of Walker's escape and two other posses went out to look for him, without success. Winters drove out to Mexican Bend in a buckboard, gave Tuttle a heavy hypodermic of morphine, dressed the wound as well as he could, and started back, over what is possibly the roughest trail in the state. It was a terrible ordeal for the injured man, and his condition was precarious for two weeks after, but he finally began to mend and was transferred to his home in Price.

Another posse was then sent to the Roost, by way of Hanksville, with the intention of catching Walker at Granite ranch, where he was staying with Jack Moore. This brave bunch of officers, like others who rode toward Robbers' Roost, "rode white horses." Halfway to Granite they met Walker riding toward Hanksville on a fine pacer. When he saw them he dismounted. Instead of charging toward him, the posse opened fire at long distance with their rifles. Their guns were new Winchesters and carried much further than Walker's old one. When bullets began striking too close for comfort, the outlaw calmly mounted his horse and rode back to the ranch. The posse, with superior numbers and better rifles, forked their horses and made a dust for Hanksville.

Apparently Walker didn't like the idea of meeting strangers in unexpected places, so he wrote Sheriff Tuttle, on May 6, in an endeavor to "patch up our differences."

"I'm sorry you got hurt," he wrote. "If you'll call it square I'll send you three good horses. You can sell them to pay your doctor bill and if there's any left over you can send it back to me." Needless to say, this generous offer was not accepted. Anyway, the horses he offered belonged to J. M. Whitmore.

After his fight with the posse on the San Rafael, Joe Walker continued his raids in the vicinity of Price. His name was placed on a list of twelve Roosters for whom Governor Wells was offering a reward of $500 each, but no one made any serious effort to collect the reward. To show his contempt for that listing, he wrote to the governor, offering a $500 reward for the body of Joe Bush, dead or alive.

Toward the end of April, 1898, Walker and three friends from the Roost made another raid on the Whitmore ranch, running off several head of fine horses. In Box Canyon the thieves found Bud Whitmore and Billy McGuire in charge of twenty-five head of cattle. After giving the two young men a terrific beating they took the cattle and the saddle horses. The boys finally made their way afoot into Price, where they told their story to Sheriff C. W. Allred.

Citizens of Price had previously looked upon the Roost gang as a bunch of wild young fellows looking for excitement. Many had relatives in Carbon County. The officers themselves had perhaps been a bit wild in their younger days; it would have been difficult to find anyone in that section who had not at some time been free with a rope and branding iron. They looked upon cattle rustling as more or less of a game. But the brutal beating of the two cowboys and the theft of their saddle horses was contrary to the accepted rules of the game; and, besides, ex-Sheriff Tuttle was still suffering from the effects of Walker's bullet in his hip. So a posse was organized, financed by J. M. Whitmore, to put a damper on Walker's playfulness.

Armed with warrants, Sheriff Allred set out from Price, accompanied by J. M. Whitmore, George Whitmore, J. W. Warf, Pete Anderson, Jack Gentry, and Jack Watson, the last-named a criminal hunter from Colorado carrying eleven bullet scars. Joe Bush, the fighting deputy U. S. marshal, took a train from Salt Lake and dropped off at Lower Crossing, then rode to Range Valley, where he picked up Jim Inglefield, Billy McGuire, and Coleman, joining the posse on Wednesday, May 11. Sheriff Allred had already picked up the trail and found a bunch of Whitmore cattle and horses, besides one of Walker's saddle horses. In Range Valley he picked up Jim McPherson, a rancher suspected of being friendly to Walker, and another unnamed man who was actually a member of the Roost gang. The former was taken along to prevent him from warning the outlaw, and the latter was forced, at gun point, to act as guide. This brought the number of men to thirteen.

Sheriff Allred had lost considerable time, having been thrown off the trail by certain "ranchers" friendly to the outlaws. The thirteenth member of the posse, however, was "persuaded" to put them right and fulfilled his position as guide with efficiency and dispatch. That night the thirteen men camped on the banks of the Green River. Thursday morning they crossed over and began climbing an extremely precipitous and narrow trail up the face of the Book Cliffs, requiring four hours to advance three miles. Arrived on top of the mesa, they rode to the head of the north prong of Florence Creek and made camp, at 2:00 A.M., within a mile of Walker's camp.

Before daylight on the morning of Friday, May 13, the posse rolled out of their blankets and, without waiting for breakfast, again took up the trail. Before advancing a mile they saw several head of horses, indicating that Walker was nearby. Dismounting, they advanced cautiously on foot. As they turned the point of a bluff they saw four men lying in their blankets on a shelf of rock protected on one side by a deep ravine.

The sheriff was a big man, with a high-pitched voice. Under the excitement of the moment, as he yelled to the outlaws to surrender, it cracked, resulting in an unintelligible squawk. The four men turned in their blankets to find themselves facing a semicircle of rifles. Joe Bush then called out in no uncertain tones, warning them to put up their hands instantly or be shot. Two of the men, who had been sleeping together a little distance from their partners, immediately stood up, pointing skyward.

Joe Walker and the other man, however, merely rolled over in their blankets and began shooting. They were armed only with six-shooters; awakened suddenly from slumber, they shot wild. The posse, all armed with rifles, were better marksmen. As they advanced, with Joe Bush in the lead, at least eleven rifles blazed. Walker's partner decided to make a run for it and was promptly drilled through the back. Joe Walker kept to his blankets and continued firing until he slumped down with a bullet in his heart. When Joe Bush turned him over, his right arm, the only part visible to the officers, was riddled with bullets. Fifty shots had been fired in less than one minute.

The posse had been traveling day and night, without sufficient sleep, and had also run out of grub. With their two prisoners and two dead outlaws, they started back for Thompson, forty miles south, across some of the roughest country outdoors. One of the possemen, J. W. Warf, told me that journey was the most distressing forty miles he ever traveled. Added to their hunger, thirst, and lack of sleep was the sight of two dead bodies strapped across their saddles, which had to be readjusted every mile or two. When the party reached the railroad at Thompson at 6:00 o'clock in the evening, they were worn out. They had been in the saddle just thirteen days!

News of the battle was wired to Price. When the posse reached there next day, they were met by the largest crowd ever assembled in Carbon County. One prisoner gave the name of Thompson; the other was thought to be Elza Lay. One of the dead men was known to be Joe Walker, and the other was believed by every member of the posse to be the famous Butch Cassidy, who had robbed E. L. Carpenter of the Castle Gate payroll just a year before.

The Pleasant Valley Coal company had offered a reward of $1,000 for Cassidy; the same offer probably held good for Lay; Joe Walker's body was worth $500, and there was probably a smaller reward for the other prisoner. The weary men could almost feel the money in their pockets before they reached home.

In due time the two bodies were placed on exhibition. Walker was well known in Price. E. L. Carpenter and a few others came down from Castle Gate and identified the other man as Butch Cassidy. The local papers announced Cassidy was dead. To make certain of the rewards, Sheriff Allred wired Sheriff Ward of Evanston to come and identify the body.

In the meantime word of Cassidy's death had reached the little town of Huntington, home of Joe Meeks, a cousin to Bob, and of a young lady called Minnie. Both straddled horses and galloped to Price.

"Is that Cassidy?" asked Sheriff Allred when Meeks arrived.

"No, it ain't," said Joe positively. "He's about the same height, same weight, same general looks; but it ain't Cassidy." Since Cassidy had borrowed his gray horse to rob the Castle Gate payroll, Joe should have known; but the sheriff was so eager for the reward he wouldn't take Meeks' word.

Late that night Minnie loped back to Huntington, exhausted by her sixty-mile ride and quite hysterical.

"They didn't get him! They didn't get him!" she shouted

over and over. "They'll never get Butch Cassidy. He's too smart for 'em. I saw the dead man and it ain't Butch!" Minnie *knew!*

When Sheriff Ward arrived from Evanston it was definitely proved the dead man was not the much-wanted Cassidy but a minor outlaw, John Herron, from the Roost. The two bodies were buried just outside the Price cemetery. Herron was exhumed a week later for another examination, then re-planted for good. Thompson and Schultz, the two prisoners, were tried at Castle Dale and turned loose.

Details of this manhunt, one of the few resulting in death or capture of any of the Roost gang, were given to this writer by J. W. Warf, a participant in the chase, who believed his bullet killed Joe Walker.

During this manhunt, Butch Cassidy was transacting certain unknown business in southern Utah. Traveling north again toward Brown's Hole, he reached the outskirts of Price, where he heard the report of his death. To talk over this interesting bit of news he rode to the cabin of his friend, Jim Sprouse, where he spent the night.

The nearest route to Brown's Hole passed twelve miles south of Price, making it unnecessary to pass through town. But Butch had a keen sense of humor and thought it would be a good joke on the posse and a rich yarn to tell his friends, if he actually passed through town while his supposed dead body lay exposed to public gaze.

Next morning Jim Sprouse drove a covered wagon through the main street of Price. In the bottom, under a generous layer of straw, lay Butch Cassidy. A saddle horse was tied be-hind. Through a crack in the wagon box, Butch watched the crowd milling about the entrance of an improvised morgue, where he was said to be lying dead. At the other end of Main Street he brushed the straw from his clothes, mounted his horse, bade Jim Sprouse goodbye, and rode on his interrupted journey to headquarters.

Back in Brown's Hole, Douglas Preston was waiting to transact certain legal business with Butch. When his business was finished, Preston rode back toward Rock Springs. In Clay Basin he met Finley P. Gridley, a mining man who was looking over a new coal prospect.

"What's the news in town?" asked Preston, who had been absent ten days waiting for Butch.

"Sheriff Allred and a posse killed Joe Walker and Butch Cassidy last week forty miles from Thompson. I saw it in the paper yesterday. Looks like you've lost a damn good client."

Preston threw back his head and laughed loud and long. "That's a good one!" he shouted; "the best I ever heard."

"What's so funny about it?" inquired Gridley.

"Nothing much," laughed Preston, "except that I talked to Butch just before I left Brown's Hole this morning!"

Gunplay Maxwell

C. L. "Gunplay" Maxwell, alias John Carter, was the black sheep of a good family who yearned to make a name for himself as a fire-spitting bad man. Like most cowboy outlaws, he began as a cattle rustler. He was a bona-fide member of the Robbers' Roost gang but conducted most of his operations in the vicinity of Preston Nutter's ranch in Nine Mile Canyon, east of Price, formerly owned by Bracken and Lee. Maxwell's brother opened a butcher shop in Price under the name of Thomas, to dispose of stolen beef.

Although he aspired to become known as leader of the "Maxwell gang," Gunplay was only a small-time four-flusher. All his stunts seemed to fall flat. On one occasion he rode into a camp of prospectors looking for Gilsonite in the Hill Creek country east of the Green River. Like any other stranger, he was invited to accept the usual hospitalities. After supper, while the men were smoking around the campfire, he tried to pick a fight with one of the smaller men, for no rea-

180

son except to demonstrate how bad he was. He kept it up for an hour; but at last the prospectors got their fill of him. They invited him to take off his guns and fight.

"I never take my guns off," Maxwell boasted.

"The hell you don't!" shouted the prospectors. Then they grabbed him, stripped off his weapons, and turned the little fellow loose. When it was all over they helped the half-dead rustler back on his horse, gave him his guns, and sent him on his way with an invitation to call again any time he felt like fighting.

The following year, 1897, some of his friends were being tried in Vernal for cattle stealing. Maxwell appeared as a defense witness and, when the evidence went against his friends, threatened the prosecutor, Sam Thurman, later Utah supreme court justice. Next day Sheriff John T. Pope stood at the door of the courtroom with a sawed-off shotgun and disarmed all spectators, including the would-be bad man from Nine Mile. When court adjourned, the sheriff allowed each man to retrieve his sidearms. Maxwell was last in line. Emptying his guns and belt of all cartridges, Pope warned him to make himself scarce before sunrise. He took the hint.

Later the same year Maxwell decided to make a reputation for himself by standing up to Butch Cassidy. Cassidy was in Vernal; Maxwell was camped just outside. He sent word to the leader of the Wild Bunch to leave town instantly or suffer the consequences. So Butch rode out to the camp, and Maxwell rode to meet him, both men with guns drawn. When the horses were neck-and-neck, Butch spoke.

"This town ain't big enough for both of us, Gunplay. You ain't a bad man; you're just a petty-larceny horse thief. I'll give you five seconds to get going; otherwise there'll be a funeral in Vernal and you'll be riding at the head of the procession."

Maxwell hesitated only two fifths of the allotted time, then turned his horse and galloped back toward Nine Mile. An irresistible force had met a very movable object, with the usual result. Such incidents did not add to Maxwell's reputation; so at last he decided to refurbish his tarnished laurels by robbing a bank in regular Cassidy style. For this job he selected a partner from Robbers' Roost named Porter and half a dozen helpers in the charge of Pete Neilson.

The "Maxwell gang" rode out from the Roost with the intention of robbing Senator Reed Smoot's bank in Provo. They made camp at the mouth of Provo Canyon, spending several days studying the lay of the town and possibilities of a safe getaway. Unfortunately certain parties who were friendly to both sides warned Smoot of what was afoot, and the bank removed most of its ready cash. Finding his plans had miscarried, Maxwell decided to strike in another place. Two of his helpers hired a team and buggy from a Provo liveryman, in which Maxwell and his partner rode through town and on south to Springville. They drove around until after dark, then sent word for their friends to move south to the mouth of Hobble Creek, as they intended to rob the Springville bank at 3:00 o'clock the next day.

Meanwhile, as the team was not returned, the liveryman swore out a warrant for the arrest of the two men who had hired it. Maxwell apparently heard of this action; at any rate he decided to pull the holdup ahead of schedule, taking for granted that his relay of horses had been brought to Hobble Creek.

About 10:00 o'clock next morning cashier Cummings of the Springville bank left his cage and started up the street. At 10:05 two rough-looking men entered. One of them presented a note to the bookkeeper, A. O. Packard, which read:

Springville, Utah, May 28, 1898

On sight pay to the order of T. S. Cerswell the sum of $200. C. H. CARTER, By T. C. Burton.

The bookkeeper started to explain that Carter had no money on deposit. Then the robber covered him with a gun and made him put up his hands while Maxwell entered the cage and scooped up $3,020 in gold, wrapping it in some red handkerchiefs.

While this was being done, Packard reached under the edge of his counter and pressed a button which rang an alarm in Reynolds' store across the street. Maxwell, thinking he was reaching for a gun, threatened him, but did not observe the hidden alarm button.

Reynolds, across the street, had received several false alarms, and did not answer the signal at once. Instead, he called up the bank on the telephone. Receiving no answer, he became suspicious and rushed out of his store with a Winchester just as the two robbers were leaving in the buggy they had hired in Provo.

Springville, then as now, appeared to be one of the sleepiest little towns anywhere in the desert. One might be misled into presuming its citizens wouldn't learn of a holdup for a day or two after it had occurred. Streets were deserted and most business houses appeared to be abandoned or locked up. But, by judging the town on its external appearance, Maxwell made a great mistake.

Reynolds, observing the robbers' exit from the bank, shouted the alarm. William M. Roylance immediately sent several men and boys on bicycles to round up horses, riders, and guns. The response was so instantaneous that within a very few minutes a large posse had formed. In the meantime, Reynolds had commandeered a team and heavy wagon tied to the hitching post in front of his store and, with a young boy driving, started in pursuit of the robbers.

Just out of town, Maxwell and his partner met Mr. Snelson riding a fine bay horse. They offered to buy it, but Snelson wouldn't sell. So they pulled their guns and ordered him off, then threw forty-six dollars on the ground and drove on, leading the animal. The transaction had taken a little time and allowed Reynolds to approach to within 150 yards. He fired two shots.

By that time the posse from town was close behind, so the two robbers abandoned their buggy and took to the brush near the mouth of Hobble Creek, four miles from town. They attempted to carry their gold with them, but it was insecurely tied and they dropped golden eagles all along the trail, making it easy for the posse to follow.

The thicket where they were hidden was soon surrounded. Joseph W. Allen, a blacksmith, offered to enter with eight volunteers to drive out the fugitives. Nine men crossed and recrossed the patch of brush, but saw nothing of the two outlaws. After some time they found another handful of money, and saw Maxwell lying on the ground nearby. They covered him with their guns and he surrendered quietly. After further searching, Allen discovered the other robber lying under a pile of leaves and ordered him to surrender. For reply, Allen received a bullet in his thigh, knocking him down. He then rolled on his side and fired into the pile of leaves, killing the robber instantly.

During the balance of the day several hundred dollars were found in the brush. Maxwell still had over $2,000 when captured. When first arrested he gave his name as J. C. Carter, his usual alias, but was soon identified by numerous persons, including Judge Dusenberry of Vernal and Sam Thurman, who had examined him as a witness in Vernal the previous year. Maxwell then admitted his identity and made quite a joke of his capture. His great mistake, he said, was in thinking he could make his getaway in a buggy. His friends had not arrived in time from Provo. Everything had gone wrong. Instead of making a reputation for himself as a rival of Butch Cassidy, he had blundered into another failure. The bank had been robbed at 10:05 A.M., May 28, 1898; at 12:45 his partner was dead and he was a prisoner. Springville wasn't as sleepy as it looked.

At his trial on September 20, Maxwell offered no defense whatever. When asked by the judge if he had anything to say, he merely stated that he had agreed with his partner not to kill anyone during the holdup and had thrown his gun away afterward. He was given a sentence of eighteen years in the pen.

Two guns used by the robbers were recovered later. Both were marked with the name "P. Nealson." Pete Neilson and Charley Lee, both from Torrey, had been arrested for stealing cattle and horses the previous year. In his home town Neilson was known as "Pete Thief." Lee was already in the pen, but Neilson had skipped back to the Roost before trial.

Governor Wells had offered a reward of $500 for the capture of Maxwell, one of twelve Roosters on his black list. Allen, who had killed Maxwell's partner and received a bullet in the thigh, had to have his leg amputated a day or two later, so the posse voted him the entire reward.

As the result of pressure brought by influential friends, Maxwell's sentence was commuted on November 21, 1903. He was hired shortly afterward as a mine guard during a strike in the Carbon County coal mines. After the strike had been broken, the company was afraid to fire him for fear he would rob their payroll as Cassidy had done previously. They finally settled the business in another way.

"Shoot-em-up Bill," then a resident of Price, was another character similar to "Gunplay" in many respects. Each tried to outbrag the other, and soon they became enemies. Word was passed to Shoot-em-up that Gunplay was out to kill him. The two invincibles met on the streets of Price shortly afterward. They were standing on opposite corners on one of the main streets when they caught sight of each other. Maxwell had been warned and was supposed to be on his guard. Both went for their guns at the same instant, but Shoot-em-up was faster on the draw. His first shot kicked up dust behind Maxwell and he thought he had missed. He fired again, and once more saw the dust spurt up. Then Maxwell crumpled to the pavement, without having gotten his gun into action. When his body was examined it was found that both bullets had passed entirely through him and hit the ground behind.

At his trial for the Springville bank robbery, Maxwell had persistently refused to identify his dead partner, stating as his reason that the man had a wife and two children who would be disgraced by the publicity. Charley Gibbons of Hanksville, who knew both, says the man's name was Porter.

Maxwell's widow soon married Pete Neilson, who later reformed and lived in House Rock Valley. His widow was living in Flagstaff in 1948, Maxwell having died a few years before.

The Law Comes
to Brown's Hole

THE operations of Bob Devine
and Sheriff Al Sproul during the summer of 1897 had caused
a great exodus from Hole-in-the-Wall. The outlaws moved
in a body to Powder Springs, a hideout in the mountains on
a branch of the Little Snake River. Old man Bender (or
Benda), posing as a rancher but actually chief of the old
Powder Springs gang, had just died of pneumonia at Baggs,
attended by one of Butch Cassidy's lieutenants who furnished
the old rustler with every comfort money could procure in
that isolated village. After Bender's death the augmented
Powder Springs gang joined the Wild Bunch under the leadership of Butch Cassidy.

George Curry and Harvey Logan, with one or two other
six-shooter aristocrats from the northern hideout, were accepted as bona-fide members of the Wild Bunch, which had
graduated from the rustling game and were sometimes known
as the "Train Robbers' Syndicate." The inner circle, however, never consisted of more than a dozen men at any one

time, and since a majority of the assembled outlaws did not
share in a division of the richer loot, they had to be content
with plain and fancy cattle rustling.

There had always been cattle thieves in that section; stockmen marked off a certain percentage each year as an expected
hazard of their business. But with so many rustlers concen-
trated in one area, losses soon became enormous. Herds of
from one hundred to five hundred head were run off at a
time. The thieves conducted regular roundups with such fre-
quency that in a short time there was scarcely a steer left on
the range within a radius of two hundred miles. Many cattlemen were forced out of business entirely and either abandoned the country or sold their remaining cattle and bought
sheep, which no self-respecting cattle rustler would stoop to
steal. Such wholesale raids killed the goose that laid the
golden egg, although the gang were too short-sighted to read
the signs. Steers brought from thirty-five dollars to fifty dollars at shipping points that year, and the rise in price was a
signal for every cowboy from Montana to Arizona who
owned a rope to go raiding. Some only stole enough to pay
their passage to the new gold fields in the Klondike; but the
Powder Springs gang had a gold mine right at home. A dispatch to the Denver *News* of February 27, 1898, describes
one such raid:

For a week news has been coming to Casper of one of the
biggest "cattle drives" ever known to Central Wyoming. It appears that Harvey Ray and other escaped Belle Fourche bank
robbers have been joined by a party of Powder Springs thieves
and together they are driving everything before them to the
Hole-in-the-Wall region. They are said to have scattered and
started their drive in a way that would be likely to create the
least suspicion, but they were discovered, and Ray, one of the
Smiths (Al) and others were recognized. There were upwards
of twenty of the riders and they were well mounted and heavily
armed.

Permanent settlers of Brown's Hole—those with families and established ranches—took it upon themselves to enforce a certain amount of order on the floating population using the Hole as a hideout. Since the law almost never entered their valley, residents were a law unto themselves and their code was seldom violated. Those who were not active rustlers had to tolerate the thieves in order to exist, but even rustlers frowned upon unjustified murder.

Valentine S. Hoy was leader of the "law and order crowd" in Brown's Hole. A native of Walker, Pennsylvania, and forty-eight years old, he had served in the Union army during the last year of the Civil War. In 1867 he crossed the plains, arriving at a point near South Pass during the gold excitement. In 1872 he went to Brown's Hole with a small herd of cattle. In 1883 he married at Fremont, Nebraska, and brought his wife and two brothers to the Hole the following year. A wound in his head received during the war had been patched with a silver plate, and this, according to Mike Nicholson, made him act a little queer at times.

The three principal characters concerned in the following tragic episode were Harry Tracy, David Lant, and Patrick Louis Johnson. Tracy, most desperate outlaw who ever entered Brown's Hole—the John Dillinger of his time—was then almost unknown. His real name, it is said, was Henry Severn, and he hailed from the little town of Pittsville, Wisconsin, where, as a boy, he had shown no particular criminal tendencies. Nothing further is known of his early history. He first appeared in Utah with four other railroad hoboes, camped in an abandoned house near the depot in Provo. While burglarizing a house he was arrested, and on July 10, 1897, was sentenced to the penitentiary. He gave his occupation as cook, his origin as Missouri, and his religion as Methodist. His number was 939. He was a moody, unsociable man of medium build, distinguished by a pair of deep-set, cruel gray eyes.

Dave Lant, twenty-seven, was born in Spanish Fork, Utah, and raised in Payson, the wild son of respectable parents. At one time he had worked for a rancher named McCoy, near Vernal. On September 27, 1897, he had been sent to the Utah pen for a burglary in Rich County.

Eleven days after Lant's arrival at the pen, he and Tracy were working with some other convicts in a quarry some distance from the prison, guarded by John Van Streeter. Tracy had whittled an imitation six-shooter from a piece of wood, covered it with tinfoil, and concealed it in his clothes. Deliberately breaking his shovel, Tracy called the guard to replace it, stepped so close that Van Streeter's shotgun was useless, pulled his "six-shooter," grabbed the shotgun, then changed clothes with the guard and made his escape with Dave Lant and two others. He and Lant kept together. They stole a horse and buggy and made their way to Brown's Hole.

At first they hid out in an abandoned cabin belonging to Larry Curtain. Later, Lant got a job near Vernal, where W. C. Lybbert taught him how to shear sheep. He soon was arrested for wounding his camp tender in a fight but was released. Later he was involved in a shooting over a woman. After that he went to Brown's Hole and hunted up Tracy, who had joined the gang at Powder Springs. Lant was not a killer like Tracy and is often spoken of by old-timers as a "gentleman outlaw." He felt indebted to Tracy for his escape, and the two became partners. Together they "smoked up a Chinaman" who ran a store near Fort Duchesne, robbed him, then hid in a cellar on the Atwood ranch. When officers came looking for them they found Mrs. Atwood knitting quietly in her rocker, which was placed over the cellar's trap door. She denied having seen any outlaws.

Patrick Louis (Swede) Johnson was a Missourian, neither Swedish nor Irish. He had come west with a partner, Charles A. Teeters. In 1892 Johnson killed a man at Thompson's Springs, Utah, and immediately joined other fugitives in

Brown's Hole. He was a rustler, of course, but sometimes worked for Valentine Hoy as cowhand. At one time he and Elza Lay ran a saloon on the Strip near Fort Duchesne.

In the fall of 1897 a prospector named Strang came to the Hole with two young sons to work some of Jesse Ewing's abandoned claims in Ewing Canyon. Strang, a native of Maine, had been a soldier, was discharged at Fort Douglas, Utah, in 1878, and was prospecting around Brown's Hole later, probably in 1890. (He was still living at Torrance, California, as late as 1941.) Running short of grub, he sent his younger boy, Willie, down below to stay with old Speck, the Negro, then operating a ferry at the mouth of Red Creek. Speck's instructions were to keep the boy away from the rough crowd. But Willie, just at the age when he wanted to be a cowboy, soon tired of helping Speck operate the ferry. When Swede Johnson rode by one day and invited him to come to Hoy's ranch and learn to rope steers, he could not resist the temptation and ran away. Speck heard nothing more of him until several weeks later.

At this time Teeters was in charge of Hoy's Red Creek ranch. He claimed that Tracy, Lant, and Johnson forced him to put them up and feed them at the ranch. At any rate they were staying there. Young Willie Strang was full of fun and having a gay time. One morning, when Johnson overslept, Willie threw a pan of cold water in his face to awaken him. A little later Johnson sent the boy out to the corral for some horses, and to hurry him up started shooting at his feet. One bullet lodged in Willie's spine, causing death within an hour. In the confusion which followed, Johnson, realizing the possible consequences of his act, slipped away and hid in the brush on Cold Springs Mountain. Tracy and Lant soon followed, not wishing to be present if officers came to investigate the killing.

All three decided it might be safer to get entirely out of the country. Putting their outfits on a pack horse, they trailed out of the mountains and started across the valley with the intention of traveling eastward into Colorado, since the mountains north and south were still full of deep snow. The date was March 1, 1898.

The three men passed through the valley without attracting attention and rode on to Vermillion Creek. There they met Jack Bennett, who informed them a sheriff's posse was scouring northwestern Colorado for cattle thieves. So they turned back along Douglas Mountain, hoping to cross the river and get out to Vernal over Diamond Mountain.

When Willie Strang died, Charley Crouse, Tom Davenport, and some others started trailing Johnson and soon found where he had been joined by Tracy and Lant. On Vermillion Creek a sheepherder friendly to the outlaws informed Crouse they had gotten out to the railroad, so he turned back.

But Valentine Hoy was not satisfied with this report and began organizing a posse of ranchers to lynch Johnson. John James Strang, older brother of Willie, then sixteen, mounted a horse and rode all over the valley to notify the men. Shortly it was reported that three men had been seen riding toward Lodore Canyon. Led by Hoy, the posse started following their trail.

The outlaws had intended to try to ride out over Douglas Mountain, just east of Lodore Canyon, but found the snow too deep and started back. On a steep, narrow trail leading up from the canyon a man was discovered by the posse. All three then dived behind some large boulders where they could protect themselves.

Having seen but one man, whom he believed to be Johnson, Hoy started climbing the narrow trail, his brothers and other ranchers close behind. Soon they were halted by a shout.

"Stop where you are, Hoy! If you come a step further I'll kill you deader'n hell!"

It was the voice of Tracy and the posse's first intimation that he was with Johnson.

"We want Johnson!" Hoy shouted back, "and we're going to come up and get him. We're not after you. Put down your gun!"

"What do you want Johnson for?" Tracy asked.

"He shot Willie Strang, and we're going to hang him higher'n a kite. You keep out of this, Tracy; it's none of your affair. Who else is with you?"

"Dave Lant is here, too," replied Tracy. "There's three of us and you're not going to take Johnson or anybody else. You think you can run this country, don't you? Well, you're not going to do it this time. Go on back, damn you, or I'll shoot!"

Tracy was a natural-born killer and gloried in the chance to wreak his vengeance on anyone who crossed his path. He automatically assumed charge of the situation and took up Johnson's fight.

Hoy was well acquainted with Johnson and Lant and did not believe either would shoot. Unfortunately he did not know Tracy. The three fugitives were well protected by boulders on the trail above and had every advantage, but in spite of that Hoy determined to go up and capture them. He had climbed to within six feet of the outlaws when Tracy fired, the bullet piercing his heart. Hoy fell in a kneeling position, with his head and arms resting on a shelf of rock.

The balance of the posse immediately retreated and kept themselves hidden for two hours. When darkness fell they made their way down to the foot of the trail, where they were joined by seven more men. Just as they were making camp, a lone rider approached, leading a pack horse, and was quickly taken into custody. He proved to be Jack Bennett with a load of supplies for the three killers. He was securely tied up for the night. In the morning he was taken back to Bassett's ranch by Deputy Sheriff Farnham of Routt County, Colorado, who had just come in from the Colorado side.

No attempt was made to follow the killers. Escape from

the top of the mountain was possible in only a few places. Men were posted at all such trails, knowing that hunger and cold would soon force the fugitives down.

Up to that time the law had been extremely unwelcome in Brown's Hole. Sheriffs from the three surrounding states had carefully avoided the place. Any outlaw entering the Hole considered himself safe from pursuit. It was well known that Tracy and Lant, the escaped convicts, were hiding there, but no effort had been made to capture them, even though a substantial reward had been posted. The killing of Valentine Hoy, however, following so closely upon the murder of Willie Strang, seems to have shaken the nerves of the hardened rustlers who formed a majority of the volunteer posse. Most of them had exchanged lead with sheriffs and cowboys, and all were familiar with the smell of burning powder. But they had never before come face to face with a born killer. The sight of Valentine Hoy kneeling against the cliff with a bullet through his heart so unnerved them that they did an unaccountable thing. They sent for the law!

On the day when Strang and Hoy were killed, newly elected Sheriff William Preece of Vernal was scouting for stolen cattle in the northwest corner of Colorado, not far from the Hole. Joe Moore, one of his deputies, rode in at sundown, having come over the mountain from Vernal that day. The settlers requested him to ride back and bring the sheriff and a posse to hunt the killers who had defeated them so decisively. Moore rested his horse until 3:00 o'clock in the morning, then started back with the message, arriving in town at 3:00 o'clock next afternoon, almost exhausted. Another messenger rode to Rock Springs.

Deputy Sheriff Fowler, in Vernal, immediately called for volunteers to return to the Hole. Twenty-five men offered their services and were instructed to be ready at daylight next morning, March 3. Sheriff Preece returned in the meantime and joined the party, which then consisted of Sheriff Preece, ex-Sheriff John T. Pope, Pete Dillman, a noted hunter, Jerry Murray, Windy Thompson, Alf Johnson, Erickson, Merkeley, Pete Neilson, and many others, besides Jack Thomas, a rustler who was forced to act as guide. The cavalcade rode hard, suffering extremely from cold on the wind-swept summit of Diamond Mountain. At Charley Crouse's ranch on the Green River they were given a drink of whiskey, then rode on to the next ranch, where Mrs. Tolliver filled them up with good strong southern coffee. With their spirits revived, they pushed on to Bassett's ranch, headquarters for the hunt, arriving late in the afternoon. They had just dismounted when Harry and J. S. Hoy arrived with the body of Valentine, which had lain where it fell since the shooting. It had been necessary to hoist the body over the top of the cliff with ropes, then pack it on a horse five miles to a waiting buckboard. Pete Dillman and John Quincy Adams, an old trapper, volunteered to prepare the body for shipment to Nebraska, but at the last minute Adams lost his nerve and Dillman had to do the job alone.

Almost simultaneously with the arrival of the Vernal posse, Sheriff Swanson rode up with a number of men from Rock Springs. In a few minutes Sheriff Neimann of Routt County came in to join the balance of his posse under Deputy Farnham.

The law had come to Brown's Hole with a vengeance!

Jack Bennett, captured while trying to take supplies to the killers, had been guarded the following night by Deputy Farnham, in the post office at Bassett's ranch. Bennett had been a bad egg as long as the oldest inhabitant of the Hole could remember. He had bootlegged whiskey to the Indians and had trafficked in squaws; he wasn't even a first-class rustler. There had previously been no necessity for a jail in Brown's Hole, and there was no place where the prisoner could be safely confined. Even if he was sent out to Vernal or Rock Springs, he would undoubtedly be released in a short time. In the opinion of the Hoy brothers he ought to be tied up—by the neck. Other settlers were of the same mind. So, some time during the night, Bennett was "taken" from the officer, apparently without any great struggle, by seven self-appointed vigilantes, whose leader is believed to have been Joe Tolliver.

No cottonwoods grew nearer than the Green River, on the opposite side of the valley, but two tall gateposts of Bassett's corral, connected across the top by a stout pole, made an excellent substitute. In compliance with the unanimous desire of those present, Jack Bennett died of an acute attack of suspended animation, at 10:00 o'clock on the morning of March 2, twenty-four hours after the killing of Willie Strang. When posses from the three states arrived, Bennett was still hanging from Bassett's gate. He was not cut down until a week later. It was the intention of the settlers to decorate the same gate with three more ropes, stretched tight by the weight of Tracy, Johnson, and Lant.

When the tri-state posse arrived, the killers had already come down from the mountain, crossed the valley, and headed for Powder Springs. After a hasty meal the officers, assisted by Isom Dart, Joe Davenport, Jim McKnight, and others from the Hole took up the trail and by sundown had followed it to the "G" horse camp in the mountains, where they camped for the night.

Next morning the hunt was continued. The trail was easily followed in the snow by blood from Johnson's feet. He was a heavy man and had worn out his boots. The trail led directly toward Powder Springs, where the killers hoped to obtain horses and supplies for a getaway. Sheriff Neimann took a few men and circled toward the northeast to head off any possible escape to the stage line and railroad in that direction.

Just beyond the horse camp the posse stumbled onto the remains of a colt the outlaws had killed the evening before. Some of it had been roasted over a camp fire, the ashes of which were still warm. Windy (Longhorn) Thompson, who had put himself at the head of the posse and had been issuing orders to the sheriffs, was first to stumble onto the remains of the colt.

"There they are! Look out for Tracy!" he yelled as he started for the rear.

The two sheriffs rode up to examine the sign, then struck out again on the trail. Johnson had cut pieces of hide from the dead colt to make wrappings for his bleeding feet, and his tracks were easily followed. Several miles further on, the trail entered a wide valley near Lookout Mountain. The floor of the valley was a playa, hard packed and blown clear of snow by icy winds. The trail disappeared. By that time Windy Thompson had recovered from his fright and caught up with the sheriffs to offer more free advice.

"It's no use," he explained loudly. "We've lost 'em. Nobody could follow a trail across that valley. They've got clean away and we might's well go back."

"You talk too much to have any guts,"·Sheriff Preece broke out. "Go on back to the rear and round up the pack mules. I think we'll be able to handle this without your assistance." Then he turned to John T. Pope.

"What do you make of it?" he asked.

"If I was making a getaway," Pope replied, "I'd head for that gap in Kinny Ridge and try to get out to the road, hold up a stage, and ride to the nearest railroad station. The trail has been leading in this same direction all day. If we keep on we'll soon pick it up across the valley."

"Sounds logical," said Preece; "let's go."

As they reached the top of Kinny Ridge, the posse saw three dark specks in the valley below and knew they were near the end of their hunt. The outlaws had traveled fifty miles from their temporary hideout on Douglas Mountain, in a night and a day, on foot, without food except what they had taken from the dead colt. They were almost exhausted;

Johnson in particular was thankful the end was near. Tracy, however, was still thirsting for blood. He herded his two companions into a deep gully and ordered them not to give themselves up without a fight.

Seeing the fugitives disappear in a wash, the posse approached carefully, leaving their horses in the rear. Crawling in the snow from boulder to boulder, they got within a few rods of the gully.

"Come out and give yourselves up!" ordered Sheriff Preece.

"Who are you?" came Tracy's voice.

"I'm sheriff of Uintah County, Utah," he replied. "We've got you covered. Come out with your hands up. You're entirely surrounded." The last statement was not wholly true, as the circle of officers was open to the north; but fourteen rifles were trained on the gully.

"Go to hell!" shouted Tracy. "If you want us, come and get us."

The officers had crept so close they could hear the conversation going on below.

"For God's sake, Tracy," pleaded Johnson, "let me go out and give myself up. I'm damn near dead. I couldn't go any further even if we did get away. I'm going out."

"Not by a damn sight!" Tracy growled. "You got me into this mess, you yellow-livered bastard, and you're going to stay with me and fight it out. Make a move and I'll plug you."

"Listen to reason, Tracy," argued Lant. "We can't possibly get out of here alive. They haven't got anything on me—it's you and Johnson they're after. I'm going to give myself up."

"No you don't, Dave, you're sticking with me whether you like it or not. Who was it got you out of the pen? It was me, wasn't it? And now you want to lay down and quit!"

There was more argument as the posse waited. Every man was under nervous tension. Lying on the cold ground behind their protecting boulders without a chance to move, they shivered—but the chattering of their teeth was not all due to temperature. They knew Tracy would kill the first man who showed himself.

"Hey, Sheriff!" came Tracy's voice from the gully after a long period of silence. "Will you guarantee me a trial in Wyoming if I come out?"

"We've got you, Tracy," Preece replied, "and we're not making any promises except that you'll not be killed if you come out with your hands up."

"Come and get me, then!" the killer returned. "Why don't you do something? Are you afraid to shoot?"

"Plenty of time for that," Preece shouted back. "It's damn cold up here after sundown, and you fellows haven't got any blankets."

More curses from the wash. An hour dragged by, yet neither side offered to begin the fireworks. The tension was becoming unbearable for both hunters and hunted.

Then a group of horsemen appeared in the distance, approaching from the north. It was the Colorado posse returning after ascertaining the fugitives had not crossed the stage road.

Suddenly Johnson appeared, climbing out of the gully, too weary to care whether he was killed or not. Then Lant leaped out with both hands in the air. "Don't shoot, Sheriff," he shouted. "I'm coming out."

Tracy cursed furiously, but for some reason did not carry out his threat. He still held out, hoping for some kind of break which would give him an opportunity to kill some of the officers. He may have been hoping for rescue by a party of his friends from Powder Springs. But the break never came. Just before the Colorado posse closed in, he came out with his hands high in the air, still cursing the officers for a bunch of nerveless cowards. The chase was over. Harry Tracy, most

dangerous killer of his period, and two other outlaws had
been captured without a shot being fired. The law had come to
Brown's Hole at last!

With their three prisoners the weary posse started back to
the valley. Tracy was tied on a horse behind Isom Dart, which
scared the black man half to death. That evening (Saturday)
Tracy, Lant, and Johnson were given a preliminary hearing
before J. S. Hoy, acting as justice of the peace, and held for
trial without bail.

Beginning with news of Willie Strang's murder on the
previous Monday, Denver papers had run daily stories of conditions in and around Brown's Hole. When the posses left
Vernal and Rock Springs, it was confidently predicted the old
hideout was due for a cleaning. When they learned Jack Bennett had been hanged, they stated as a fact that the other three
outlaws would suffer the same fate when captured. No one
expected the prisoners to be brought out alive.

If left to their own inclinations, the settlers would certainly
have added three more decorations to the pole over Bassett's
gate. It is greatly to be regretted, in the light of Tracy's later
career, that they did not have their way. But the Wyoming
and Colorado sheriffs insisted on taking the prisoners out for
trial. There was some dispute as to which state should claim
them. Sheriff Preece wanted to return Tracy and Lant to the
Utah pen; but the other two officers overruled that desire, believing the men would certainly be hanged if tried for the two
murders. It was finally agreed that Johnson should be taken
by the Wyoming sheriff, since he had killed young Strang in
that state, while Sheriff Neimann took Tracy and Lant for the
killing of Hoy in Colorado.

Sheriff Swanson left the Hole with Johnson on Sunday
afternoon, arriving in Green River the next afternoon at 4:00
o'clock. He put Johnson in jail at the latter place for safekeeping, as a lynching party had been formed in Rock
Springs, where the body of Valentine Hoy had just arrived on

its way to his wife's old home in Fremont, Nebraska. Johnson was given a preliminary hearing in Green River, principal witness for the defense being William Pigeon, close friend of Jack Bennett, who had been arrested while trying to escape to Colorado. Johnson was held for trial without bail. Teeters, his partner, who was present at the killing of Strang, was found in Green River, and since it was thought he was also trying to leave the country, was thrown in jail. "Queen Ann" Bassett says he had merely gone there to pick up mail from his girl friend.

Sheriff Neimann had started for Hahn's Peak, Colorado, on Sunday morning, with Tracy and Lant. Three days later, Denver papers had heard nothing of him, and excitedly predicted the prisoners had certainly been hanged somewhere along the route. As a matter of fact, Neimann had taken an unfrequented trail to avoid any attempt at rescue by the Powder Springs gang, and arrived in Craig on Friday, March 11. From there he proceeded on to Hahn's Peak, where the two prisoners arrived safely next day.

In the meantime the governors of the three interested states were bickering for possession of the outlaws. Governor Wells insisted Tracy and Lant should be returned to Utah to finish serving their sentences. He also wanted Johnson for the old murder at Thompson's Springs. But Governor Adams argued that since Tracy and Lant would certainly hang for the murder of Hoy in Colorado, there was no use taking chances on another jail delivery. J. S. Hoy, Valentine's brother, then entered the discussion with a letter to the Denver newspapers which, although long, is well worth reproducing here:

Lodore, Colo., Mar. 6, 1898—The three outlaws and murderers of Valentine S. Hoy and Willie Strang are captured and lodged in jail "according to law."

We all know here that these men committed these two black malignant murders and justice could only be done by killing them when captured. They gave their victims no chance to tell why they should not be murdered. We know positively that these men murdered two of our citizens, but we are equally sure, after costing the counties thousands of dollars, they will be off with a few years of imprisonment, if not cleared, and set free to murder more good citizens. There is talk of sending militia to destroy or rid this country of criminals. To we people living here, knowing the country and knowing the habits of these desperadoes, it is to our minds the very best way conceivable not to capture them. Might just as well send a lot of schoolboys to do the work, to get lost or killed themselves. Hunting men in a thickly settled country or on the plains or open country is one thing, but to hunt them in these mountains snowcapped in sections the year around, cut by impassable canyons, unfordable rivers, gulches, gullies, and where nearly every section of land affords a hiding place, is another proposition. To round up the whole country is impossible, nor can any considerable number of men enter the country without their presence being known to the criminals. If these outlaws are to be gotten rid of it will be done by the men living here or by men knowing the country and acting in concert with resident citizens of good reputation.

A reward of $1,000 apiece dead or alive offered by the authorities of the three states, Colorado, Wyoming and Utah, and paid by the state where the capture is made, will do the work. One or two men on the trail of a criminal will succeed where 100 men will be sure to fail. They must be hunted like wild animals, once on their trail stay on it, camp on it, until the scoundrels are run down, and there are men who will do it, men just as brave, determined and cunning as the outlaws themselves. Knowing they will be paid for their work will be inducement enough for them to devote their whole time to the business.

Another thing, the public in general is misled in regard to the habits of these desperadoes. They think and talk of a Robbers' Roost as if they had a permanent stopping place from which as occasion or inclination moved them, they sallied forth to rob and kill. In the very nature of things a permanent abode is impossible. If such were the case they could be easily surrounded and captured by sieges if in no other way. This Harry Tracy and

Dave Lant escaped from the Utah pen last fall and have been on the move ever since. A few days in a place and fear of capture forces them to move on and keep moving. There is no permanent gang that infests any particular section for any length of time. The Roost at Powder Springs consists of a dugout and a corral. The first of March the snow still covered the ground to the depth of a foot around and on the sides of the hills of the country known as Powder Springs. This gang consists of Tracy, Lant, Johnson, who were trying to secrete themselves until the snow was gone, while such men as Bennett, Teeters and others, known and unknown, against whom no particular complaints were lodged by the authorities kept them supplied with information and food. Johnson, Tracy and Lant expected Bennett, signals were arranged so that the whereabouts of both could be made known. Bennett was captured and hung unknown to the three outlaws, their condition was made desperate being without food, overshoes and bedding and they were compelled to come down and out of the rocks, cedars and snow to the more or less open country where they were taken. Two men could have followed and killed them where a posse failed with the loss of a valuable life.

Desperadoes who are now in New Mexico this winter may be in the wilds of Montana next winter, paying this section a visit on their way, terrorizing the people, robbing camps and stealing horses en route. They are migratory criminals, here today, there tomorrow, changing their names when they change locality. The names of these men, so far as known, should be sent to the different sections, giving a minute description of each by the authorities of every state from British Columbia to Mexico, so that the work of extermination would continue until they could find no resting place. $1,000 reward for the capture of every known member of the band will put an end to them and restore peace and security to many a long-suffering and terrorized community. They are criminals by instinct and glory in their calling and the more bold and murderous an individual is, the higher he rises in the estimation of his comrades. To become a member one must be an outlaw or at least to have com-

mitted crimes that some member knows of. Then and not till
then are they entitled to the support and confidence of the
brotherhood.

J. S. HOY

This letter, published in the Denver *News* on March 11,
was eagerly read by members of the gang still at Powder
Springs. They deemed it an insult, a distinct breach of
etiquette on the part of J. S. Hoy, their neighbor, on whose
ranch they had often been employed and entertained. It was
distinctly against the code to steal from settlers in the Hole;
but Hoy's unfriendly attitude prompted them to teach him a
lesson in manners. So on March 14 they rode out in a body
to one of Hoy's cattle camps, over the line in Colorado, and
stole everything in sight—cattle, horses, wagons, camp equipment, and grub—destroying what they could not pack off.

Tracy and Lant languished in separate cells of the Hahn's
Peak jail until March 24. On that morning Lant succeeded in
breaking through to Tracy's cell. When Sheriff Neimann entered with their breakfast, he was struck over the head with
some heavy object, falling unconscious to the floor. The prisoners secured his keys, unlocked the cell door, then continued
to beat the officer for some time, robbing him of ninety dollars and leaving him tied in bed. When they left, they locked
the outside door, threw away the key, and started on foot
for Steamboat Springs.

After a time the sheriff recovered his senses, worked himself loose, and hammered on the door for help. When the lock
had been pried off he immediately started in pursuit, in spite
of his injuries. He followed the trail to Steamboat Springs,
then took a stage running southwest, hoping to head off the
fugitives before they reached the railroad.

At Larimer's ranch, six miles out of Steamboat, two men
hailed the stage, asking for a ride. Neimann squeezed into a
dark corner until they had stepped inside. He then covered
the two men, who proved to be his former prisoners, with a

sawed-off shotgun and invited them to have a free ride with him back to Hahn's Peak. Neither was armed, as they had not had time to purchase or steal any guns. The sheriff recovered his money and watch. Said the Denver *News:* "They expressed their surprise and disgust at anyone from Hahn's Peak being abroad at such an early hour."

(The 12 x 12 metal "tank" in which Tracy and Lant were confined was later moved to Steamboat Springs when that town became county seat, and in 1943 prevented two other desperate criminals from making a jail break. At that time Sheriff Neimann was still living.)

In course of time Tracy and Lant were taken to the jail at Aspen, Colorado, for safekeeping. Tracy whittled out a wooden gun, covered it with tinfoil, and with that dummy weapon again made his escape with Lant, setting a precedent for the late John Dillinger. They were not recaptured.

The two men, partners in a murder and three prison breaks, split up after their last escape. Although he was a wild young buck, Lant did not want to get mixed up in any more killings. After separating from Tracy he volunteered for the war and served in the Philippines, distinguishing himself for bravery in action, returned to Utah, and thereafter lived peaceably.

Tracy soon made his way to Oregon, and in Portland met David Merrill, another outlaw. The two resembled each other enough to be blood brothers. Tracy is said to have married Merrill's sister, Mollie Robinson. If he did, the honeymoon was short, for the two outlaws soon started a crime wave which for pure, cold-blooded killings excels the record of any other pair of the West. After a series of robberies they were arrested, but shot their way out of jail. They were finally landed in the Oregon pen, but in some manner secured two rifles and shot their way out in a nervy, spectacular, bloody prison break. They were persistently hunted for months. They stole horses, trains, and steamboats in eluding various posses. They killed at the slightest provocation or with none at all. Tracy finally accused Merrill of treachery and shot him in a duel. He then continued his killing rampage alone. He was finally surrounded in a wheatfield and, after a long, bloody battle, shot himself rather than submit to capture.

If the Brown's Hole posse had hanged Tracy beside Jack Bennett, as they planned to do, more than a score of lives would have been saved. During the siege north of Brown's Hole, Joe Davenport, who was in the posse, once had a bead on Tracy's head, but for some reason did not pull the trigger. He always regretted his leniency.

Patrick L. Johnson, killer of Willie Strang and instigator of all the trouble, was tried in Rock Springs. Since he had no attorney, the court appointed David G. Thomas, a young lawyer who had just hung out his shingle. It was his first case. Young Thomas knew he was up against a hard job, but was determined to do his best. A careful questioning of defense witnesses seemed to indicate the shooting had been accidental rather than intentional. When the jury was polled, eleven were for acquittal and one for conviction. Johnson went back to jail while the case went to the supreme court of Wyoming. That tribunal finally ruled the trial court had erred in refusing to admit Willie Strang's dying testimony, to the effect that Johnson had not intended to kill him. Johnson was released from the Rock Springs jail, after two years' confinement, but was immediately rearrested by the sheriff of Routt County and taken to Aspen for trial on the charge of being an accomplice in the killing of Valentine S. Hoy. He was convicted and served two years. He then returned east and as recently as 1938 was supposed to be still living in Iowa. Charles A. Teeters ran a hotel in Rock Springs until his death in 1945. John James Strang, older brother of Willie, was known to be living in Torrance, California, in 1949.

Two Wars
Are Declared

THE killing of Willie Strang and Valentine S. Hoy in Brown's Hole on March 1, 1898, the hanging of Jack Bennett, the operations of posses from three surrounding states, and the escape of Harry Tracy and Dave Lant from jail at Hahn's Peak, Colorado, released a flood of publicity concerning activities of the Wild Bunch, the Powder Springs, Hole-in-the-Wall, and Brown's Hole outlaws. Deplorable conditions existing at Three Corners, where rustlers and outlaws had defied the law for years, were brought to public attention and created a furore of indignation which finally prodded the governors of the three states into some semblance of action. Denver papers were especially active in calling attention to the matter. On March 4 the Denver *News* said:

The gang of outlaws now pursued by the posse is but a small detachment of the greatest organized band of thieves and murderers that ever rendezvoused in the west. These men have a line of strongholds extending from Powder Springs, Wyoming, in a southwesterly direction across the entire state of Utah and down into Arizona, giving them easy access to Mexico.

This strip of country is rugged and broken and almost impregnable by a stranger, and abounds in caves, deep gorges, and strongholds from which it is impossible to dislodge the outlaws who have trails unknown to any except themselves.

The number of outlaws operating from these headquarters is variously estimated at from 50 to 500 and the correct number is somewhere between these two extremes. Whenever a convict escapes from the Utah penitentiary or a murder is committed, the criminal heads for this outlaw strip and once he reaches it he is safe from pursuit . . .

The gang planned the robbery of a Union Pacific train last summer but their plot was revealed to the officers by the capture of a letter in the mails. Since that time they have written no more letters, but communicate with each other by a regular system of couriers and cipher dispatches. The extermination of this band is a problem with which the authorities of the states interested seem unable to cope.

Since failure of the famous "Invasion" of 1892, stockmen had done little to curb rustler activities. Occasionally one was arrested, but no convictions could be had. A few had been shot by sheriffs or cattlemen; but no organized effort to exterminate the gangs had been made for some time. Cattlemen merely marked off a certain percentage of expected losses and let it go at that.

Rising prices for cattle in 1898, however, had caused an alarming increase in rustling. The gang assembled at Powder Springs from both Robbers' Roost and Hole-in-the-Wall were sweeping the country clean and many stockmen had been forced to abandon that section of county. On March 6 the Denver *News* said:

For three or four years there have been several gangs of outlaws in the western district who defied the authorities. They were in league and had several retreats wherein they felt secure from invasion by deputy sheriffs and common officers. The more prominent of these dens are "Robbers' Roost" and "Hole-in-the-

Wall." The gangs have almost depopulated the ranges within 200 miles of their retreats, and travelers, farmers and freight wagons have been robbed so frequently as to cause little comment. Murder has been frequent. The large cattle companies have been almost driven out of business. Their herds and flocks have been run off, brands changed, and stock sent out almost under the eyes of the officers. The local police are terror stricken. The ranchmen are either open friends of the outlaws' or else are so terrorized as to be compelled to give them help. Thieves, murderers and burglars from all over the country have joined the gangs and radical measures are needed to get them out. Ordinary measures will not do and much blood will undoubtedly be shed before the three states are rid of the pests.

The large companies have been quietly laying plans for a war of extermination for a year past. One of the large detective agencies of the country has been employed to gather evidence and there have been men in the dens for months past quietly gathering together such data as will enable the authorities to make a clean sweep not only of the ordinary bandits but of the alleged ranchers who act as spotters and guards on the outside. That this information is nearly complete is shown by the activity on the part of Governors Adams and Wells. During the recent cattle convention a resolution was adopted calling on the governors of Colorado, Utah and Wyoming to assist in ridding the country of the desperadoes. The resolutions were presented by a man near the head of the councils with the secret service department, and they went through without much discussion, only the real leaders of the convention being aware of the details connected with the future movement.

Several days ago a secret meeting of parties interested was held in the private office of Governor Adams. At that meeting were representatives of the large cattle companies, Governor Richards of Wyoming, as well as an unofficial representative of Governor Wells of Utah. A man in possession of the reports of the secret service men gave a résumé of the evidence at hand and it was sufficient to startle the state executives. It was shown that a state of terror existed, the like of which does not bear a parallel in western or eastern history. Nothing short of a combined military movement will have any effect, and it is possible that troops from Fort Duchesne will be called upon to aid the civil authorities. Only the establishment of an impregnable cordon around a vast stretch of territory, the declaration of martial law within the lines and then a gradual closing in will get what the people of the district declare they must have. They are afraid of mere arrests, for it will then be only the matter of a short time until every man will be out on bail. Martial law and death to those who resist authority only will suffice, and the outcome promises to be one of the most sensational affairs in the history of the state since the Custer Massacre.

The meeting of cattlemen referred to took place in Denver, when a resolution was passed demanding concerted action by the three interested states. All three governors promised cooperation when a workable plan had been formed, and the convention adjourned. But delegates had scarcely left Denver before newspapers were filled with stories of the Strang and Hoy murders, which came at just the right time to stir the states to action. The plan decided on at the Denver convention was to be carried out with great secrecy, in order to prevent a flight from Powder Springs and Brown's Hole, and for that reason the three governors were reticent about furnishing bulletins to the press. However, a persistent demand for action by the Denver *News* brought these responses:

Cheyenne, Wyo., March 4, 1898

Rocky Mountain News, Denver: Wyoming will cooperate with Colorado or any adjoining state in the suppression of lawlessness.

W. A. RICHARDS, Governor

Salt Lake City, Utah, March 4, 1898

Rocky Mountain News, Denver: Am doing everything within my power to assist in their arrest and extermination. My authority to offer rewards is limited to escaped convicts and felons.

Recent murders were committed in Wyoming and Colorado. Will cooperate in every way possible.

HEBER M. WELLS,
Governor of Utah

The plan as originally outlined required the militia of three states to surround Brown's Hole, then to begin closing in, arresting or killing every man who could not give a good account of himself. But the letter from J. S. Hoy, brother of the murdered Valentine, published in Denver papers (see page 201), discouraged such a plan as being impracticable. Hoy suggested a small force of experienced officers who would camp on the trail and eliminate outlaws one by one. Hoy's idea seemed sound, and for that reason the governors began considering a force of fifteen officers, five from each state, who would have authority to kill on sight, and who could be employed for $100 a month each. Such a force, it was thought, would be more effective and much less expensive. Governor Wells of Utah proposed to furnish Joe Bush and ex-Sheriff Fowler of Utah County, who had already led two expeditions into the Roost country, as part of his contribution to the army of fifteen. This plan had already been suggested at a secret meeting of cattlemen and detectives held in Rawlins on February 15.

On March 14 Governor Adams of Colorado and Governor Richards of Wyoming journeyed to Salt Lake City for a conference with Governor Wells of Utah, to determine final action and set a date for the opening of warfare. The meeting was held behind closed doors. Governor Stunenberg of Idaho was also invited to cooperate.

During this conference of governors John H. Ward of Evanston, Wyoming, most fearless and efficient sheriff of his period, visited Salt Lake City, where he was interviewed by a reporter. Ward was at that time on the outs with the Wyoming governor, because of the latter's pardoning of so many rustlers and outlaws he had risked his life to capture. Ward denied his presence had any connection with the conference.

"I have an idea," he said, "of the proper method to be pursued in capturing outlaws, but I don't feel like telling it for publication. Whenever I happen to want one of those men, I'll demonstrate my idea to you; that's better by far than sitting in an easy chair here in the city and telling how men should be caught."

The conference of governors finally ended as the biggest social event of the season in Salt Lake, with nothing definite accomplished. When interviewed, the three executives looked secretive, smiled knowingly, and finally admitted that the matter had been turned over to their various legal departments in order to determine their powers. To search the statutes of the various states required considerable time. Meanwhile they gave newspapers to understand that something might happen any minute.

Something did happen! On April 25, 1898, the United States declared war on Spain. The outlaws of Brown's Hole were instantly forgotten and the men who might have formed the tri-state militia for extermination of outlaws immediately volunteered to help exterminate Spaniards in Cuba.

Then occurred another incident still more surprising. All rustlers on the Outlaw Trail were American citizens, as patriotic toward their flag as any other group. They enjoyed fighting and were accustomed to the odor of burning powder. When news reached Brown's Hole, Robbers' Roost, and Hole-in-the-Wall that the *Maine* had been sunk, they forgot their old enemies—sheriffs and cattle barons—in their anxiety to fight Spaniards.

Word went out on the underground telegraph that the boys were to meet at Steamboat Springs, Colorado, to form a troop of cavalry to be known as the "Wild Bunch." On the appointed day, hard-riding, quick-shooting buckaroos began drifting in from all directions. It is not unlikely that Butch

Cassidy himself passed the word, and it goes without saying that if a company had been formed he would have been elected leader. The Wild Bunch might have contested for honors with the famous "Rough Riders." But fate willed otherwise.

When the meeting got under way, enthusiasm ran high until some of the older heads began asking embarrassing questions. What would be the status of an outlaw in the army? Would he be arrested when he showed up for enlistment? Or would he be thrown in jail after being discharged? Would his service in the army wipe out his past deeds, or would his description in army records betray him to civil officers after the war?

Younger men who itched to try their marksmanship on Spaniards favored taking a chance and volunteering in a body. They pictured themselves returning home covered with medals and glory, their past all forgotten. But older men were more cautious. Cattle rustling might be overlooked, but some had blood on their hands which might not be easily washed away. Unfortunately for history, the final vote was "No."

That decision, however, did not prevent many from volunteering. None of the outlaws who enlisted, so far as the record shows, ever returned to the Outlaw Trail.

Various reports claim that Butch Cassidy also enlisted in the army and served in the Philippines, but no proof has been found. Bob Calverly, who arrested Butch Cassidy in Wyoming, was a lieutenant under Theodore Roosevelt in the Rough Riders.

General J. P. O'Neil, of Portland, Oregon, told me an interesting story of his experiences in the Philippines while in command of a detachment of fifty mule packers recruited from the Southwest, three of whom were apparently former members of Cassidy's Wild Bunch. In San Francisco, after having loaded five hundred mules efficiently and with despatch, they were given shore leave and "took in" the old Barbary

Coast. Sixty policemen escorted them back to their ship. After that final spree they behaved with credit during the balance of their enlistment, and before being discharged gave General O'Neil a gold ring which he has worn constantly ever since. The general said:

The reputation of these fifty packers had preceded them to Manila. In the island of Mindanao the pack trains could hardly get through on account of the constant forays of fierce Moros. When these fifty packers were assigned to this district the Moros jumped them as they had the others. After the first three or four pack trains had gone over the trail, complaints began pouring into headquarters that the packers were killing large numbers of Moros and leaving their bodies on the trail. Not a single pack train of which these packers were in charge failed to arrive at its destination. These packers were also responsible for many an insurgent and many a fierce ladrone arriving at the happy hunting ground, or wherever dead Moros go.

Major Frederick H. Sparrenberger, retired army surgeon, confirmed this and added some interesting personal experiences in a letter dated September 10, 1940:

On Dec. 2, 1899, I was assigned to duty as surgeon aboard the U.S. army transport *Centennial* to sail for Manila. We left San Francisco July 6, 1900, with 350 horses and some 50 packers and muleskinners. Capt. Lewis H. Koehler was commanding officer on this trip. He was known in the service as "Toughy" Koehler.

This bunch of packers were a pretty tough crew from the Southwest; had a fine time on the Barbary Coast before sailing. We were told that some of Butch Cassidy's crowd were present. They behaved remarkably well until we got to Honolulu, where we went into camp for some thirty days awaiting the arrival of a ship, the *Addenian*.

The packers came aboard the *Addenian* after loading the horses pretty well liquored up with Honolulu's "swipes," and within eight hours after leaving got into a fight among themselves in their quarters. The captain of the ship came to the quarters of Capt. Koehler and myself scared to death. Koehler and I went down to the packers' quarters and it was a mess; broken furniture, gunplays, men hurt and bleeding. Believe me, the old West never had such a party as we ran into then.

We landed at Manila, and these packers, with several of the horses, were sent down to Mindanao in the Moro country. The Moros, prior to arrival of this band of packers, had killed two or three packers on the old Camp Vicors-Malabang trail; but this bunch of packers told the Moros to keep off and it took some time for this to sink in. Thereafter, when the bell on the bell mare was heard on the trail the Moros left the country. A soldier escort was sent with the pack train, not to protect the packers but to protect the Moros. The pack train never had any more trouble. I personally have ridden over that thirty-two-mile trail alone, without an escort, but I took it on a lope.

The Battle
of Roost Canyon

Because of the excitement prevailing during the Spanish-American War of 1898, no attempt was made to interfere with the activities of rustlers in Robbers' Roost that year; but the rising price of cattle had made rustling a very profitable business, and raids on stock ranches increased alarmingly.

Caustic newspaper comments and insistent protests of cattle owners finally forced Governor Wells into action. Utah sheriffs were paid only $500 a year at that time, little inducement for them to risk their necks trying to capture desperate criminals. To overcome this difficulty, Governor Wells offered a reward of $500 each for a list of twelve well-known rustlers using the Roost as headquarters. The list included Silver Tip, Blue John, Jack Moore, Pete Neilson, Charley Lee, Tom Dilley, and Mrs. Jack Moore.

In the latter part of February, 1899, Blue John and Silver Tip visited the town of Moab. After their departure a number of fine horses were missing. Sheriff Tyler suspected the pair and decided to go to the Roost after them. Up to that time no sheriff had ever entered the Roost. Joe Bush had arrested Blue John once previously and had scouted around the edges. A posse had come in looking for Joe Walker but got no further than a few miles beyond Hanksville. The Roost itself was—by reputation—impregnable.

With half a dozen deputies, Sheriff Jesse M. (Jack) Tyler left Moab, rode to Greenriver, turned south, crossed the San Rafael, and gradually climbed the summit of the Swell. He was guided by a man who had been in the hideout and knew the country. This guide led him directly to Roost Canyon. The stolen horses were grazing on the mesa above. That night the posse made a dry camp, prepared for an early-morning assault on outlaw headquarters.

Roost Canyon proper is a long, deep sandstone gorge running north from the Dirty Devil River. Its walls are perpendicular and there is no way to get in or out of the canyon except through its mouth on the Dirty Devil. Above the blind northern end of the gorge and south of what is now called Roost Ranch, is a secondary canyon, several hundred feet above the main gorge. In that upper canyon are several wind-hollowed caves, two of which were frequently used by outlaws. Across the opening of one large cave was built a rough rock wall for defensive purposes. A stratum of white sandstone carried water and made the place an ideal camp. The caves were a considerable distance below the surface of the surrounding country.

Early on the morning of March 5, 1899, Tyler and his men crawled to the edge of the cliff and looked down into Roost Canyon. The large cave below was occupied by Silver Tip, Blue John, Ed Newcomb (a halfbreed Indian from Oklahoma formerly associated with the outlaw Henry Starr), and another unnamed. Newcomb was on his way to the spring with a bucket; the other three were still in their blankets. Glancing upward, the halfbreed saw a Stetson hat against the skyline. Dropping his bucket he rushed back to the cave, grabbed a rifle, and started shooting. The other three rolled out of their blankets and followed his example.

The wall across the cave's opening furnished temporary protection against the officers' bullets which began pouring down from above. After the first fusillade the posse began taking more careful aim but could not make a direct hit, as the outlaws were close behind the wall. But when some of the better marksmen began shooting against the slanting cave roof, causing the bullets to ricochet back toward the wall, it became evident to the four below that their hideout would soon be too hot for comfort.

The outlaws' horses were feeding on the mesa above, across from the posse's position. A steep trail zigzagging from ledge to ledge up the canyon wall was the only exit. To escape from the cave and reach their horses, the four men were forced to climb that narrow trail, exposed to the officers' fire.

"I'll stay here behind the wall," said Silver Tip, "and keep up a hot fire while you fellows make a run for it. If you get to the top, start blazing away until I come up. Maybe we can keep 'em too busy dodging bullets to do any shooting."

Blue John went first, covered by the blazing guns of the other three. Then the unknown man ran for the top, followed by the Indian. While the three above distracted the posse's attention, Silver Tip made his escape. The Indian received a bullet through the leg; otherwise there were no casualties.

The posse could not cross the canyon because of the steep cliff on their side. Once out of the trap and mounted again, Silver Tip felt quite brave. Besides, he was thoroughly mad. Sheriff Tyler had ventured where he had no business. Didn't he know the Roost was impregnable? Unless he was taught a lesson, no rustler would be safe. The more Silver Tip thought of it the madder he got.

"Let's run the bastards clear back to Moab!" he suggested to Blue John. "If we take after 'em they'll run like jackrabbits."

"Go ahead if you feel like it," said Blue John, "but I'm movin' outa here pronto. It's lucky we got out of that cave alive. Come on, I'm headin' for Dandy Crossing."

"Damn your soul, Blue John, you're yellow as hell. I always thought so; now I know it."

"Get yourself killed if you want to, I'm on my way."

"Goin' to run like a coyote, eh? How about the rest of you? Goin' to stick with me?"

The halfbreed hung his head. That bullet in his leg hurt, and all he wanted was to get away from Roost Canyon.

"Go to hell, then, all of you," cursed Silver Tip, "and don't let me see hide nor hair of you again!"

Blue John and the Indian headed for Dandy Crossing. Silver Tip rode south toward the Henrys. The route of the other man is unknown. At the crossing of the Colorado, Ed Newcomb, the halfbreed, forded the river and was last seen going up White Canyon. Blue John borrowed a leaky old boat from Cass Hite and started downstream. A day or two later he camped with Arthur Chaffin and some other miners on California Bar. They warned him about the boat but he seemed to be in a hurry. Since he was never seen again, they believe he was drowned somewhere below.

Sheriff Tyler and his posse, after seeing the outlaws escape, might have been expected to circle the canyon and continue the chase. Instead they mounted and—according to one old-timer—"busted their cinches" trying to get back to Moab in record time. The famous Battle of Roost Canyon had passed into history!

The results of Tyler's expedition were worse than negative. He had proved the place was not impregnable and had shot away two hundred rounds of good ammunition, only to see the outlaws escape before his eyes almost without a scratch. He excused his failure by saying the Roost was full of dangerous criminals and he did not want to risk the lives of his men by pursuing them with such a small force.

In view of another circumstance, his excuse sounded logical. C. L. Maxwell, confined in the Utah pen for the Springville bank robbery, wrote a letter to Governor Wells about that time, containing "complete information" on the Roost and the men who occupied it. According to Maxwell, the gang consisted of two hundred desperate men, well protected by a series of fortifications, tunnels, and mines, with supplies enough cached in their caves to last indefinitely. Maxwell offered to betray his old pals and guide an expedition to the Roost in exchange for his freedom. The letter made quite an impression on the governor and may have been one of the reasons why Maxwell was pardoned in such a short time. His imaginary description of the Roost has remained a classic among writers of fiction to the present day.

After Governor Wells issued his offer of $500 each for twelve Roosters, Joe Bush decided to go back and clean out the place. He outfitted at Torrey, where he picked up Ott Thompson and Cox, then rode on to Hanksville and added Jack Cottrell to his posse. The four men rode out to Granite ranch, which was to be their operating headquarters.

Joe Raleigh, a Salt Lake deputy sheriff, had little faith in Bush's efforts. He didn't believe there were any outlaws in the Roost worth catching. He thought Bush was manufacturing stories of rustler activities in order to draw four dollars a day and expenses. So Raleigh went to Governor Wells with an offer to investigate the facts. He proposed to enter the Roost with three other men disguised as prospectors and report on what he found. The governor agreed to the proposition and gave him instructions to pass through the Roost, learn what he could, then report to Joe Bush at Granite ranch.

With Andrew Burt, ex-sheriff of Salt Lake County, and ex-Sheriff Fowler of Utah County, Raleigh went to Moab, where he outfitted and picked up a guide who knew the country. The horse that Raleigh hired for his trip was a roan called Suze— the same horse Bill McCarty had been riding when he was killed by W. Ray Simpson after the bank robbery at Delta, Colorado. The animal was one of three race horses the Mc-Cartys had brought from Iowa and trained for the business of bank robbery. She would stand perfectly motionless while her rider shot between her ears. She had been traded off by Tom McCarty a short time before, at the mouth of Oak Creek, east of Boulder Mountain. Raleigh was warned it was bad luck to ride old Suze, but he took a chance.

Dressed as prospectors, Raleigh and his three companions left Moab, arriving in Greenriver two days later. In a saloon there they met Jack Cottrell, half drunk, telling all and sundry about the imminent invasion of the Roost! Cottrell left Greenriver early next morning to join Bush at Hanksville.

Raleigh and his men rode leisurely southward across the San Rafael Desert to Hanksville. From here they rode to Dandy Crossing, where Raleigh spent two or three days visiting with John Hite. The other three men crossed the river in search of outlaws. Seeing none, they returned, picked up Raleigh, and rode back to Granite ranch, where they joined Joe Bush. On their entire trip they had not seen a single outlaw!

News reached Bush at Granite, however, that Silver Tip had stolen a bunch of horses and was headed for Arizona. With the combined posse of eight he started in pursuit. The trail was fresh and plain. They followed it south through the roughest kind of country to Salt Wash, known locally as "Sopeye," on the Pariah River twenty miles above Lee's Ferry. The posse made a dry camp and prepared for an early morning attack.

Silver Tip was camped in an abandoned cabin just above the Wash. Bush ordered two men to approach the front and shout. He and Ott Thompson hid themselves in the wash below. With guns drawn, the first two men leisurely began closing in. At their shout, Silver Tip jumped out a back window, lit out down the wash and ran plump into the arms of Joe Bush.

Bush had drawn his six-shooter; but when he tried to cock

it the hammer stuck, because of a defective primer. Thompson, scared half out of his wits, was trembling like a leaf. In his excitement he accidentally discharged his gun, narrowly missing Bush. Silver Tip was armed with a very fancy gun but did not have an opportunity to use it. Bush stepped up and relieved him of the weapon, then snapped on the handcuffs.

"Well," said Bush with a sigh of relief, "we finally got you, Silver Tip. But I was worried for a minute. My gun jammed and I couldn't have shot you if you had made a break."

"Hell's bells!" cursed the outlaw. "If I'd a-knowed that, you'd never have put the bracelets on me. Thompson here was skeered stiff. I could have got both of you. Damn the luck!"

With Silver Tip, the only outlaw caught on the entire expedition, Joe Bush and posse returned to Hanksville, where they arrived on June 6. On their way, Bush stopped at Granite ranch and picked up J. B. Buhr and Mrs. Jack Moore, charging them with harboring criminals. In this arrest Raleigh and his companions refused to take part.

Mrs. Moore and Buhr were tried in Hanksville. The trial lasted two or three days. During the proceedings Buhr bought a barrel of beer with which to treat his friends—including Joe Raleigh—but not including Joe Bush. Both he and Mrs. Moore were discharged.

Bush then went on to Torrey, where he turned his prisoner over to John Hancock, twenty-two-year-old sheriff of Wayne County. Hancock, who did not own a gun, kept Silver Tip in his own house several days, unguarded, the outlaw making no effort to escape. Later he was transferred to the Provo jail for safekeeping.

On September 18, 1899, Silver Tip was returned to Loa for trial, charged with "assault with intent to commit murder" on Sheriff Jesse M. Tyler. Such a charge, it was thought, could be more easily proved than the crime of horse stealing and would draw a longer sentence. It looked like a cut-and-dried case.

The boys in the Roost took up a collection and hired Colonel Tatlock, an able lawyer from Salt Lake, to conduct the defense. Testifying in his own behalf, Silver Tip swore he did not know that the men who fired at him were officers of the law. They had not called on him to surrender, had not even shown their badge of office. He thought he was being attacked by a gang of robbers, and naturally defended himself as well as he could. He was just an ordinary cowhand, he said, working for J. B. Buhr, and had never seen any suspicious characters in the Roost. On examination, Sheriff Tyler admitted he had no warrants for Silver Tip.

"Do I look like a horse thief?" asked the outlaw from the witness stand. "I could point out a dozen men in this courtroom who look more like outlaws than I do." The court admitted that to be a fact. Silver Tip's friends had dressed him in a new outfit of clothes. With his well-trimmed beard and his soft voice, he looked less a horse thief than any man in the courtroom excepting possibly his attorney.

But in spite of the testimony Silver Tip was found guilty and received a sentence of ten years in the pen. His lawyer then petitioned for a new trial. The petition was granted. On rehearing, the prisoner was discharged. Gathering up his band of stolen horses, he changed his name and continued his interrupted journey to Arizona, where he was later killed by an Arizona sheriff.

As an aftermath of this affair, Mrs. Jack Moore started suit against Joe Bush in the amount of $2,100 damages for seizing the horses found in possession of Blue John and Silver Tip!

Thus the law came to Robbers' Roost!

The One-man Army

Tᴏᴍ Hᴏʀɴ has been dead more than fifty-five years, yet the mere mention of his name still sends cold chills coursing down the spines of all those who remember the old days in Brown's Hole.

Horn's earlier history, written by himself while awaiting execution for an alleged murder, is a rare item of Americana and an exciting tale of Indian warfare. It tells how he came west as a boy, fell in with Al Sieber, a famous Indian scout, learned all the Indians' tricks, and had no inconsiderable part in finally subduing the Apaches in one of the most spectacular and futile campaigns in the history of American Indian warfare. In his capacity as scout, Tom Horn earned a well-deserved reputation for endurance, bravery, and dependability.

After the Apache campaign, Horn tried various ways of making a living. He ranched, he mined, he took any employment he could find, but none of his subsequent occupations provided the excitement and thrills that were his bread and meat. The autobiography brings his story down to the year 1903 but unfortunately omits one of the most exciting periods

of his life. For the following facts we are principally indebted
to William G. Tittsworth and Albert "Speck" Williams.

After organizing their association, the cattlemen of Wyoming tried various methods of ridding the country of rustlers. They hired detectives and reported thefts to county sheriffs, but juries of "nesters" seldom convicted their neighbors.
They had finally organized the "Invasion," but it proved an
almost total failure.

In desperation, certain members of the association agreed to
try one more scheme. The idea was to hire some fearless man,
a stranger to the thieves, who would secretly and quietly pick
off the rustlers one by one, striking where least expected and
without warning—an Unknown Terror.

The operative finally selected for this hazardous job was
Tom Horn, whose temperament and earlier experiences perfectly fitted him for such a commission. He was absolutely
fearless, could follow any kind of trail, knew how to protect
himself and live off the country when necessary. With the exception of two or three cattle-association officers, no one knew
who had been selected for the undertaking. Absolute secrecy
was essential.

Tom Horn had checked off plenty of Apaches in his time
but had never been known as a gunfighter. At the time of his
employment he was down and out, had been drinking heavily,
and was known as a saloon bum. His activities for the association previous to his operations in Brown's Hole are clothed in
utmost secrecy. No records were kept, for obvious reasons.
But when certain well-known rustlers were mysteriously
found dead—"dry-gulched" in the language of the range—the
association quietly passed the information that the killer was
Tom Horn, a name which had previously meant nothing.

In an incredibly short time the mysterious Tom Horn
gained a wide and unenviable reputation. His name was
spoken in whispers by every rustler in Wyoming, Colorado,
and Utah. No one knew what he looked like or where he

would strike next. It was rumored—and is still believed—that he received $500 for every dead rustler, and that belief made him the most hated man in the West. As an officer of the law he might have accepted rewards for dead outlaws without criticism, but as a hired killer, at $500 a head, he was thought to be "lower than the shadow of a snake's belly." Yet every guilty man, believing his life worth $500 to Tom Horn, trembled in his sleep.

When Horn entered Brown's Hole in 1900, he had already become a legendary monster. Hundreds of cattle thieves, it was said, had been "dry-gulched" without a chance to defend themselves—without any warning—without seeing their enemy. It was the horrible uncertainty of his methods that threw the outlaws into a panic. Their secret terror was not less than the terror inspired in earlier days by Porter Rockwell, Avenging Angel of the Mormon Church, whose methods Tom Horn had adopted.

Under the name of Tom Hix, Horn entered Brown's Hole in the spring of 1900, posing as a horse buyer, in order to gather evidence against rustlers. His first stop was at the Bassett ranch, where he was entertained with frontier hospitality. There he met young Joe Davenport and inquired if his father had horses to sell. He then went to the E. H. Rife ranch, where he boarded for a time, and during the early summer visited all ranches in the Hole. For two or three weeks he made his headquarters with Albert Williams, the "Speckled Nigger," who particularly warned this writer before his death not to mention the fact. After weeks of careful investigation his suspicions rested on two men as being leaders in the rustling of cattle. Their names were Matt Rash and Isom Dart, who have been introduced to the reader earlier in this book.

Matt Rash was from Cleburne, Texas, and has been described by his contemporaries as a likable, friendly young man. He had come to the Hole in 1883, followed a year later by Isom Dart, the Negro. Rash had worked as a cowhand for the Middlesex outfit, Tim Kinney, and the 2-Bar ranch on the Little Snake River. In revenge for being fired, he stole seven hundred head of Kinney's cattle to start a ranch of his own on Cold Springs Mountain, five miles from the Mexican Joe Trail. At Summit Springs, on the same mountain, Isom Dart had his ranch, also stocked with stolen cattle. During his investigations Tom Horn learned of the smoldering feud between Rash and Dart caused by the reported murder of Mincy, the halfbreed Indian girl, who had been befriended by the Negro. Toward the end he had in view, Horn quietly passed word that each had threatened to kill the other.

To be absolutely sure of his men, Horn hired out to Matt Rash as cook during the spring roundup in the Hole, and later agreed to stay on as cowhand. Matt liked his new employee so well he made him a present of a fine saddle horse. As an employee, Horn probably assisted in some of Rash's rustling activities, thereby gaining positive evidence.

Sam Spicer (who died in 1947) owned a very troublesome bull which had taken such a personal dislike to Isom Dart that the Negro threatened to kill it. One day Matt Rash rode to Dart's place at Summit Springs and found the bull killed and dressed, with the burned hide still lying on the ground. Matt embraced this opportunity to give the Negro a cursing. A wordy battle ensued during which the whole story of the Indian girl and various other shady activities were thoroughly aired, in Tom Horn's hearing. This quarrel furnished all the evidence needed, besides an almost perfect alibi for Horn, who advised Rash to "kill the damn nigger." Becoming frightened, Dart went to Spicer and arranged to buy the troublesome bull which, unknown to its owner, had already been quartered.

Shortly after this incident, on June 20, Tom Horn left Matt Rash and took a job with the 2-Bar outfit on the Little Snake River. Rash went to Rock Springs to attend the Fourth of July celebration and had his picture taken with Mike Nicholson and Billy Harris. He started home on the fifth, camping with Willis Rouef and James Taggart on Red Creek, and the following night slept at Bassett's ranch. At 4:30 on the afternoon of July 7 he started for his cabin, nine miles away, and that is the last time he was seen alive. He was thirty-five.

When the fatal hour arrived, Matt was alone in his cabin, his horse tied nearby. To draw his victim from the shack, Horn shot the horse. At the sound, Matt rushed to the door, where he presented a perfect target and instantly received three bullets from Horn's .30-.30 rifle—one in the lung, one in the hip, and one in the back as he fell. The killer then rode back to the 2-Bar ranch.

On July 10, Felix Meyers and Uncle Billy Rife were riding past Rash's cabin. Meyers threw open the door and gave an Indian war whoop, his customary greeting, before his eyes accommodated themselves to the dark interior. In a moment he noticed the floor of the cabin covered with dried blood, and in another instant discovered the body of Matt Rash lying in a bunk four feet from the floor. He immediately called to Billy Rife and together they examined the cabin. There were no signs of a struggle. Rash had evidently been killed as he stood in the door and the killer had then lifted his body onto the bunk. His pocketbook and watch were found on one of the logs over the bunk. Robbery was not the motive.

Rife remained at the cabin while Meyers rode to Bassett's with the gruesome news. He returned later with John Dempshire, A. L. Sparks, and George and Eb Bassett, when a consultation was held. Eb then rode to Rock Springs, George started for Craig to notify the sheriff and coroner, while Larry Curtain notified residents of Brown's Hole. No one had any idea why he had been killed.

J. S. Hoy, who seems to have been a self-appointed justice of the peace, held an inquest, since the body could not be kept longer, then rode to Hahn's Peak, Colorado, to report. Matt was buried on Friday, July 13, near his cabin. As a matter of historical record his mourners were John Erickson, Sam

Spicer, Charley Sparks, Larry Curtain, W. H. Blair, Carol Blair, John Dempshire, William May, Claude Casebeer, O. Rosewold, Bale Herndon, Joe Davenport, Chris Bevin, W. Amidon, Sam Bassett, and Speck Williams.

To avert suspicion, Tom Horn remained in the Hole, stopping at Speck's place, among others, to spread the rumor that Rash had been killed by Isom Dart. It was a logical theory, in view of their previous relations, especially after their quarrel over Spicer's bull.

Matt Rash, like other young men in the Hole, had been courting the Bassett girls and had formed a special attachment for "Queen Ann." The depth of this attachment was not realized until after his death, when, according to newspaper reports, Ann Bassett filed a will in which she was named beneficiary of his estate. In August, Matt's father came from Cleburne, Texas, with Bledsoe, a lawyer, to claim the estate. Charley Crouse was appointed administrator and Judge David Reavill was retained to handle legal details.

On the day appointed, all interested parties started for Hahn's Peak, seat of Routt County, in which the killing had occurred. Ann Bassett and her brother Eb were on the road also, and all took dinner at Mrs. Walihan's. It had been the intention to fight Ann's purported claim; but somewhere along the road a compromise was reached whereby the girl accepted $300 for her claim and returned to the Hole.

At the time of this compromise Ann charged Tom Horn, who was present, with the murder of Matt Rash; but the charge seemed so absurd that others of the party passed it off as a joke. Tom was so cool and so amused that even Ann and her brother seemed to have some doubts and let the matter drop.

When the elder Rash and his lawyer returned from the county seat they stayed at Bassett's ranch. A few weeks later Charles Neimann, ex-sheriff of Routt County, who was among those present when the law came to Brown's Hole, bought

Matt Rash's cattle; the estate was settled and Matt's father returned to Texas.

One morning in September the cattle thieves of Brown's Hole arose to find notices tacked on their cabin doors warning them to leave the country within ten days or suffer the consequences. Similar notices, they all knew, had been posted previous to the "dry-gulching" of many of the mysterious Tom Horn's victims in other parts of Wyoming. These new warnings seemed to be definite proof that Horn was in the Hole and meant to exterminate all rustlers. "Tom Hix," the cowhand, had been successful in diverting suspicion from himself even after the killing of Matt Rash, except for the half-hearted accusation of Ann Bassett. After the notices had been posted it was discovered Tom Hix had disappeared; the Bassetts' suspicions seemed to have been confirmed, and general sentiment in the Hole agreed that Tom Hix was none other than the terrible, deadly, mysterious Tom Horn, who received $500 a head for dead rustlers. The killing of Rash was then explained —he was number one on Horn's list. Who would be next? Several young men closed their affairs and left the Hole during the next few days, but the majority were not yet convinced the warnings were genuine.

Tom Horn, it was afterwards learned, went to Ogden, staying there several weeks. Early in October he took a train for Rawlins, then quietly worked back to the 2-Bar ranch on the Little Snake River, where he stayed until the ninth.

When daylight broke on the morning of October 11, Isom Dart, the Negro rustler, stepped from his cabin door to answer the call of nature. He had taken not more than a dozen steps when a rifle cracked and Isom fell, shot through the heart. Three young men who had started to follow the Negro trampled each other in their hasty endeavor to get back inside.

Five men had spent the night in Isom's cabin at Summit Springs: Con Dresher, Gail Walker, Joe Davenport, George and Eb Bassett. They were as brave as any other five men in the Hole and had defied the mysterious warning to leave. No one had seen the killer who fired the fatal shot, but Isom's dead body was definite and convincing proof that Tom Horn was a man who meant business. They firmly believed they were all marked for slaughter, and their blood turned to water. Barricading the door, they remained inside all that day, not even daring to go to a nearby spring for water. After sundown they sawed a section out of a log on the side away from the aspen grove from which the shot had come, crawled silently through the brush, and made their way singly back to their friends in the valley below. No one remained to cover the face of the dead.

Ten days later—on October 21—a procession cautiously climbed back to Summit Springs to see if anything remained of the dead rustler. They found Isom's body just where it had fallen, preserved by the cold. They dug a grave and interred the remains of Isom Dart, early resident of Brown's Hole and one of its most famous characters. Those who paid their last respects were Josie Bassett, Joe Davenport, Bale Herndon, Willis Rouef, Con Dresher, Larry Curtain, Billy Morgan, Carl Blair, George and Eb Bassett, and Speck Williams.

Following the funeral there was a large and hurried exodus from Brown's Hole. Two of Tom Horn's bullets had found their mark, and none craved to become a third victim. Most of those who left at that time never returned. Joe Davenport never saw his old home again until the summer of 1934.

From that time on, Brown's Hole began to be civilized and law abiding. Rustling was not entirely abandoned, but the organization broke up when its principal leaders were killed or left the country. Butch Cassidy used the Hole as a hideout during the next year or two, but the good old days were numbered, and the Hole never again saw the rip-roaring times of former years, when it was a rendezvous for all bandits on the Outlaw Trail.

Singlehanded and with the killing of only two men, Tom

Horn had done more to bring law and order to that isolated
section of wilderness than the combined militia of three states
could have done if the original plans of the governors had
matured. Tom Horn was a one-man army!

On November 20, 1903, Tom Horn was hanged at Cheyenne for the alleged murder of Willie Nickell, a fourteen-year-
old boy. He had been found guilty by a jury of "nesters," and
there are many, including this writer, who believe he was
framed because of his success in eliminating cattle thieves.

The foregoing information on Tom Horn is reproduced
substantially as it appeared in the first edition of this book.
No part of the book has received more bitter criticism. Hundreds of letters have been received in which Tom Horn is represented as the lowest character who ever lived in the West,
not to be compared with other men, like Harvey Logan, who
killed for somewhat larger sums. Such outlaws, these writers
declare, took their chances and shot it out face to face, while
Tom Horn never gave a man a break. But if a sheriff was
paid $500 a year, the average salary in those days, to hunt
down outlaws, he could take them in any manner he chose,
even shooting from ambush if necessary, and it was considered
praiseworthy. The greatest objection against Horn is founded
on the fact that he received $500 for each man he killed. No
one contends, however, that he ever killed an innocent man.
The critical letters, as one might easily guess, have all come
from small ranchers, nesters, ex-outlaws, and their friends.

One protest was received from the Wyoming Stockgrowers
Association, stating that the association never at any time paid
Horn $500 each for dead cattle rustlers. This protest, I think,
is justified. Russell Thorp, for many years secretary for the
association, in a letter dated October 10, 1939, says:

Tom Horn was brought up to this country by our association.
. . . Horn worked for a comparatively short time, but was not

particularly successful as a livestock detective from the association's angle. He did submit a proposition to the association, through a prominent cattleman of that time, that he would ambush and kill those rustlers that were blacklisted at $500 each. When the proposal was made, Horn was immediately dismissed from the service of the association. Later he made private arrangements with private parties, and did kill several men, including Willie Nichol [Nickell] and Isom Dart.

The association, naturally, could not afford to be implicated in any such deal; individual members or groups were free to make their own arrangements. Frank Beckwith, of Delta, Utah, says his father, A. C. Beckwith, donated to a pool in Evanston that was to be paid to Tom Horn. Queen Ann Bassett says Hi Bernard, then manager for Haley, paid Horn $1,000 for killing Matt Rash and Isom Dart. She later married Bernard, but left him when he told her about that deal. Beckwith and Haley were both members of the association, but these deals were privately arranged.

While this method of eliminating cattle thieves seems cold-blooded and mercenary, it was, in my opinion, necessary under the circumstances, since all other methods had failed. By putting a chill in the hearts of rustlers and would-be outlaws, Tom Horn was responsible for the reformation of a good many wild young bucks who otherwise would have ended up in the pen or on the long end of a short rope. Similar methods had to be employed by the F.B.I., later, in eliminating Dillinger and his gang. Legal procedure in our muddled courts, then as now, had no power to restrain lawbreakers. But one cannot argue with hot lead. It carries a powerful psychological effect.

⊓⊔⊓⊔⊓⊔⊓⊔⊓⊔⊓⊔⊓⊔⊓⊔⊓⊔⊓⊔⊓⊔⊓⊔⊓⊔⊓⊔⊓⊔⊓⊔⊓⊔

Two Failures

Aₗₜₕₒᵤ𝓰ₕ Butch Cassidy was almost uniformly successful in every robbery he undertook, in two instances his plans misfired.

Because his friend Bob Meeks had been sentenced to the pen from Evanston, Cassidy decided to get revenge on that town by pulling a robbery there. His intended victim was the Beckwith bank, founded by Ashael C. Beckwith, one of the biggest stockmen in Wyoming.

Camping just outside town with some of the Wild Bunch, Butch Cassidy walked into Evanston one evening to study the lay of the bank and make his plans. Meeting some of his old friends from Brown's Hole, he foolishly gave them to understand that the Beckwith bank was about to suffer a loss. There were a number of men in Evanston at that time who had been close to the Wild Bunch, if not actually members, but had settled down and quit their wild ways. One of those learned of Cassidy's plans. Being also a friend of Beckwith, this man—who later rose to high office in Wyoming—passed the word to Bob Calverly, who warned Beckwith to be prepared for a holdup.

Beckwith's first move was to send nearly all his cash to a bank in Salt Lake City. His second was to hire an expert marksman and place him in a vacant store across the street from the bank. He also armed the cashiers—his two sons, Fred and Frank—with six-shooters, and stood loaded rifles within easy reach.

Every day for the next week, as noon approached, everyone was alert. Every customer who entered the bank was carefully scrutinized. No one in the institution knew Cassidy by sight.

A week passed, however, without incident. The friend who had tipped off Beckwith also warned Cassidy of the preparations being made to receive him, and he was too wise to risk death or capture in such a trap. In a few days the Bunch rode back to Brown's Hole, leaving Bob Meeks unavenged. It was one of the wisest things Cassidy ever did.

His second failure occurred at Rock Springs. The coal mines were then booming and large payrolls were being disbursed semimonthly. Most of the money was in the form of checks, which were worthless to the outlaws. However, Finley P. Gridley, manager of one of the Union Pacific mines four and a half miles from Rock Springs, always paid in cash so that his men would have no excuse to patronize the numerous saloons.

The Wild Bunch learned of this custom and decided to hold up Gridley with the payroll on his way to the mine. It appeared to be an easy job. The superintendent usually carried the coin in a leather bag under the seat of a buckboard, without guard, and made the trip on the same days each month.

Gridley was well known and liked by everyone in Rock Springs. On October 18, 1896, while he was standing at the bar of a saloon he was approached by a stranger.

"Goin' to the mine with the payroll tomorrow?" the stranger asked.

"Yes," replied Gridley. "Why?"

"I wouldn't do it, if I was you," the man replied confidentially.

"Why not?"

"Can't tell you exactly, but don't do it. I'm an old-timer around here and I've seen things. Goodbye."

Gridley thought the matter over and decided to take the stranger's advice. There might be something in the wind. Instead of loading his coin on the buckboard, he got an engine from the railroad yards, put a steel car ahead of it, put the money on the car with a guard of four men armed with rifles, and started it downgrade to the mine. He then climbed into a buckboard, put his empty leather bag under the seat and started to drive to the mine as usual. The driver was a green Swede from the livery stable. Two other men rode in the back seat.

Halfway to the mine the road passed through a narrow cleft in the rocks. If there was to be a holdup, it would occur at that point. Gridley instructed the driver, in such an event, to stop the team and put up his hands.

As they neared the narrows a masked man with a rifle rose from behind a boulder and shouted, "Hands up!" Gridley and the two men immediately complied; but the Swede driver, frightened out of his wits, gave his horses the whip and started down the canyon at a gallop. The outlaws hidden on the canyon sides then opened fire and the team dropped dead, pierced with nine bullets. The buckboard piled on top of the dead horses, throwing the occupants violently to the ground while bullets kicked up dust in every direction.

The next thing Gridley remembers, he was behind a boulder at the top of the ridge. The other men were out of sight. No one had been hit. The robbers searched the buckboard, found the empty bag, cursed their luck, and rode away.

After that, Gridley always took the payroll to the mine in a steel car. The engineer, Mike Nicholson, believing speed was the best safeguard, almost jumped the track going around sharp curves, and Gridley was more frightened of the engineer than he had been of the robbers. On one trip a twelve-inch railroad timber had been laid across the track at one end of a trestle. There was no time to apply the brakes, so the engineer opened the throttle and hit the obstruction with all possible force. Fortunately, the timber was thrown a hundred feet out of the way and the engine remained on the track.

The most prominent attorney in Rock Springs at that time was Douglas A. Preston, who later became attorney general of Wyoming. Whenever any of the outlaws were in trouble it was Preston who defended them—always with success. On account of his intimacy with Butch Cassidy, Preston was suspected of being the tip-off man in Rock Springs. One day Gridley met Preston in a saloon.

"You're a smart lawyer," said Gridley, "but you're not smart enough to keep from being mixed up with a bunch of outlaws. Everyone knows it; people are saying that Cassidy splits with you on every job he pulls. It's not doing you any good, Preston, and if you were wise you'd quit defending them every time they get in a jam. Let the law take its course; they all ought to be in the pen, and you with them."

Preston seemed rather upset by Gridley's remarks. He left the saloon and seemed to be in a sulk for several days. At last he went to the mine to see Gridley.

"You're a friend of mine, Grid," he began, "in spite of the things you told me the other day. I like you, and I want you to get the straight of this business. I'm guilty, as you say, of defending the Wild Bunch whenever they get caught, but there's a reason for it. Butch Cassidy once saved my life. I can't tell you just how, but it's a fact. I promised then to defend him or any of his friends whenever they got into trouble, and I can't go back on my word."

"All right, Preston," said Gridley. "I think I can understand your attitude, although I don't approve of it. You tell Butch to lay off my payroll and I'll say no more about either of you."

"I'll do it," Preston agreed, "and I hope we can still be friends."

Preston left Rock Springs within a few days after this conversation and was gone two weeks. Then one day he appeared in Gridley's office.

"I just talked with Cassidy in Brown's Hole," the lawyer announced, smiling, "and he gave me his word he would let you alone. You can depend on that, Grid, because he wouldn't dare break his word to me."

"Thanks," replied Gridley. "I'll feel a lot better about the payroll."

Cassidy kept his word. There never was another attempt to hold up the payroll of No. 2 mine.

Shortly after this incident Gridley obtained a photograph of Cassidy. One day in Denver, at a meeting of mine superintendents, he met E. L. Carpenter, who had been held up by Cassidy at Castle Gate. Carpenter was sitting at the opposite end of a long mahogany table. Without a word Gridley took Cassidy's picture and spun it down the table toward Carpenter, where it landed right side up. Automatically Carpenter threw up his hands.

"For God's sake, Grid," he grinned, "don't ever give me another scare like that!"

Wilcox
Train Robbery

Two years after Douglas Preston's interview with Butch Cassidy in Brown's Hole, Finley P. Gridley went east to accompany his two young daughters from their school to Rock Springs for summer vacation. On his return he met an old acquaintance in Omaha who was then working for the Union Pacific as railroad detective.

"Grid," warned the friend, "watch your step. Hell's going to bust loose right soon somewhere along the line. I can't tell just when nor where, but it's going to pop, and it won't be long. Keep your eyes peeled."

"How do you know?"

"I lived in Rock Springs a long time and I can read the signs."

The train continued on its westward way. When night came everyone retired. At 2:30 o'clock in the morning Gridley awoke to find the train stopped and everything quiet. He pushed a button for the porter.

"What happened, George?" he asked.

"Don't know, boss, guess they's a wreck up ahead somewhere."

Gridley tried to go back to sleep, but the continued silence aroused his curiosity. Again he rang for the porter.

"Any news, George?"

"No suh, I ain't heerd any news, but 'pears like the whole side of the baggage car is blowed out; leastways that's what somebody said."

Gridley jumped into his clothes and went forward along the coaches in the dark. He found that his train, second section of the Overland Flyer, had been stopped just behind the coaches of the first section. The engine and express car of the first section had been run across a small bridge some distance up the track, and the bridge blown up. Questioning trainmen, he learned what had happened.

The first section had been flagged just before crossing the bridge. As it came to a stop two masked and armed robbers had covered the engineer and fireman, ordering them to un-couple the express car and move on across the bridge. En-gineer W. R. Jones had hesitated to obey the order and was struck over the head with the barrel of a six-shooter by one of the two bandits. The other, apparently the leader, about fifty years old, ordered his partner not to kill the engineer.

After moving a short distance up the track the engine was stopped. Four more masked men then appeared, two on each side of the express car, and began hammering on the door, or-dering the messenger to open up. Instead of complying, mes-senger Woodcock turned off the lights, bolted the doors more securely, grabbed his gun and stood ready to kill the first man who forced an entrance.

Finding that the messenger refused to open the door, one bandit placed a stick of dynamite on the door sill, lit the fuse, and stepped back. The resulting explosion blew the door to bits and threw Woodcock against the iron safe, knocking him unconscious. The robbers then climbed inside, rolled the mes-senger out on the ground, and began rifling the car.

The big iron safe was locked and the messenger was too

dazed to remember the combination, so they opened it by placing ten pounds of dynamite on top and lighting the fuse. The explosion that followed blew a ten-inch hole in the strongbox, blew off the door, and completely wrecked the car. When the dust had settled, the ground was covered with fragments of paper money and splashed with what looked like blood.

When Gridley arrived on the scene the robbers had taken their loot and ridden away. As the crew stood around exchanging notes on their experience, the sky in the east began to lighten and it was found that the "blood" on the ground was all that remained of a shipment of red raspberries. Near the track lay a burlap bag containing fifty pounds of dynamite. A third of a mile further along, Gridley found the place where the robbers' horses had been tied, with horse biscuits still steaming in the cold morning air. A mile from the right-of-way he found where the men had camped. They left several sacks of grain and some blankets.

The train had been stopped at 2:18 A.M., June 2, 1899, between the little settlements of LeRoy and Wilcox, Wyoming, nine miles west of Rock Creek (one hundred miles south of Casper). The train crew gave a fair description of the six bandits. Their leader answered the description of Flat Nose George Curry; one with dark skin and black hair was Harvey Logan; another was Elza Lay. They were all gentlemanly, said the trainmen, except the one who struck the engineer, who was very profane.

Just as Gridley turned to go back to his Pullman, he came face to face with Douglas Preston, Butch Cassidy's attorney. Before Gridley had said a word, Preston threw up his hands and said: "Don't shoot, Grid! Don't shoot! I can prove an alibi!"

This unsolicited statement from the lawyer convinced Gridley there was more than an accidental connection between the holdup and Preston's presence on the train.

This job, known as the Wilcox train robbery, netted about $30,000 in unsigned bank notes. It was planned by Butch Cassidy and executed, like most of his jobs, without loss of life or molestation of the passengers. Because of his promise to Governor Richards there has been some doubt that Cassidy personally participated on this occasion; but there is good evidence he shared in the loot, and there is positive evidence, as will be shown later, that he immediately left the country with Harvey Logan and Elza Lay.

After having been delayed two hours, engineer Jones drove on into Medicine Bow, nearest telegraph office, where he notified railroad officials. Posses were immediately organized to run down the bandits. A special car loaded with men and horses arrived at Wilcox at 8:30 and the men rode out to pick up the trail. Another posse was organized at Medicine Bow, and still another at Dana. Sheriffs of all surrounding counties were notified. The first group of officers took up the trail eight hours after the holdup, and within twenty-four hours a hundred men joined the hunt. A reward of $1,000 was offered by the railroad company for each of the robbers. Bloodhounds were sent by special car from Omaha, but the heavy rain which fell immediately after the robbery rendered them useless.

The trail picked up by the first posse ran north and indicated there were but three bandits, while the train crew distinctly saw six. It was predicted they would easily be captured, since the North Platte River was in flood and all bridges heavily guarded. A. J. Mokler, in his *History of Natrona County*, gives some details of the chase:

Word was received in Casper to be on the lookout for the men, and W. E. Tubbs, with six men, was sent to Alcova to guard the bridge at that place. These men were on guard thirty-six hours, nearly all the time being exposed to a heavy downpour of rain.

On Saturday afternoon a special Union Pacific train arrived

in Casper over the Northwestern tracks with a half dozen railroad detectives, and Sheriff Josiah Hazen, of Converse County. Sheriff Hazen, Sheriff Oscar Hiestand of Natrona County, and Detective Vizzard of the Union Pacific were put in charge at this point. No trace of the robbers was discovered until Sunday morning, when Al Hudspeth came in from the north and reported that three men were camped in a cabin on Casper Creek, about six miles northwest from town. He said he rode up toward the cabin and two men came out with rifles in their hands and told him to "hit the road and hit it quick." Hudspeth came to town and reported the occurrence. It was learned afterward that the three men were in Casper Saturday night and secured food and provisions, and undoubtedly were assisted by friends in making their escape out of town and across the Platte River bridge. . . .

A posse of men composed of Sheriff Hiestand and Sheriff Hazen, Dr. J. F. Leeper, E. T. Payton, Al Hudspeth, J. F. Crawford, Sam Fish, J. B. Bradley, Lee Devine, Tom McDonald, and Charles Heagney immediately left in pursuit of the outlaws.

The robbers had left the cabin, but their tracks were followed to a point about five miles west from the horse ranch on the Salt Creek road. At this point the robbers dismounted behind a hill and when the pursuers were within half a mile of them fired about twenty shots at the officers. A horse belonging to one of the posse was shot, and while Sheriff Hiestand was adjusting his rifle, with the bridle rein thrown over his left arm, a bullet struck the ground in front of his horse and the animal broke loose and ran away. The sheriff walked fifteen miles to secure another horse and then came to town to get a better mount and to order provisions for the men on the chase, who had been in the saddle from Sunday noon until Monday night without anything to eat. Sheriff Hazen and the other men kept on the trail of the bandits all Sunday night, and on Monday in the forenoon Sheriff Hazen and Dr. Leeper dismounted and were walking up a draw, following the track of the outlaws' horses. The sheriff and the doctor were about one hundred yards apart when the sheriff called that he was on the trail. Dr. Leeper came up to

within about six feet of Sheriff Hazen when the robbers, who
were concealed behind a rock, opened fire on the two men.
Sheriff Hazen was hit in the stomach and the bullet went through
his body. Dr. Leeper fell to the ground to avoid being hit by
the bullets that were being shot at him by the bandits, the
firing continuing for about ten minutes. The doctor ministered
to the wounded man as best he could when the firing ceased
and the robbers took this opportunity to make their escape to
Castle Creek, which was only a short distance below. They
waded down this stream for several hundred yards in order to
throw the posse off their trail. They left their horses and some of
the plunder they had taken from the train. Their horses were
caught and were ridden by some of the posse in pursuit of them.
(This place later became nationally famous as Teapot Dome.)

Sheriff Hazen was brought to Casper and from here he was
taken to Douglas on a special train, and on Tuesday morning
at about 5:00 o'clock he died from the effect of his wound. By
that time more than fifty men were scouring the country in
pursuit of the outlaws, and all kinds of reports were brought in
by the men who came from the range after provisions and
ammunition. . . . It was finally learned that the three bandits,
after shooting Sheriff Hazen, went north down Castle Creek and
the next morning ate breakfast at Jim Nelson's sheep camp,
which was located on Sullivan's springs. (John C. DeVore cooked
for them. He recognized Flat Nose George Curry and the Logan
brothers but had not heard of the train holdup.) From here they
went into the Tisdale Mountains and then made their way to
Hill's ranch on the north fork of the Powder River, near Kaycee,
where they secured a change of clothing, and with fresh horses
made their escape further north.

By this time the United States Marshal, with a number of
deputies, ten picked men from the Buffalo militia, a dozen railroad detectives and at least a hundred men, and half a dozen
bloodhounds, had joined in the hunt, but the outlaws were now
among friends and they were furnished with food, shelter, and
horses, and their trail was covered up by their friends, and they
made good their escape, probably to the Hole-in-the-Wall country, and from there they scattered in different directions.

Popular opinion of the Hole-in-the-Wall hideout was aptly expressed by the Denver *News:*

If the robbers succeed in reaching the Hole-in-the-Wall they will find friends who will fight for them and stores of food and ammunition. The region is so wild that nothing less than a systematic attack by a large number of men will drive out the bandits.

Every effort had been made to prevent the robbers from reaching Hole-in-the-Wall. Large rewards had been offered, the railroad company stating it would spend $25,000 to run them down if necessary. Between fifty and seventy-five men were scouting the country. But when the trail was definitely found to be nearing Hole-in-the-Wall, all posses turned back, abandoning the chase. They had lost one good man and did not hanker for a meeting with the entire gang in their own hideout.

After obtaining fresh horses and supplies at Hole-in-the-Wall, the robbers rode on to the Lost Cabin country. A group of officers from Thermopolis started out that way but returned to town when the bandits notified them by letter they would be pleased to meet the law at "Lost Cabin No. 2."

The three men who rode north were positively identified by John DeVore. Unfortunately, no effort had been made to follow any other trail except that leading north. Three other robbers rode south, but their trail was not discovered until some days later. Sheriff Swanson of Rock Springs followed it a few miles, but prudently returned to his bailiwick when he found that it led through Horsethief Canyon to Brown's Hole.

According to the story told to Frederick Bechdolt by Will Simpson, of Jackson, Wyoming, Butch Cassidy was present at Lost Cabin No. 2 when the loot was divided, and received his share. Simpson says he met Cassidy shortly afterward and asked him why he had violated his promise to Governor Richards. Butch denied any part in the Wilcox affair, explaining he had come to the rendezvous to confer with Harvey Logan about leaving the United States.

But there is still further proof that Cassidy led the Wilcox train holdup. Mr. A. G. Rupp, living as recently as 1938, was operating a general store connected with post office at Welling, Wyoming, three miles south of the present Manderson, in the 1890s. Post-office officials had sent him a circular containing Cassidy's picture, which he posted on the door. A bunch of men rode up one day on lathered horses, all heavily armed. One of them, whom he recognized as Cassidy, asked if he might have the circular, then tore it into small fragments and stamped it in the mud. The men used his corral that night, washed the lather from their mounts, bought a few supplies, and gave Mr. Rupp a twenty-dollar gold piece for his hospitality and to aid him in forgetting his visitors. News of the Wilcox train robbery arrived the following day.

In connection with this affair William L. Simpson writes:

The last time I saw Cassidy was immediately after the Wilcox robbery. I met him on the Muddy between Fort Washakie and Thermopolis, Wyoming, and spent an hour with him. I told him he had been accused of being in the Wilcox robbery; that he had promised Governor Richards, Jesse Knight, and myself that he was not to turn a trick in Wyoming, and he assured me that, while he was on his get-away, he had nothing whatever to do with the Wilcox robbery or the killing of Sheriff Hazen, and I know this to be true, because a few days later he turned over to Tom Skinner, in his saloon in Thermopolis, a considerable volume of gold coin. It is known that no gold was obtained from the Wilcox robbery and that the currency was blown to pieces and of no value to the robbers.

With due respect to Mr. Simpson, who certainly knew Cassidy well, there is plenty of evidence that Butch at least shared in the loot. Not all the greenbacks were blown to bits, and it later got all the outlaws into difficulty.

After the loot from the Wilcox robbery had been divided, the Wild Bunch began one of the spectacular rides for which they were famous. George Curry temporarily remained in Wyoming; but Butch Cassidy, Harvey Logan, and Elza Lay started south before officers had given up the chase. At Brown's Hole, Lay buried part of the loot, giving his girl friend Queen Ann a map of the location and asking her to send it to his mother if he did not return within a year. Here Cassidy picked up a dozen other long-riders and continued south by way of Hill Creek and the town of Greenriver, Utah, to Robbers' Roost, where the gang was increased to about a score.

Cassidy's money belt was bulging with greenbacks taken from the express safe at Wilcox; being an honest robber, he made a special trip from the Roost to pay a debt owed to Charley Gibbons, Hanksville storekeeper and his former employer. On his way he met Harry Ogden, the boy he had once befriended. Cassidy's horse was done up, so he asked Ogden to trade with him, giving him a one-hundred-dollar bill and his worn animal. Ogden later turned the bill over to his father, who suspected that it might have been part of the unsigned currency taken in the Wilcox robbery. It proved to be good money, however.

On Ogden's horse, Cassidy rode on into Hanksville, where he paid his old debt, amounting to a considerable sum. Feeling flush, Gibbons decided to take his wife on a trip to Salt Lake City, where he spent Cassidy's money freely. Soon he found he was being followed. Sensing something wrong, he took a train back to Richfield but was arrested when he stepped off the train and returned to Salt Lake City. There he was questioned for some time but finally satisfied officers he was not a member of the Cassidy gang. The money he spent in the city was part of the shipment of unsigned bank notes taken at Wilcox, and it had been quickly spotted by bank tellers.

Two weeks after the Wilcox robbery, Charles A. Siringo, a famous Pinkerton detective, was put on the outlaws' trail. Through conflicting orders from his office he got off to a bad start, following a false scent to Mississippi. But he did trail Harvey Logan (Kid Curry) as far as the Carlisle ranch near Monticello, Utah, where Logan and Bob Lee had slept one night in a haystack. W. E. (Latigo) Gordon, who died in 1947, was then foreman of the ranch. He remembered the two fugitives, also Siringo's visit two weeks later. Another member of the gang followed a week behind Logan. All were riding hard toward the south.

The manhunt following this robbery was the most extended and thorough ever conducted up to that time in Wyoming; but, as usual, the Wild Bunch made good their escape.

```
ПППППППППППППППППППППППППППП
```

Folsom
Train Robbery

Fʀᴏᴍ the Roost, Cassidy and his friends traveled south by way of the Carlisle ranch, continuing on into Arizona. They threaded some of the most magnificent canyons in the southwest and crossed some of its worst deserts during the hottest season of the year. They arrived in Alma, New Mexico, just over the line from Arizona, in such a short space of time that it seemed impossible they could have been present at the Wilcox robbery. It was one of the longest rides they ever made. By traveling so far and so fast they discouraged any possible pursuit and made it easier to pass some of the hot money taken in their last escapade. The date of their arrival was almost an alibi.

Following his usual custom, Butch Cassidy immediately began looking for a job on a ranch. The largest outfit in the vicinity of Alma was the WS, owned by Mr. Wilson, a non-resident Englishman, and managed by Captain William French, an Irishman.

The WS ranch had suffered increasing losses for some time past, and French suspected that some of his own cowhands had a hand in it. He was contemplating a change in personnel. When Cassidy, Logan, and Lay rode in one day looking for work, they were immediately hired. They made such an instantaneous hit with the manager and his foreman that the old crew was dismissed and their places filled with new men who, curiously, kept drifting to the ranch. These new arrivals posed as strangers but were, of course, members of the Wild Bunch. Within a very short time Cassidy practically ran the WS. He was known there as Jim Lowe; Elza Lay went by the name of William H. McGinnis, and Harvey Logan called himself Tom Capehart.

Rustling of WS stopped immediately. Jim Lowe and McGinnis expressed supreme contempt for the "petty larceny" crowd, as they called the rustlers, and worked whole-heartedly for the interest of their employer. French says he never saw two men who could handle stock like Lowe and McGinnis. Cassidy handled the cattle while Lay had charge of the remuda. They worked together perfectly. They drove a herd of cattle out to the railroad, three hundred miles away, across deserts sometimes seventy-five miles wide, without losing a head. There was never any tail to their herd.

"Jim Lowe," says French, in *Reminiscences of a Western Ranchman*, "was a stocky man of medium build, 'fair complexioned.' He had a habit of grinning and showing a row of small, even teeth when he talked." McGinnis was somewhat younger, taller, darker, a good-looking young fellow with somewhat of a swagger. The "cowhands" they picked up to help on the ranch were an orderly crowd, never shooting up the saloons when they went to town. Lowe seemed to command an unlimited supply of help, all good men; but the turnover was surprisingly large. Men were always quitting to go on some urgent business, but there were always new men to fill their places. Tom Capehart (Harvey Logan) was Jim Lowe's right-hand man in handling cattle.

Tom "Black Jack" Ketchum and his brother Sam, friends of Tom and Bill McCarty, left their outlaw ranch west of Milford in Millard County, Utah, having graduated from the rustling game. They moved south into Arizona and later into New Mexico where, during two or three years previous to 1899, they made a reputation for themselves by robbing stores, post offices, and trains. They were already badly wanted in both states and at the moment had scattered to avoid arrest after a spectacular train robbery. Black Jack was working on a ranch. Sam went to Alma, where he met some of the Wild Bunch and was invited to assist in a new job.

After about a month on the WS ranch, Elza Lay (William McGinnis) asked for his time, explaining that he was a horseman, not a cowhand, and since he had broken all the wild horses on the place his services would no longer be needed. French paid him off reluctantly. Another outlaw, known as Red Weaver, quit at the same time.

A few days later—on July 11, 1899—a train on the Colorado Southern was held up and robbed near Folsom, New Mexico. French claims he heard the news from the telegraph operator at Springer, seventy miles west of Folsom. One of the men, said the message, had been identified as a former employee of the WS. If his story is to be believed, French rode on toward a friend's ranch and on the way met special officer Reno, a railroad detective, who had been in the posse which followed the robbers. Reno had lost a horse, had walked fifteen miles through the cactus, and his coattails—so he claimed—had been riddled with bullets.

When details of the affair became known, it was found the robbery had been pulled off in regular Cassidy style. The engine and express car had been detached and run some distance up the track, and the express car blown up with dynamite. When they found that the safe contained nothing, the disgusted bandits rode away in the direction of Cimarron

Canyon. Principals in this affair, as was proved later, were
Sam Ketchum, Elza Lay (McGinnis) and Harvey Logan,
the latter using a new alias, G. W. Franks.

A posse was organized at Trinidad, consisting of Sheriff
Edward Farr of Huerfano County, Colorado; special officer
W. U. Reno of Denver; F. H. Smith of New York, a volun-
teer; H. N. Love, a cowboy from Springer; James H. Mor-
gan; Captain Thacker of Wells Fargo; Perfecto Cordova, and
Miguel Lopez.

The outlaws had previously established camp in Turkey
Canyon, ten miles above Cimarron, where they had several
horses and a good supply of grub and ammunition. After the
holdup they immediately returned to their camp, where they
seem to have felt perfectly safe.

The posse had no difficulty in picking up the trail, following it directly to Turkey Canyon and arriving at 5:00 P.M. on
July 16. The outlaws were preparing supper; Elza Lay was
on his way to the creek, fifty yards distant, with a canteen
when he was hit in the shoulder by a bullet and almost immediately shot through the back by another bullet from the
posse. According to his testimony, he fainted and remained
unconscious until dusk. Other accounts state that when Sheriff Farr shouted "Hands up!" Lay raised a rifle to his shoulder
and both men fired at the same instant, the outlaw being hit
in the shoulder and the sheriff being wounded in the wrist.
Members of the posse said Lay was shot through the body
during the hail of lead which followed but that he succeeded
in rolling into a protected position from which he returned
their fire and killed Sheriff Farr. Bullets began flying so thick
for the next few minutes that no two accounts agree as to
exactly what happened. The robbers were cornered and fighting desperately. The posse was brave and determined. It was,
in fact, the best fight ever staged by any posse against the
Wild Bunch, who had become accustomed to little or no
resistance from Wyoming or Utah officers. Judging by pre-

vious experience, they believed one round of shots would scatter any posse. In this instance they were badly mistaken.

Sheriff Farr, after receiving a bullet through the wrist, calmly bandaged it with a handkerchief and continued the fight until killed by a shot assertedly fired by Lay. Sam Ketchum received a bullet through the left arm, which seems to have satisfied his appetite for fighting. But Harvey Logan found the scrap just to his liking. He fought like a pair of demons against odds of eight to one and got away without a scratch. He hit Smith in the leg and killed Love, the cowboy, with a shot through the breast. The battle lasted 45 minutes.

Harvey Logan kept up a fusillade of bullets and managed to get Lay on a horse, carrying him to a safe hideout in the mountains. But, according to Lay's testimony, it was the posse which retreated with its dead and wounded. He said he lay unconscious from the beginning of the fight until dusk —probably 8:00 o'clock or later. When he came to his senses, he heard loud cursing. "Damn you both!" Harvey Logan was saying; "you're neither of you fit to hold up an ox team!" Together they examined Sam Ketchum, who was lying among some rocks, and decided he was unable to mount a horse. They left him, Logan helping Lay to make his getaway, in spite of his opinion and the fact that Lay was in a very dangerous condition from his wounds.

After his capture five days later, Sam Ketchum made this statement:

They placed me on the horse twice but I could not sit there. I was the first one shot. When I saw I could not ride I told the kid [Logan] to pull out and leave me. If you want my gun and ammunition it is hid up in the mountains and you can have them if you can find them. When they commenced firing I threw up my hands and then I was shot. . . . After they left me I was wet through. I could not get kindling to build a fire, the matches were all damp and I could not light one after trying the whole box. I am a brother of Tom Ketchum, the original Black Jack.

Sam was taken to Santa Fe for safekeeping but died of blood poisoning on July 24.

In revenge for his brother's death, or because nothing had been obtained in this holdup, Tom Ketchum made a single-handed attempt to hold up another train near the same place on August 16. The trainmen were ready for him this time and succeeded in shooting him through the right arm. Shifting his rifle to the left shoulder, Tom wounded both the conductor and the express agent. Weak from loss of blood, he was easily captured next day and lodged in the same prison where his brother died and where doctors amputated his arm. After being convicted, he was hanged at Clayton, New Mexico. The long drop jerked his head off.

If the posse had steadfastly held its ground and pushed its advantage at Turkey Canyon, Logan would not have escaped, taking with him his badly wounded partner. The posse had made a good fight, to be sure; their casualties were one dead, one fatally wounded, and one shot in the leg. But there were still five sound men against one outlaw—unless we believe French's story that special officer Reno wore out his coattails in his haste to be somewhere else.

After escaping from the scene of the fight, Harvey Logan turned his injured partner over to Red Weaver—according to French—then rode on east to Lincoln County. Weaver nursed Lay for some time, moving him to the vicinity of an isolated cabin occupied by a rancher named Lusk. The rancher became suspicious and rode to town to notify the sheriff.

On August 22, M. C. Stewart, sheriff of Eddy County, with two deputies, J. D. Cantrell and Rufus Thomas, went to the ranch to arrest the two suspicious strangers, guided by Lusk. Lay was in the cabin at the time, eating breakfast, while the other man was out hunting horses. The posse made a slight noise while tying their horses to a wire fence, alarming Lay, who dashed out the door intending to get his rifle from his saddle. He saw Deputy Thomas approaching the cabin and fired with his .45 Colts, striking Thomas in the shoulder. Seeing Lusk in the posse and knowing the rancher had tipped off the sheriff, he fired again, wounding Lusk in the wrist. By that time the sheriff had gotten his rifle into action and fired a shot which struck Lay on the side of the head, stunning him. He was then quickly disarmed, handcuffed, and tied on a horse for the return to town. His partner, who was watching proceedings from a hill about a mile away, disappeared and was never captured.

Harvey Logan—according to French—was three hundred miles away when he heard of Lay's capture. Three days later he arrived at the WS ranch to ask if Captain French would furnish bail. The Irishman had taken a great liking to the Three Musketeers of the Wild Bunch and says he would have come to Lay's assistance if the offense had been bailable. He claims he appeared as a character witness for Lay at the trial, but court records fail to show that such was the case.

Elza Lay, under the name of William H. McGinnis, was brought to trial on October 6, 1899, charged with the murder of Sheriff Edward Farr, before Chief Justice W. J. Mills. Seventy-five veniremen were examined before a jury was accepted. The defendant insisted he had been rendered unconscious by his two wounds and had not fired any shots at Sheriff Farr. At first he refused to identify his partners, but later admitted they were G. W. Franks (Harvey Logan) and Sam Ketchum. Being charged with murder only, he refused to answer any questions in regard to the train holdup.

The jury, after deliberating three hours, preferred to believe the testimony of surviving possemen and found William H. McGinnis guilty of murder. Under the laws of New Mexico he was sentenced to the penitentiary for life, on October 10.

There is no evidence that Butch Cassidy took a personal part in the Folsom train robbery and he was never accused of the crime. But he was recognized leader of the gang that made its headquarters at the WS ranch and at Alma. His two principal lieutenants took part in the affair, and it may be presumed that he laid the plans. At the time of the holdup—according to French—Cassidy was at a cattle camp twenty miles from ranch headquarters. French sent him word of Lay's capture, but he already knew of it. So far as the law was concerned, Cassidy was only a cowhand, performing his usual duties on the WS.

Detectives all over the country had been watching for unsigned bank notes taken in the Wilcox robbery. Cassidy was too wise to pass any in Wyoming, but of course the stuff was no good unless it could be put in circulation. After several months at the WS, one of the gang, going under the name of Johnny Ward, bought a horse with some of the bills, which were afterward spent in a saloon in Alma and immediately spotted by an alert bank cashier. A government detective was put on the trail. It led directly to the WS ranch.

Captain French was asked by the detective if he had seen any of the bills or knew who was passing them. Johnny Ward was called in from the corral and after questioning admitted he had received some of the money from an unnamed cowhand. The officer took the numbers of all bills in Ward's possession but did not take the bills themselves. He then exhibited a photograph of the Wild Bunch. French immediately recognized one of the figures as "Jim Lowe" and another as "Tom Capehart." The detective then gave a detailed history of the various men and the crimes for which they were wanted. He made no effort, however, to arrest any of the outlaws, stating he could not do so unless backed by a company of soldiers. When Cassidy returned to the ranch, French told him of the detective's visit and what he had learned.

"Thanks for the tip," said Cassidy with a grin, "but that's not news to me. I met your friend the detective a few days ago in Alma. In fact, I bought him several drinks. We all knew who he was and what he wanted, but he didn't offer to start anything, so we let him go." M. E. Coates, who named the town of Alma, was present at the time and remembered the circumstances. The detective was Frank Murray, assistant superintendent of the Pinkerton agency at Denver.

About that time French's foreman decided to quit. French offered the job to Cassidy, believing the outlaw intended to settle down and go straight. Butch thought the matter over but finally decided that sooner or later he would have to hit the trail again. He declined the offer in the interest of the ranch, which would acquire a bad name when it became generally known it was headquarters for the Wild Bunch. French parted with him several weeks later with regret. The boys had been loyal to the WS and had stopped the depredations of the "petty larceny crowd." When Cassidy rode away he was accompanied by Red Weaver and Harvey Logan.

A few days later the sheriff rode a sweating horse up to the WS corral.

"Where's Jim Lowe and Tom Capehart?" he asked.

"They left several days ago," replied French. "What's up?"

"Nothing much," replied the sheriff; "only they took every horse on the Holoman place. Holoman had to walk ten miles to a neighbor's for a horse to ride to town."

The Holoman outfit, although posing as honest ranchers, had been rustling cattle from the WS for years. Cassidy's loyalty to French and his contempt for the "petty larceny crowd" had prompted him to run off their horses—not because he needed the animals but as a good joke on the hypocritical "honest rancher." The sheriff finally caught up with Cassidy and Logan at St. Johns and put them under arrest. After questioning he released Cassidy, and some time later also released Logan—if French's story is correct—for reasons which are not apparent at this time. Both went back to Alma, where they remained some weeks, then drifted north.

About the middle of January, 1906, Elza Lay, alias William H. McGinnis, rode into the WS ranch for a visit with Captain French. He had put on weight, lost his sunburn, was dressed in a long-tailed black coat, and looked more like a minister of the Gospel than an outlaw. French was flabbergasted.

"How in the hell did you get out?" he asked when he had recovered his breath. "I thought you got a life sentence."

"I did," replied Lay, "but you gave me such a good character that they decided to turn me loose." So says French in his *Reminiscences*. This is questioned by Miguel A. Otero, former governor of New Mexico, who told me:

I was present at the trial of William H. McGinnis at Raton, New Mexico, in 1899, before Chief Justice William J. Mills. . . . William French I knew very well. He was not at the trial. Mrs. Lay also wrote me that McGinnis did not visit Captain French after leaving the penitentiary.

H. O. Bursum—afterward Senator Bursum of New Mexico —was warden of the penitentiary while Elza Lay (McGinnis) was a prisoner there. In a letter written especially for this record he says:

A mutiny occurred at the penitentiary about 4 o'clock in the morning, as I recall, about 1899 or 1900. Two prisoners, one who was serving a sentence for train robbery, another under sentence for murder, while being brought from the cellhouse through the keyroom into the administration building hall, enroute to work in the bakery shop, attacked the deputy warden, locked him up in the keyroom, and, equipped with pistols and ammunition which had been smuggled into the prison by a discharged convict, proceeded to capture the prison armory, which brought resistance from the prison guards. The night captain of the guard was seriously wounded, also a guard named Pedro Sandoval. The mutiny was suppressed; the two principals who started and led the rebellion were shot, one dying in the fight and the other expiring several days later in the hospital.

During this trouble McGinnis was night engineer at the power plant and remained thoroughly loyal to the penitentiary authorities and was helpful in preventing a more serious situation.

Some years later, while I was absent, another mutiny was attempted. The prisoners used a young lad, a brother of Mrs. Bursum, as a shield to keep the guards from shooting. The prisoners were armed with knives and had surrounded the cellhouse keepers, demanding the keys to the armory. The women folks, Mrs. Bursum, Mrs. James and Mrs. Martin, from the top story of the administration building, saw the whole proceeding and called to McGinnis, who was then a trusty, to get help. McGinnis jumped on the gray pony belonging to Billy Martin and flew to Santa Fe, and in short order a squad of the militia was on the ground, and everything was quiet. At the time of the first mutiny Tom Ketchum, or "Black Jack" was a prisoner for safekeeping from Union County.

It had long been a custom in New Mexico for the governor to commute the sentence of some deserving prisoner on national holidays each year. Because of his loyalty, McGinnis was recommended for consideration, and on July 4, 1905, his sentence was commuted by Governor Miguel A. Otero to ten years. He was released on January 10, 1906.

Continuing the use of his alias for the balance of his life, McGinnis (Elza Lay) lived in Alma for two years after his release, then returned to Wyoming and went into the saloon business.

By that time the Wild Bunch was scattered, many of its members dead. Butch Cassidy and Harry Longabaugh were in South America. So Lay, one of the original members and Cassidy's closest friend, wisely decided to quit the outlaw trail. His first wife, Maude Davis, whom he had married on Diamond Mountain, had seen little of him for a number of years and probably got a divorce. At any rate, soon after he was released from the pen, he married Mary Calverly, whose father owned several ranches in northwestern Colorado, and for a time was manager of his wife's interests. Later he became watermaster for a section of the International

Canal in southern California. He died in Los Angeles in 1933, without his grown children knowing he had ever been a famous outlaw.

Through the operations of the Wild Bunch at Alma, New Mexico, another station had been added to the outlaw trail. So far as records show, Cassidy himself never operated south of Alma; but the Ketchum brothers had gone as far south as Nogales and made occasional forays into Old Mexico, thus extending the trail from Canada to Mexico. Principal members of the Ketchum gang who joined Cassidy were Bill Carver and George and Ben Kilpatrick.

After the Folsom train robbery various members of the Wild Bunch scattered temporarily to various parts of the country. On New Year's Day, 1900, Lonny Logan arrived at the home of his aunt in Dodson, Missouri. Mrs. Lee, it is said, had no knowledge that her nephews were outlaws. But when bills from the Wilcox train robbery began to appear in the vicinity of Dodson, detectives soon picked up the trail.

On February 28, 1900, officers surrounded the Lee cabin. Lonny Logan, possibly to prevent his aunt from being hit, left by the kitchen door and dived behind a mound of snow. For twenty-five minutes he battled the posse without hitting an officer. When it was over, his body was found to be riddled with bullets.

At almost the same time that Lonny was killed, his cousin, Bob Lee, described in Pinkerton files as being a halfbreed, was convicted of rustling and sent to the Wyoming pen. But Harvey Logan, last survivor of the wild Logan brothers, was still at large.

George Curry Cashes In

"F LAT NOSE" GEORGE CURRY, identified as one of the Wilcox train robbers, did not accompany the Wild Bunch to New Mexico. For some reason he left them at Robbers' Roost and shortly afterward made his appearance in Castle Dale, below Price, Utah, posing as a cattle buyer while actually operating as a rustler.

A wild young cowboy by the name of Tim Dilley had attempted to fill the position left vacant by the sudden demise of Joe Walker in 1898. While employed by the P. V. Coal company, Dilley became involved in a couple of fights; in one he had killed Stephen Chipman, a halfbreed Mexican—allegedly in self-defense—and in the other he had struck Sam Jenkins over the head with a six-shooter. Warrants had been issued for his arrest, but he fled to the Roost, where he was safe for the time being. Word came that he was stealing cattle in the vicinity of Greenriver, Utah, so two sheriffs—Preece of Vernal and Tyler of Moab—went out to look around.

About that time Mr. Fullerton, manager of the Webster Cattle company, north of Thompson, discovered a man altering the brand on one of his cows. Riding toward Greenriver to notify Sheriff Tyler, he met Sheriff Preece, who immediately took up the chase while Fullerton rode on to get Tyler.

Preece found a rustler at the place described by Fullerton and started in pursuit. There was a running fight for six miles. The rustler swam the Green River and took up a defensive position on the further bank behind some large boulders, while Preece continued to fire at him from time to time. Meanwhile, Sheriff Tyler rode up from the opposite direction—on the rustler's side of the river—and, taking careful aim, shot the outlaw through the head. Sheriff Preece then crossed over and the two officers examined the dead man. To their great surprise it was not Tom Dilley, as they supposed, but Flat Nose George Curry, for whom the Union Pacific Railroad had offered a reward of $3,000, dead or alive. Preece claimed to have killed him before Tyler arrived, but the latter insisted the fatal bullet had been fired from the rear and claimed the reward.

Curry's body was taken to Thompson and packed in ice, and word of his death wired to Casper, where he had relatives. John C. DeVore, who had cooked breakfast for him one morning after the Wilcox train robbery, was sent down by the Union Pacific Railroad to identify him. Curry was killed on April 17, 1900. On May 9 his father arrived from Chadron, Nebraska, to claim the body, taking it back to Chadron for burial.

Ever since the Folsom train robbery of 1899, Harvey Logan and other members of the Wild Bunch had remained in New Mexico. Logan still traveled under the name of Tom Capehart, or sometimes Tom Wilson. He was accompanied by Bill Carver, from Bandera County, Texas, formerly a member of the Black Jack Ketchum gang; a man calling himself Black Jack, or Franks; another going by the name of Mack Steen, also alias Franks; and another unnamed. The two "Franks" were probably George and Ben Kilpatrick. The Black Jack gang had killed Frank T. Leseur and Gus Gibbons in Arizona and were on their way to Hole-in-the-Wall at the time George Curry was killed.

Curry had been leader of the Hole-in-the-Wall gang when the Logan brothers first arrived. When Harvey Logan learned of his death, he immediately started north to avenge his old leader by killing Sheriff Tyler.

Tom Dilley was still at large; Sheriff Allred of Price had talked with him at Sunnyside, where they were both attending a ball game. Tyler, through the newspapers, asked Allred why he hadn't arrested Dilley at that time. Allred replied, through the same medium, that he didn't know Dilley was wanted and that he was "not in cahoots with the rustlers," in case anyone wanted to know. It was common knowledge that Dilley had a ranch near Woodside stocked with three hundred head of stolen cattle.

Learning that Dilley was out after more cattle in the vicinity of Hill Creek, fifty miles north of Thompson, Sheriff Tyler went after him in company with Sam Jenkins (the man Dilley had assaulted with a six-shooter), Herbert Day, a deputy, and Mert Wade, a young boy.

Riding along on the morning of May 27, 1900, Tyler saw a small bunch of horses. Nearby he also observed three men wrapped in blankets squatting around a camp fire. Believing they were Indians who might have some knowledge of Dilley's movements, he rode up to the group with Sam Jenkins, leaving Day and the boy in the rear. Day watched them as they approached the camp; he saw them speak to the men and start to dismount. Just at that moment three guns barked and both Tyler and Jenkins fell to the ground. They had unwittingly walked into Harvey Logan's camp.

At the sound of the shots the boy disappeared in the brush. Herbert Day, believing from the number of horses that there must be twenty outlaws in the vicinity—so he says—rode madly back on the trail he had come by, and within four miles met Sheriff Preece and four men who were also looking for Tom Dilley. Preece had previously made a good record as a brave officer, but on this occasion he was thrown into a panic by Day's report of the shooting, and instead of following the killers turned back to Moab for reinforcements.

Next morning two men brought in the bodies of Tyler and Jenkins. Tyler had been shot twice through the back, while Jenkins' body was riddled with bullets. Day thought he heard Jenkins yell "Dilley!" as he fell, and believed Dilley was one of the gang and had taken advantage of an opportunity to get even with his old enemy. The fact that both men had been shot in the back caused a strong resentment in the minds of the public in general and officers of the law in particular. As a result of that feeling the greatest manhunt in the history of Utah was set in motion.

When he learned the details, Governor Wells wired the governors of Colorado, Wyoming, and Arizona. All three responded by sending posses into the field and guarding every known trail into Brown's Hole, Hole-in-the-Wall, Robbers' Roost, and all other sections frequented by outlaws. Sheriffs from all surrounding counties of Utah joined in the hunt—the entire Outlaw Trail was lined with men. It was confidently predicted the killers could not possibly escape.

Preece's delay, however, had proved a fatal mistake. Men and horses were shipped from Salt Lake City, with guns and ammunition, but the small army did not get started, because of poor management, until thirty-six hours after the killing. The trail was easily followed to Turner's ranch, twelve miles from where Tyler was killed. There the three outlaws had secured fresh horses and supplies. The trail led north toward Brown's Hole, outlaw mecca, where it was believed they would certainly be captured.

Joe Tolliver, formerly one of the Brown's Hole gang, was then marshal of Vernal. In Sheriff Preece's absence he was instructed to search the Hole with a posse. He did so but, as might have been expected, found nothing.

Sheriff Preece and four men rode ahead of the main posse and reached Ouray, Utah, in the Uintah Basin, after a twenty-four-hour ride of one hundred twenty miles. While they were catching a wink of sleep their horses were stolen by friends of the gang. No fresh horses could be found with which to continue the chase. Preece finally commandeered a mount, leaving the balance of his posse scattered along the trail or stranded at Ouray.

The other posses fared in like manner. Within a week, scattered over some three hundred miles of desert, they had run out of supplies and ruined their horses. County officials refused to run up any more expense. Sheriffs fell out with each other and the hunt was definitely abandoned on June 9.

Harvey Logan had avenged the death of George Curry!

The five outlaws who had come up from Arizona split after the killing of Tyler. Two returned; the other three kept on north over the Outlaw Trail they knew so well and were safe in Hole-in-the-Wall almost before the hunt got under way.

Tod Carver, giving his real name as T. C. Hilliard, was arrested and arraigned in justice court at Moab, on August 20, 1901, for the murder of Sheriff Jesse Tyler. He was ordered held for the district court, but the records do not show what disposition was made of his case. He probably broke jail before his trial came up.

Cassidy Wants
to Reform

W<small>HEN</small> Butch Cassidy rode
away from the WS ranch near Alma, New Mexico, in the fall
of 1899, he was headed back to Utah, his home state, on a peculiar errand. Operations of the Wild Bunch that year had
been rather unsatisfactory, even disastrous, to some of the
boys. Elza Lay, first lieutenant, had been badly wounded,
captured, and sentenced to the pen. Black Jack Ketchum and
his brother Sam were both dead, their gang broken up. Three
of Ketchum's men—Bill Carver and the Kilpatrick brothers—
had joined the Wild Bunch but had already gotten themselves
in hot water through three or four killings. Cassidy realized
that sooner or later the gang would meet its Waterloo.

Cassidy himself had not taken an active part in the train
robbery at Folsom, although he was still the gang's recognized
leader and undoubtedly planned the job. Captain French, his
employer on the WS ranch, was of the opinion he had definitely decided to leave the Outlaw Trail, and his opinion was
proven correct by the outlaw leader's next move.

Judge Orlando W. Powers, Utah's most prominent criminal lawyer, who had helped defend Matt Warner in 1896, was sitting in his office one day in 1900 when a stocky, well-dressed man entered and asked for a private interview.

"I want to ask you some questions, Judge," the stranger began, when they were alone. "I understand that anything I may tell you will be held in strict confidence; is that right?"

"Correct," replied Powers. "You may feel perfectly free to discuss your case with me in confidence. What seems to be the trouble?"

"My name," he began, "is George LeRoy Parker, better known as Butch Cassidy. You've probably heard of me."

"Yes, certainly," replied the Judge. "Almost everyone has heard of you in these parts. Judge Preston often spoke of you during our association in the Matt Warner case. In fact, newspapers claimed you furnished the money for Matt's defense and tried to make trouble for Preston over the affair."

Cassidy laughed. "Well, Judge," he said, "maybe I did and maybe I didn't. That's all water under the bridge anyway, and Matt's been released from the pen. What I came to see you about is something different. I'm not in any trouble just now, but I want your advice. I want to quit this outlaw business and go straight."

Powers turned halfway around in his swivel chair and leaned toward Cassidy, boring the outlaw with his piercing gaze. He was a good judge of human nature, this shrewd lawyer, and his scrutiny seemed to satisfy him that Cassidy was not joking.

"It's this way," Cassidy continued. "I realize now that it's a losing game. Matt just spent two years in the pen; Bob Meeks lost his leg trying to escape; Elza Lay nearly got killed and was sent to the pen. Some of the other boys are dead. George Curry cashed in this spring. Sooner or later it'll be my turn. I figured it was a good time to quit before I got in any deeper. You know about some of the jobs I've done. But I'm not as bad as I'm painted. I never killed a man in my life,

Judge, and that's gospel. I never robbed an individual—only banks and railroads that have been robbing the people for years. There's no charge against me in Utah that I know of, unless it might be for the Castle Gate business, and they can't prove I did that."

"What do you want me to do?" asked Powers.

"Just this, Judge. You're the best lawyer in Utah. You know who's who and what's what. You've got a lot of influence. I thought maybe you could fix things with the governor to give me a pardon or something so I wouldn't be bothered if I settle down and promise to go straight. I'll give you my word on it. Is there any way it could be fixed?"

Powers rose from his desk and began pacing the floor, the long black cape he always wore swinging from his shoulders. After a few moments he turned to face his client.

"I'd like to help you if I could," he said, "but I'm afraid it's impossible. The governor has no power to give you a pardon until after you have been convicted of a crime. He has no power to grant any sort of amnesty, nor to guarantee you against prosecution. He has no jurisdiction over any acts committed in other states. The chances are, Mr. Cassidy, that as soon as it was known you had settled down somewhere on a ranch, every man or corporation with a charge against you would begin hounding you and it would keep you broke trying to defend yourself. For instance, there is nothing to prevent the Telluride bank from having you arrested for that job in 1889. The governor of Utah can't even promise you immunity for the Castle Gate job, and Carpenter swears he can identify you. You might get a pardon, after conviction, but Wyoming officers would be standing on the courthouse steps waiting to take you back for the Wilcox train robbery. No, Cassidy, I'm afraid you've gone too far to turn back now, at least to settle in any of the western states. The best advice I can offer you is to leave the country and make a new start some place where you are not known."

"Thanks for the advice," said Cassidy. "You know the law and I guess you're right; but I'm sorry it can't be fixed some way. You'll never know what it means to be forever on the dodge."

Cassidy left the office a disappointed man. But after thinking things over he decided to make one more attempt and appeal directly to Governor Wells. He knew the governor had "pardoned" two young men in Manti under similar circumstances, through the intercession of Parley P. Christensen, sheriff of Juab County. So he sent word to his friend the sheriff, asking him to come to Salt Lake City.

On the appointed day both proceeded to the governor's office. Introducing Cassidy, the sheriff explained the circumstances, cited the previous case of immunity from arrest guaranteed the Manti boys, recommended Butch, and asked for similar action in his case. Governor Wells, after listening to the plea, stated he believed the matter could be arranged, provided Cassidy was not guilty of murder. The outlaw insisted he had never killed a man and Christensen verified his statement, so far as his knowledge extended. Wells promised to look into the matter and make his decision in a few days.

When Cassidy and his friend again met the governor they were informed that clemency or immunity could not be extended. The attorney general, he said, had searched the record and found Cassidy guilty of murder in at least one instance, which made him ineligible for a pardon.

The sheriff protested in vain. He believed Cassidy was innocent of murder and was sincere in his determination to quit the Outlaw Trail. He believed Governor Wells' refusal to act was responsible for the many bold robberies Cassidy committed after that time. This writer has been unable to find any charge of murder against Butch Cassidy during his entire career. If the case had come up years later, while one of Cassidy's cousins was attorney general of Utah, the outcome might have been different. But from a legal viewpoint the governor had no authority to grant any such amnesty for untried past offenses, and it is certain that Cassidy would have found life on a ranch rather dull after the excitement of an outlaw career and would have sooner or later drifted back to his old trail.

Judge Powers had been deeply impressed by the outlaw's apparent sincerity and continued to ponder the matter several days. He wanted to help the man if it could be done. Finally he formed a plan he thought might work and proceeded to carry it through on his own initiative. His first move was to interview officials of the Union Pacific Railroad.

"Butch Cassidy was in my office not long ago," Powers told the railroad men. "He says he wants to quit the outlaw game and go straight; but he's afraid you fellows will hound him with old charges. I advised him to leave the country; but now that I've had time to think it over, I believe there is a solution. If Cassidy continues his train holdups it will cost you fellows a lot of money and possibly some lives as well. You stand to be the biggest losers.

"Here's my proposition: If the railroad will agree to forget all past offenses, I will try to see Cassidy again and with your permission will offer him a permanent job as express guard on your trains, at a good salary. If he was in your employ I believe he would perform his duties faithfully, and if other outlaws knew he was riding in the express car they would never attempt to rob it. Cassidy's salary would be a sort of robbery insurance, and cheap at twice the price. What do you say?"

After some discussion the railroad officials agreed to the plan and authorized Powers to get in touch with Cassidy. Powers wrote to Douglas A. Preston, Cassidy's attorney at Rock Springs, who carried the message to the outlaw in Brown's Hole.

"That sounds good to me," said Butch. "You meet me in ten days from today, at Lost Soldier Pass, and bring the U.P.'s chief detective and some official with power to make an agreement. I'll be there alone. Tell 'em not to pull any funny stuff. This is on the level. If they promise not to prosecute I'll take the job."

Preston rode back to Rock Springs and telegraphed the railroad, which sent two officials at once. Lost Soldier Pass was forty-five miles north, on the Rock Springs cutoff of the old Overland Stage Road, in a wild section of country but little traveled. Cassidy figured that even if the proposition was a trap he would still have a good chance to escape.

With a hired team and buckboard Preston and the two railroad men started for the rendezvous. They had allowed plenty of time under ordinary conditions, but were unfortunately delayed by a storm, lost the trail, and arrived twenty-four hours late. Cassidy had waited for them all day; then, becoming suspicious, he left for Powder Springs.

When the three men arrived the next day they found no Cassidy. After half a day of suspense they decided to return. Just before they climbed into the buckboard, Preston, disgusted with his fruitless effort, savagely kicked at a flat stone lying under the lone cedar where the meeting was to have taken place. Underneath he found a piece of paper. On it Cassidy had written:

Damn you, Preston, you have double-crossed me. I waited all day but you didn't show up. Tell the U.P. to go to hell. And you can go with them.

Preston rode to Brown's Hole to see Butch shortly after this episode, but Cassidy wouldn't talk to him. It took him six months to square himself for what the outlaw believed was an act of treachery.

In the meantime Judge Powers, learning that Preston's efforts had failed, had another idea. Matt Warner, recently released from the pen, was as close to Butch as any living man. He would never be suspected of treachery. So Powers went to Governor Wells with the proposition of sending

Matt to Butch direct with the railroad's offer and an explanation of why the previous appointment had not been kept. They assured Matt it was on the level and gave him $175 expense money.

Matt took the train out of Salt Lake City for Rock Springs, hoping to find Cassidy at Powder Springs or Brown's Hole. At Fort Bridger, east of Evanston, the conductor handed Matt a telegram. It read:

All agreements off. Cassidy just held up a train at Tipton.

Tipton
Train Robbery

Tipton, Wyoming, was a little settlement along the tracks of the Union Pacific Railroad fifty miles west of Rawlins and not more than two days' ride from Lost Soldier Pass. Table Rock, a prominent landmark, was two and a half miles west of Tipton.

The engineer on the second section of train No. 3, Henry Wallerstein, was pulling upgrade past Tipton toward Table Rock at 8:00 o'clock on the evening of August 29, 1900, when a masked figure came sliding over the tender and stuck a big black .45 Colts in his ribs.

"Slow down when you see a fire along the track," the masked man said, "and don't try any funny stuff." There was nothing for him to do but comply. Within a mile he saw a fire beside the rails and brought his train to a stop. Three other masked men then appeared from the darkness and took charge of affairs.

As the wheels ceased grinding, Conductor Ed J. Kerrigan stepped off the day coach and started forward to see what had caused the delay. He was covered by one of the bandits and ordered to uncouple the mail and express cars from the train. Stepping forward, he started to climb onto the platform of the first coach.

"Here!" yelled one of the robbers. "What you trying to do? Uncouple them cars and be damn quick about it. We ain't got all night!"

"I'm going to set the brakes first," said Kerrigan, stubbornly. "This train's on a grade and if I uncouple the coaches from the engine they'll start rolling downhill and everybody'll be killed. I'm not going to cut this train till the brakes are set."

"All right then," said the leader, "go ahead, but don't do anything foolish. And tell the passengers to keep inside. We don't want to have to shoot anybody."

Kerrigan went through the train setting all brakes and warning passengers to keep quiet and not stick their heads out of the windows. Most of the windows were open, and one deaf old man who hadn't heard the conductor's warning stuck his head out, but drew it back quickly when he saw the flash of a gun. Another curious passenger, who had dropped off to investigate the trouble, was hit over the head with a gun. When all brakes were properly set the conductor returned and cut the train. With others of the crew he was herded into the cab and the engineer was ordered to pull on about a mile up the track.

While one of the bandits held the crew under guard, the other three began work on the express car. Woodcock, the same brave messenger who had to be blasted out of the express car during the Wilcox holdup, was still on the run. Again he locked the door and refused to open up on command. He was finally persuaded to open, however, by Kerrigan, the conductor, who was afraid Woodcock would be killed.

Herding the crew away from the express car, the bandits began blasting the safe. They set off three blasts before breaking it open, wrecking the car. When they had sorted over all contents of the strongbox they returned to the crew.

"What time is it?" asked one of the bandits. Kerrigan pulled out his watch, gave them the time, and held out the watch.

"I suppose you want this too," he said.

"Keep it," replied the leader, "we don't want anything from the railroad boys." The four robbers then mounted their horses and rode into the darkness. The delayed train finally pulled into Green River two hours late and gave the alarm.

First reports were that the bandits had taken $55,000 from the express car. But when a complete check had been made it was found that the safe only contained $50.40, complete extent of the loot.

Rewards of $1,000 each were immediately posted, and U. S. Marshal Frank Hadsell left Rawlins with twenty-five men in a special car which had been equipped for just such emergencies by Timothy T. Keliher, chief of the "Union Pacific Mounted Rangers." In the posse were Deputy Marshal Joe LaFors, Sheriff McDaniels of Carbon County, and Sheriff Swanson of Sweetwater County.

On September 5 Hadsell and his men returned, having lost the trail entirely. Swanson found that the four original bandits had been joined by a fifth, their trail leading directly toward Powder Springs, a place he did not crave to visit. So he returned to Rock Springs, reporting that his horses had given out and he was compelled to abandon pursuit.

One of the robbers, reported the train crew, was a "sandy complected," smooth-shaven man with gray eyes, five feet ten inches tall, who had a quick way of speaking. That was Butch Cassidy. One of the others, they said, was very profane and resembled the profane member of the gang which robbed the train at Wilcox. That was Harvey Logan. The third member was undoubtedly Harry Longabaugh. The fourth and fifth men cannot be identified.

Railroad officials later admitted that a shipment of $100,-000 of government money destined for the Philippines should have been on that train but had been delayed. Cassidy apparently had inside information on the shipment and had planned to make one big haul before leaving the country.

Winnemucca
Bank Holdup

Cassidy's original purpose in robbing the express car at Tipton was to obtain money for a new start in South America. But his failure to obtain anything of value made it necessary to get the money elsewhere. Following his policy of never pulling two jobs in the same vicinity, he chose for his next attempt the bank at Winnemucca, Nevada.

His companions in the Winnemucca holdup were Harry Longabaugh, alias the Sundance Kid, and Bill Carver. The loot was to be split only three ways.

These three outlaws—cream of the Wild Bunch—rode into town one afternoon to study the lay of the bank. They then rode back to camp on the banks of the Humboldt River. Next day, September 19, 1900, at noon, they again rode into town, tied their horses to a hitchrack back of the bank, and went into a nearby saloon for a last drink. Carver carried a carbine concealed under a blanket.

From the saloon the three walked to the First National

Bank and entered the front door. Covering cashier McBride with the carbine, they ordered him to open the vault. McBride said the vault could only be opened by the president, who was in his office at the rear. The president, Nixon, was then brought out at the point of a gun, forced to open the vault and put the money in a sack. The robbers took the sack and left by the back door, herding Nixon, McBride, bookkeeper Hill, stenographer Calhoun, and a horse buyer named Johnson before them, to prevent any alarm being given.

Mounting their horses, the three robbers left town in a cloud of alkali dust, firing their guns in the air. It was all over in five minutes. No one was hurt. The loot was $32,640.

Carver, carrying a small bag of gold, accidentally dropped it in the street. He dismounted to pick up the coins, but his horse was anxious to follow the others and he had considerable difficulty in remounting. Nixon rushed into the street and began firing a revolver to attract attention. Johnson, the horse buyer, grabbed a shotgun and in his excitement shot both windows out of the saloon next door.

Franklin Reynolds, in *All-Western* magazine, gives the details of the chase which followed, obtained from Judge Edward A. Ducker of Winnemucca. Ducker was then studying law in the office of C. D. Van Duzer, across the street from the bank. Hearing the shots, he ran out in time to see three men disappearing in a cloud of dust. A posse was organized and pursuit started within a few minutes. A switch engine was also requisitioned to follow the robbers, who were escaping on a road parallel with the railroad track. After firing a few ineffectual shots, the engine posse returned.

The posse, of which Judge Ducker was a member, continued until they came to the outlaws' camp at a ranch along the river owned by Nixon, president of the bank. Three ordinary plugs ridden by the robbers out of Winnemucca had been abandoned, and the fugitives changed to three fine saddle horses, one of which was a beautiful black stallion belonging to

Nixon. The trail led toward Lost Soldier Pass. By the time they reached that place the posse was fifteen miles behind.

News of the holdup had been telephoned to Golconda, seventeen miles east of Winnemucca, and a posse had been formed there to head off the outlaws; but they were half an hour too late. They then joined the Winnemucca posse and all proceeded together.

Riding through the narrow pass with caution, the pursuers reached Silve's ranch a few miles beyond. Cassidy and his two pals had left four magnificent gray horses at the ranch some days before, in charge of an unnamed confederate. Stopping to change mounts and saddles, they lost time, and when they rode away the posse was only a mile behind. They left word with Silve that it would be unhealthy for the sheriff to follow them further. The robbers rode leisurely to warm up their horses and the posse gained ground. An Indian from Golconda on a good horse came up with them, but dropped back when Carver dismounted to take a shot at him with a rifle. By that time the posse was forty miles from Winnemucca. It was getting dark and most of their horses were winded. They rode on to Clover ranch, from which place most of the pursuers returned next day.

In the morning Judge Ducker, Shorty Johnson, Jack Lowrie and Burns Caldwell secured fresh horses and pushed on. In Squaw Valley, twenty miles north, they found where the outlaws had divided the money and thrown away some canvas sacks. Continuing on day after day, they followed the trail north into Star Valley, Wyoming, but were finally forced to turn back without contacting Cassidy or his friends. They found that the four gray horses had been stolen from a man named Moore, at Three Creeks, Idaho, more than a month before.

Since eyewitness stories are always more interesting, here is one written by Wallace Lyman, of Omaha, in 1939, specially for this record:

Our outfit was camped for the night at the Squaw Valley stone house. We did not camp in the house. We pitched our tents, set the grub wagon and cooked on our own camp kitchen. It was about 2:00 o'clock in the morning and we had all been asleep for hours.

The posse came galloping into camp, making a lot of noise. We all piled out, built a big fire for light and listened for half an hour to the recital of the bank robbery. The only road out of Winnemucca to the north ran parallel to the railroad track, with a quarter mile of barbed wire fence on the other side, so the robbers had to ride down this lane to get out. The switch engine was sitting on the track with steam up, and the engineer and a couple of men with guns started in pursuit. The engineer had to throttle down quite a bit to avoid cornering them and having them get mean.

When the posse reached our camp their boss was Ed Cavanaugh. He had arrived unarmed at Clover, our ranch headquarters, the day before with the posse, so Frank Noble, our ranch manager, had given him my 303 Savage and a box of shells.

Shorty Johnson was a genial Swede bronco buster. He was called Shorty because he was 6 feet 11 inches tall. It was impossible for a bronco to throw him because he tied his legs together under the horse's belly.

We started out next morning, about twenty of us, and picked up the tracks of the bandits almost immediately. Jim Boyle, our roundup boss, and I were riding up in front. No one suggested hurrying up. The sun was just showing over the hills. All at once Jim put up his hand to stop the procession. Then he pointed down to the road ahead of us where lay a little pile of horse droppings not over an hour old. "By God," said Bill, "we've got a hell of a lot of cattle to work today and if we don't get going we won't get done by dark."

So we all bunched up and Jim sent us out in pairs to the east, west and south. Then he let out a real laugh and said, "I just found out there ain't no cattle of ours out to the north." The posse held a council of war that lasted about an hour, then they took up the chase.

My recollection is that all but Ed Cavanaugh and one other man gave it up after a few days more. Ed hung doggedly on the trail at $10 a day and didn't get back for two months. He reported the gang had finally disappeared in the Hole-in-the-Wall and he privately reported to me when he returned my gun that it was a hell of a good shooter and he had knocked over plenty of game.

On his ride from Winnemucca to Star Valley, Butch Cassidy passed through Robbers' Roost, where he once more traded horses with Harry Ogden, the young cowpuncher. That was the last time Ogden saw him before he left the country.

With their loot from the Winnemucca bank, Cassidy, Longabaugh, and Carver headed for Fort Worth, Texas, to hide out for a time in "Hell's Half Acre." There they met Harvey Logan and Ben Kilpatrick.

Flush with money, the five outlaws planned to paint the town. Their first step was to buy new outfits of expensive clothes, including derby hats. The change from overalls and Stetsons made them feel so proud they decided to have their pictures taken in a group—a bit of foofaraw which almost got them into serious trouble.

Fred Dodge, a Wells Fargo detective masquerading as a gambler, happened to stroll into the photograph gallery where the group picture was on display and immediately recognized Bill Carver. Taking the photograph to headquarters, he identified all the others. The hunt was on.

Getting wind of trouble, the gang went to San Antonio, where for three months they made headquarters in Fanny Porter's sporting house. Here Harvey Logan fell for one of the girls, named Lillie, while Butch Cassidy amused himself by buying a bicycle and joining the new bicycle craze. Bill Carver picked up Laura Bullion, said to have been part Indian, who was later passed along to other members of the gang.

Wagner
Train Robbery

THE last exploit of the Wild Bunch in the United States was the holdup of a Great Northern train near Wagner, Montana, 196 miles east of Great Falls, at 2:00 P.M. on July 3, 1901. On this occasion Cassidy was assisted by Harry Longabaugh, Harvey Logan, and Camilla Hanks.

Hanks, fourth man in the Wagner holdup, was from De-Witt County, Texas, and had operated occasionally with Bill Carver and the Kilpatricks. Very little is known of his early history. His first name is sometimes spelled Comelio. He had probably met Cassidy in San Antonio and joined him in Montana for this job.

Cassidy had planned to leave for South America after the Winnemucca job, but for some reason his departure was postponed. He wanted Longabaugh and Logan to accompany him. Longabaugh was enthusiastic over the idea, but Logan was harder to convince. It was probably Logan who induced Cassidy to pull one more big robbery before they left the country. He probably chose Wagner because it was near his old hideout, and he may have wanted to show the people of Landusky that he was now a "big shot." At any rate Cassidy agreed.

The plan used at Wagner was identical with that used in the Wilcox robbery. When the train stopped at Malta, seven miles from the scene of the holdup, Harvey Logan climbed aboard the blind baggage. Harry Longabaugh boarded the same train as a paying passenger. Butch Cassidy awaited his two partners near the Mike O'Neill ranch, three miles from Wagner. Camilla Hanks guarded the horses.

At the proper moment Logan climbed over the tender into the engineer's cab, covered the trainmen with his six-shooters, and ordered them to stop just before crossing the next bridge. Tom Jones, engineer, could do nothing but obey.

As the train came to a stop, the conductor and some passengers became curious, sticking their heads out of coach windows. Longabaugh jumped to the ground, ordering everyone to keep inside. He sent a bullet or two into the woodwork of the cars as a warning. Logan then ordered the engineer to uncouple the express car and pull it across the bridge. At the appointed spot Cassidy stepped out and took charge of operations.

About that time Sheriff Griffith, of Great Falls, a passenger on the train, opened fire from the rear coach. Longabaugh returned his shots and no more was heard from the Great Falls officer. A curious sheepherder who rode up to see the excitement had his horse shot from under him. Otherwise there were no casualties.

Cassidy, with a bag of dynamite, entered the express car, placed a charge against the safe, lighted the fuse, and jumped to the ground. The explosion demolished the car. Two or three more shots were necessary before the strongbox was opened, and to keep him from getting into mischief, Cassidy made Fireman Mike O'Neill carry the bag of dynamite while he set the charges. When it was all over, the four outlaws rode away with $65,000 in paper money.

When the delayed train finally arrived at Wagner, a message was sent back to Malta, and two cowboys, Byron Hurley and Tim Maloney, mounted their horses to cut off the robbers. In their excitement they forgot to take their guns and had to return to Malta. Glasgow, county seat of Valley County, was seventy miles from Wagner. A large posse was organized by the sheriff, but it never caught up with the Wild Bunch, being encumbered with a regulation chuck wagon. None of the bandits were arrested.

The loot on this occasion consisted of unsigned bank notes consigned to a bank in Helena, Montana. As in the case of the Wilcox robbery, it was easily traced and in a very short time all four outlaws were on the dodge.

According to Lillie, Logan's San Antonio girl friend, who was interviewed at Fanny Porter's place by detectives, the gang first went to a Wyoming hideout after the Wagner job (probably Star Valley). She said they had seven sacks of gold and large bundles of paper money. When Logan later returned to San Antonio, he generously gave her $167 as expense money for a visit to her home in Palestine, Texas. She claimed to be ignorant of how they got the money. "If I had known who they were," she told officers, "I would have taken them for all they had."

When bills from the Wagner job began circulating in San Antonio, detectives were put on the job and the Wild Bunch donned their chaps and Stetsons for another long ride. Cassidy and Longabaugh probably rode to Star Valley to cool their heels while hounds of the law bayed on their cold trail. Hanks was almost caught in Nashville when he tried to pass one of the Wagner bills in a clothing store, but escaped into the canebrakes along the Cumberland River, on October 26, 1901.

Ben Kilpatrick was spotted riding in a carriage in Knoxville, by an alert detective on November 8. He was followed to a hotel, where he was arrested with Laura Bullion, who was on the point of leaving with $7,000 stuffed in a suitcase. After ten days of questioning, Kilpatrick confessed and on December 12, 1901, was sentenced to fifteen years in Atlanta. Laura got five years.

Harvey Logan, wildest and toughest member of the Wild Bunch, was not yet ready to leave for South America, as Butch tried to persuade him to do. Moving from one small town to another, he exchanged all his Wagner bills for good money, then went to Knoxville to spend it. In a pool-hall fight he wounded two officers and was badly wounded in the side. Jumping down thirty feet from a back door, he commandeered a cab, rode to the edge of town, then walked almost to Jefferson City, where he hid in the woods. Next morning he staggered into town, was recognized, and returned to the woods, where Knoxville officers soon surrounded him. At 6:30 that night, December 15, he surrendered and was taken to the Knoxville jail.

In November, 1902, Logan was convicted and sentenced to twenty years in the pen at Columbus. An appeal was prepared and heard in the Circuit Court the following spring, but it was turned down. Preparations were then made to transport him to Columbus. But he was not quite ready to go.

It was 4:15 P.M. of Saturday, June 27, 1903, when Harvey Logan went to the front of his cell to speak to his guard. When the guard turned his back for a moment, Logan slipped over his head a loop made from broom wire. In a few seconds he had securely tied the guard with more wire and secured two pistols. He then called a second guard and forced him to unlock the cell. Jumping on the sheriff's horse, tied outside, he was soon on his way out of Knoxville.

The sheriff seemed in no hurry to catch his escaped prisoner, and the guard could not show any marks of the wire around his neck. After an investigation the Pinkerton office declared there had been collusion in Logan's escape.

On July 7, 1903, a train was held up near Parachute, Colorado, in Butch Cassidy style. The express safe was dynamited but it contained nothing of value. Two days later a posse came up with the robbers and a gun battle took place, in a gully not far from Glenwood Springs. All the bandits escaped but one, who had been wounded. The posse then heard a single shot—followed by silence. The dead outlaw was declared to be a man known in Glenwood Springs as Tap Duncan. But Pinkerton agents later had the body exhumed and photographed. It was then positively identified by an operative, Lowell Spence (still living in 1949) as the remains of Harvey Logan, most desperate member of the Wild Bunch.

The outlaw Logans were finished.

In South America

In all his outlaw activities, covering half his lifetime, Butch Cassidy had served only one short term behind bars, and that for horse stealing. He had managed to escape every trap set for him, had outsmarted pursuit, and never fought a gun battle with the law. His uncanny judgment told him the jig was about up, the game played out, and it was time to quit. Against that judgment he had pulled the Wagner train holdup, a job that ended disastrously for every man concerned except himself and Harry Longabaugh. These two remained together in some wild hideout until the attention of officers was diverted elsewhere.

Butch Cassidy was now ready to leave for South America. He had accumulated enough to make a good start in a new country, and I believe he fully intended to quit the outlaw trail permanently. Of all his former pals, only Longabaugh agreed to go with him. They separated somewhere in the West and met again by appointment in New York City on February 1, 1902.

But when the Sundance Kid arrived in New York, he was accompanied by a woman. This may not have been a surprise to Butch, who probably knew Longabaugh's plans. If he had been planning further banditry in the south he would never have consented to her company; but since both men intended to settle down and start a ranch, there could be no objection to the woman's presence.

Her name was Etta Place, and Pinkerton files contain a description. "She is about 27 years old, five feet four inches in height, weighing about 110 pounds, medium complexion and wears her brown hair on the top of her head in a roll from forehead. She appears to be a refined type." In her photograph with Longabaugh, also found in Pinkerton files, she looks like a Sunday-school teacher. But wherever she had learned it, she was already an expert rider and a crack shot.

In New York, Cassidy, Longabaugh, and Etta Place took rooms in a boarding house with Mrs. Taylor at 234 West Twelfth street. Cassidy registered as Jim Ryan and the other two signed their names as Mr. and Mrs. Harry D. Place. As soon as they were comfortably settled they visited Tiffany's, where Harry bought a fine watch for himself and a beautiful lapel watch for Etta. After outfitting themselves in new clothes, Harry and Etta visited De Young's photographic studio at 826 Broadway and had their pictures taken together. The pair looked like a young minister and his wife. Butch was then thirty-eight, and Harry must have been about the same age.

For nearly three weeks they enjoyed the sights of New York, where they were almost as safe as in Brown's Hole. Then, on February 20, they took passage for Buenos Aires on the freighter S.S. *Soldier Prince*.

Some time in March the three landed at their destination, where they took rooms at the expensive Hotel Europa. A day or two later Longabaugh deposited $12,000 in the London & Platte River bank. With this backing they filed application in a government office for land and were given "four square leagues" in Cholilo, Province of Chubut, District 16 de Octubre. They reached their allotted holdings some time in May, traveling by steamer and mule train, where they found their nearest neighbor to be Dr. Newberry, a dentist of Buenos Aires. According to reports, they bought cattle and horses to stock the ranch and gave their neighbors every reason to believe they were honest and law-abiding. I think there is no doubt they intended to be at that time.

Some months after their departure, Pinkerton operatives traced them to New York and thence to Buenos Aires. One of their operatives in the latter city was asked to apprehend them, but since it was the rainy season he could not follow them inland. The police of Buenos Aires were sent photographs and descriptions and warned that Cassidy and Longabaugh might begin operations there at any time. The police agreed to watch for them if they attempted to leave the country.

From all reports, the two last survivors of the Wild Bunch worked their ranch quietly and with success until 1906, when rumors reached them that United States officers were closing in. Whether this was the case or whether they tired of the monotony of ranch life, is not definitely known. In any case, they saddled their horses and hit the outlaw trail once more, with Etta Place riding between them and operating with as much coolness, daring, and physical fortitude as Butch himself. Sometimes they picked up some other wandering Americano as temporary assistant.

Their first exploit of record occurred in March, 1906, when the three, assisted by an American fugitive named Dey, robbed the bank at Mercedes, Province of San Luis. While Etta held the horses, the other three entered the bank, where it is said they obtained $20,000. During the robbery one of them killed the banker. Making a fifteen-day ride back to their ranch they sold their stock, split the profits, and temporarily separated. After this time Cassidy apparently had no permanent headquarters.

The next bank holdup occurred a few months later at Bahia Blanca, four hundred miles from Mercedes, where they again took about $20,000. One of the robbers was described as a slim young woman. A posse followed but gave up the chase when Cassidy shot their horses.

Next they went to Bolivia and held up a pay train at Eucalyptus, using the old Cassidy system. An outlaw named McVey is said to have accompanied them on this expedition, but he may have been the man Dey who rode with them at Mercedes. After this exploit they are said to have hidden out in the abandoned Jesuit mission of Cacambaya on the Andes' eastern slope.

Although Butch Cassidy occasionally wrote to friends in Utah, his activities in South America were generally unknown until publication of an article, "Butch Cassidy," by Arthur Chapman in *Elks Magazine*, April, 1930. The facts were furnished by Mr. Siebert, a mining man who was in the country at the time, and are believed to be authentic.

In Wyoming, Cassidy had been a valued employee of many large cattle ranches, because it was known he would never rob an employer. His wages were found to be good insurance against rustling. The climate of South America did not change that trait in his character. He once went to the Huanuni mines in Bolivia, owned by the Scotch firm of Penny & Duncan, to pick up information in regard to their payroll shipments. The Scotch owners received him with such hospitality and made his visit so pleasant that he finally went to work for the firm, being put in charge of their crew of watchmen. Needless to say, the mine payroll was never stolen. In fact, when a plot was hatched by another band of outlaws to kidnap Mr. Penny and hold him for ransom, Cassidy sent him word of the plan and even sent a trustworthy personal guard.

Mr. Siebert, quoted by Arthur Chapman, said:

All over the pampas of Bolivia, Cassidy seemed to have the friendship of the Indians and halfbreeds. As soon as he arrived at an Indian village he would be playing with the small children, and he usually had candies and other sweets in his pockets to give them. Because of this friendship the natives looked upon him as a sort of Robin Hood, and when he was hard pressed by the authorities, Cassidy could always find a hideout among the native population.

When Cassidy worked for me at the Concordia mines, where I was manager in 1908, on coming into the sitting room he would invariably take a seat on a small sofa which was placed between two windows. This seat gave him a survey of three doors and one window. He always seemed to be cool and calculating, and protected his back very well. Although he always went armed with a frontier model .44 Colts, this weapon was usually stuck in his trouser belt in such a way as to be inconspicuous. I never saw him under the influence of whiskey except once, and then he seemed to be very much ashamed of himself because he could not walk straight.

When our camp was visited by two embryo American bandits on horseback, horses being very rare in the high altitudes of Bolivia, Cassidy promptly approached them and told them to get out of camp. He informed them that he did not want them or any other would-be bandits to cause people to get the impression that our camp was a rendezvous for outlaws. These unwelcome visitors informed Cassidy that they realized that they had not done right in coming into camp mounted on horses, but as they had to have food, there was no alternative for them. I afterwards learned that Cassidy gave them one hundred dollars, with a warning never to appear in camp again.

One night at the Concordia mines my predecessor, Mr. Rolla Glass, and I had on the office table several hundred pounds sterling in gold, which we were counting out to pay our gold payroll men, when Cassidy came in. He jokingly remarked that it was the easiest money he had ever seen, but we continued our work and he finally asked us if we would give him the gold in exchange for paper currency. We told him that we would gladly accommodate him, but we would have to fulfill our obligation to certain of our men and pay them in actual gold. Cassidy then volunteered to see these men and get their consent to the exchange. This he did within an hour or two and when he came back we made the exchange, much as we disliked being a party to such a transaction.

Mr. Siebert says Longabaugh was somewhat distant and did not make friendships easily. But Cassidy seemed to be good-natured, pleasant, and entertaining. He used good language, was never vulgar, and was liked by all the women who made his acquaintance. To Mr. Siebert he talked freely of his former outlaw career in the States, stating that he had come to South America to make a new start because he knew it was only a matter of time before he was captured or killed in his former territory, as the officers were getting familiar with his tactics and his hideouts. Harvey Logan, he said, was the bravest man he ever knew. In Bolivia, Cassidy traveled under the names of James Maxwell or Jim Lowe.

Harry Longabaugh had previously obtained employment at the Concordia mines to spy out the land for a big payroll holdup. Cassidy arrived later and went to work as a packer. In this work he was often entrusted with large sums of money, but his accounts were always correct. As in the old days in Wyoming, he was loyal to those who gave him their confidence. This cordial relation continued until Longabaugh, who had taken aboard too much liquor, bragged of his exploits as an outlaw in the States. His boasts came to the ears of the authorities, so, rather than embarrass their employers, both men left the Concordia mines.

W. L. Bell, of Butte, Montana, in a letter written to Struthers Burt in 1938, says:

In 1907, I think it was, I was in Peru and had charge of some mining operations which resulted in some $50,000 monthly in gold bars. These were transported about 150 miles to the railroad. While in La Paz on a visit I was told by an American who had worked for me that the next shipment was to be held up by a trio who would ride across the border from Bolivia into Peru to meet the guard in charge. He said these men were bad men, with accent on the "bad," and had been driven out of Wyoming where they belonged to the Hole-in-the-Wall gang.

I returned to Peru via Lake Titicaca and then was advised by the superintendent at the mine that a newcomer in camp had gotten drunk on July 4th, shot up the camp, and talked to the effect that he was going out with the next shipment as a guard. He was disarmed but pulled a knife from his boot and made a jump at the office man, who pulled an automatic from under his high desk and emptied it into him. I sent out fifty mounted men who got reports from Indians of two men, mounted, along the border, but did not catch them.

Late in 1907, Cassidy, Longabaugh, and Etta Place went to the town of Rio Gallegos, Argentina, where they stopped at the best hotel. Harry and Etta registered as Mr. and Mrs. Lewis Nelson, while Butch took the name of Henry Thompson. They arrived on Patagonian ponies and wore fancy English riding clothes. Posing as wealthy ranch owners, they mingled with local society and spent freely, visiting the local bank almost daily.

At 2:00 P.M. on December 7, 1907, Cassidy and Longabaugh again entered the bank; but this time they were dressed in rough clothes. Cassidy had a six-shooter in each hand while Longabaugh carried a gun and waved a razor with which he threatened the cashier. They backed banker Bishop against a wall, then scooped $10,000 into a sack and rode away in a driving rain. Several miles out of town they met Etta Place with a relay of horses. A posse followed, but gave up when some of their horses were shot.

Their next appearance, according to the old records, was on December 27, 1910, when they entered a store in Arroyo Pescado, District 16 de Octubre, killed the manager, broke open the safe, and forced employees to load their horses with supplies. But there are good reasons to doubt this statement. The action does not represent Cassidy's usual style; and both Cassidy and Longabaugh are believed to have been dead on this date.

The reports listed here are, of course, only a few of the many robberies committed in South America by that odd trio, Butch Cassidy, Harry Longabaugh, and Etta Place. Cassidy had already proved himself the most daring and successful outlaw in the United States; in South America he maintained that reputation by committing the greatest and most successful series of holdups ever known there. Knowing the country intimately, he was able to escape all pursuit. Hideouts were more numerous and safer than in western deserts of the United States. Perhaps officers of the law were not so efficient nor so well organized in the south; certainly trails were more difficult to follow. But in any case, so far as records show, he never, up to this time, had any gun battles with the law.

It seems a little strange that Butch Cassidy, who had never allowed women to distract his attention from the business in hand, should have allowed Harry Longabaugh to take a woman with him when they left for South America. My theory is that his intention at that time was to quit the outlaw trail, in which case a woman's company in the new venture would be acceptable. But when he finally decided to quit ranching and return to the excitement of his former activities, Etta Place rode with him as a full-fledged, dependable member of this second "Invincible Three." Surely this woman, who from appearances would have been more at home in a schoolroom or as a leader in charitable work, must have been an extraordinary character. Any woman who could ride with Butch and Harry was made of tough stuff, with a hair-trigger mind. At Arroyo Pescado she disappears completely from the picture, to remain forever a mystery. But what a book she could have written!

Cassidy's
Last Stand

CASSIDY and Longabaugh
had gone to South America in 1902. For seven years, except
for the time they were in the cattle business, they terrorized
the country on both sides of the Andes and became the most
wanted outlaws in South America. George LeRoy Parker,
the Mormon cowboy, had set out in the very beginning to
make a reputation for himself. He had succeeded even beyond
his expectations and had become the most celebrated outlaw
of his time in both the Americas. As a result of his coolness
and careful planning, quick judgment of human nature, and
ability to make friends, he had, except for one short term in
the Wyoming penitentiary, escaped entirely from the law's
clutches. Although never a killer, he was more feared than
any other bandit who ever held up a train or robbed a bank.
The law had long since come to the conclusion that Butch
Cassidy could not be captured.

But there must be an end to all things. Even Cassidy's luck
could not last forever. To Arthur Chapman, author of that
immortal poem "Out Where the West Begins," is due the

credit for preserving the real story of his last stand, a thrilling climax to a life of thrills:

The payroll remittance of the Aramayo mines, near Quechisla, in Southern Bolivia, was held up early in 1909. A few weeks after this holdup two heavily armed Americans, on jaded mules, rode into the patio of the police station at the Indian village of San Vicente, Bolivia, and demanded something to eat.

It was not an unusual demand, for the police station was also an inn, and there was no place else in the village where wayfarers could find food and shelter.

After making it known that they intended to pass the night at the station, the strangers stripped their saddles, blankets and rifles from their mules. They piled their equipment in a room at one side of the little courtyard which was soon to become a shambles. Then they sat at a table in a room across the patio and called for a speedy serving of food and liquor.

One of the men was Butch Cassidy and the other was Harry Longabaugh. After the Aramayo mines remittance holdup, the bandits had proceeded to Tupiza, where they took employment with a transportation outfit. Learning that they had been identified as the perpetrators of the Aramayo holdup, they hurriedly departed for Uyuni, Bolivia.

The constable in charge of the station at San Vicente happened to catch sight of one of the strangers' mules, then rolling in the dust of the courtyard to relieve his saddle-galled back. He recognized the animal as having belonged to a friend of his—a muleteer who was helping transport the Aramayo mines' remittance when the holdup took place.

How did these Americans across the courtyard come into possession of that mule? They were rough-looking fellows, with stubby beards and battered clothes. Maybe they had something to do with the holdup. If they were bandits, they were careless, as their rifles were leaning against the adobe wall in the room which held their saddles. It would be easy to capture these hungry gentry and inquire into matters. There was a company of Bolivian cavalry just outside of town. The constable would send an Indian messenger to the captain. Then the Americans would have to explain how they came into possession of that mule.

On receipt of the message the Bolivian captain brought up his command and quietly surrounded the station. Then the captain himself walked into the room where Cassidy and Longabaugh were eating and drinking.

"Surrender, señors," came the demand from the brave captain.

The outlaws leaped to their feet. Longabaugh was drunk, but Cassidy, always a canny drinker, was in complete command of his senses.

The captain had drawn his revolver when he entered the room. Before he could fire, Cassidy had shot from the hip. The captain fell dead and Cassidy and Longabaugh stationed themselves where they could command a view of the patio.

A sergeant and a picked body of cavalrymen rushed through the gate, calling upon the outlaws to surrender. Revolvers blazed from door and window, and men began to stagger and fall in the courtyard. The first to die was the sergeant who had sought to rescue his captain.

Cassidy and Longabaugh were firing rapidly and with deadly effect. Those of the detachment who remained on their feet were firing in return. Bullets sank into the thick adobe walls or whistled through the window and door. Other soldiers began firing from behind the shelter of the courtyard wall.

"Keep me covered, Butch," called Longabaugh. "I'll get our rifles."

Shooting as he went, Longabaugh lurched into the courtyard. If he could only reach the rifles and ammunition which they had so thoughtlessly laid aside, the fight would be something the outlaws would welcome.

Blood was settling in little pools about the courtyard. The sergeant and most of his file of soldiers were stretched out dead. A few wounded were trying to crawl to safety. The mules had broken their halters and galloped out of the yard, among them the animal which had been the indirect cause of the battle.

Soldiers were firing through the open gate and from all other vantage points outside the wall. Longabaugh got halfway across the courtyard and fell, desperately wounded, but not before he had effectively emptied his six-shooter.

When Cassidy saw his partner fall, he rushed into the courtyard. Bullets rained about him as he ran to Longabaugh's side. Some of the shots found their mark, but Cassidy, though wounded, managed to pick up Longabaugh and stagger back to the house with his heavy burden.

Cassidy saw that Longabaugh was mortally wounded. Furthermore, it was going to be impossible to carry on the battle much longer unless the rifles and ammunition could be reached. Cassidy made several attempts to cross the courtyard. At each attempt he was wounded and driven back.

The battle now settled into a siege. Night came on, and men fired at the red flashes from weapons. There were spaces of increasing length between Cassidy's shots. He had only a few cartridges left. Longabaugh's cartridge belt was empty. So was the dead Bolivian captain's.

The soldiers, about 9:00 or 10:00 o'clock in the evening, heard two shots fired in the bullet-riddled station. Then no more shots came. Perhaps it was a ruse to lure them into the patio within range of those deadly revolvers. The soldiers kept on firing all through the night and during the next morning.

About noon an officer and a detachment of soldiers rushed through the patio and into the station. They found Longabaugh and Cassidy dead. Cassidy had fired a bullet into Longabaugh's head, and had used his last cartridge to kill himself.

In the pack saddles of the bandits was found intact the money that had been taken in the Aramayo mines remittance holdup, besides a large sum in pounds sterling, gold, which had been taken in the holdup of the Bolivian railway. Also in the equipment of the bandits was found a considerable quantity of antiseptic drugs, field glasses, and a beautiful Tiffany watch which Cassidy was known to have bought in New York when enroute for Buenos Aires.

Cassidy and Longabaugh had made good soldiers out of twenty Bolivians, and had wounded twice that many. Two men with six-shooters against a company of soldiers with rifles! It was just the sort of finish one might have expected—the sort they would themselves have desired. But it was not a Bolivian bullet that finally ended the career of Butch Cassidy, the Mormon boy from Circleville, Utah!

It was the irony of fate that this leader of the Wild Bunch, successful in a hundred forays, who had taken hundreds of thousands of dollars in cash during his lifetime at the point of a gun, should finally die for the theft of a mule!

Since the story of Butch Cassidy speaks for itself, it seems unnecessary to evaluate his personality or analyze his psychological processes. Most famous outlaws, like Jesse James, Cole Younger, Harry Tracy, or John Dillinger, were possessed of twisted minds, full of uncontrolled hatred for all mankind, with a lust to kill just for the sake of killing. They were mad dogs in human form.

But Butch Cassidy was cast in a different mold. By ancestry he was as English as Robin Hood; by environment a typical American cowboy. To him, monotony was deadly and adventure the tonic of life. He entered the Outlaw Trail looking for excitement, with his eyes wide open, and followed it to the end, with few if any regrets. He had a sense of fair play even when robbing trains and banks. He made many friends and few enemies. While he never consciously robbed the rich to feed the poor, he did perform many acts of generosity. So far as we know, he never killed a man during his entire career, until his last stand. That in itself makes him outstanding among outlaws.

Finis to
the Wild Bunch

AFTER Butch Cassidy went to South America the Wild Bunch quickly disintegrated. Without their leader they were helpless. There was not one left with the ability to plan, organize, and execute. They never again gathered for a raid, and their previous spectacular exploits soon became history, kept alive by hundreds of legendary tales repeated wherever cowboys gathered. Although Cassidy had become, within a few short years, the West's most famous outlaw, he left behind no personal enemies. The cowboy outlaw era ended with him.

Tom Horn, with two well-placed shots, had made good boys out of the Brown's Hole rustlers. Most of them left the Hole, never to return; others became respectable ranchers almost overnight. Joe Bush had proved that Robbers' Roost was not impregnable. He had killed Joe Walker and Herron and had run Blue John, Silver Tip, and their friends out of the state. The Roost was soon deserted. Sheriff Sproul, Joe Devine, Joe LaFors, and a few other determined men continued raiding Hole-in-the-Wall until they drove out the outlaws and opened the country behind the Red Wall to settlement by law-abiding ranchers.

But the law was not alone responsible for the disappearance of those men who had ridden the Outlaw Trail for so long. They were in fact being gradually crowded off the trail by thousands of flocks of woolly sheep which began filtering into every corner of the desert, eating the grass on which cattle had formerly grazed, leaving in their wake a real desert, the like of which had never been seen before.

Where, in the old days of the Wild Bunch, a hundred cattle grazed in knee-deep grass, a thousand sheep came to tear out by the roots all vegetation and kill even the sagebrush by constant nibbling. Under such conditions, erosion began its deadly work. After the sheep had passed, even jackrabbits were hard put to it to find a living. Cattle and horses disappeared from the ranges, and rustling died a natural death. Herders guarded their woolly flocks—but only from coyotes. The vilest epithet one rustler ever applied to another was "sheep thief."

Sam's Mesa, the sandy plateau on which Robbers' Roost was perched, never was intended by nature for ranching purposes. However, Joe Biddlecome squatted at Roost Spring after the outlaws had abandoned the place. He built a cabin, brought in a few cattle, and started ranching. After his death the business was continued by his daughter, Pearl, who kept the poison feet of encroaching sheep from her domain. In comparison with other parts of the desert not so protected, she developed one of the best cattle ranges left in that section of Utah. She was a worthy daughter of her pioneer father, who may have carved this inscription over Roost Spring:

BEWARE!
14 Notches on my gun
J. B.

An ancient cabin built of mountain cedars stands on the Biddlecome ranch, a replica of one built by Blue John at Blue John Spring. On its door is painted "Robbers' Roost Headquarters." On the door casing is pasted a fragment of a poem, said to have been written by Joe Biddlecome. It reads:

ROBBER'S ROOST

In the eastern end of Wayne county
  There is a lovely spring,
The Robber's Roost is its name,
  To it fond memories cling.
One drink of it, you lose your hope,
  Two, your religion's gone,
Three, you want to rob a bank
  Before another dawn.
Old Blue John and Old Silver Tip
  Lived here for many years,
They spent a very busy time
    . . . Sam shed tears
      . . . . took a bunch . . .

Robbers' Roost Ranch, as the Biddlecome place is known, lies at the absolute end of the trail, sixty-five miles south of Greenriver, Utah. Its nearest neighbor is the Chafin ranch, forty miles north. The trail, unworthy of the name "road," climbs gradually up the north slope of the San Rafael Swell, much of the way through sand almost impassable for automobile travel. The canyon of the Dirty Devil River cuts off all access from the south. Cataract Canyon of the Colorado River lies just to the east. It is the most isolated ranch in Utah.

The outlaw cave from which Blue John and Silver Tip made their escape during the "Battle of Robbers' Roost" is just as it was left by the outlaws. On its walls are carved two or three names, among them that of Ella Butler. Its roof still bears the marks of Sheriff Tyler's bullets.

On July 24, 1934, this writer arrived at Greenriver, Utah,

after having visited Torrey, Hanksville, the Henry Mountains, Poison Springs Wash, Robbers' Roost, and the San Rafael Desert. I had been out of contact with the "outside" for more than a week. Pulling into the nearest station to have the car serviced, I asked the attendant for any late news of interest.

"Did you know that John Dillinger has just been killed?" he asked.

John Dillinger dead! What could have been more appropriate after a visit to Robbers' Roost? Dillinger was the No. 1 outlaw of modern times, as Cassidy had been during his day. Yet, what a difference! In comparison with Dillinger, Cassidy was a gentleman. Over a period of thirty-seven years even outlaws have degenerated to unspeakable depths. Robbers' Roost was a thousand times preferable as a hideout to anything found in our modern cities, and the worst of its old-time characters were infinitely to be preferred to the best variety of 1934 gangster.

Charley Gibbons, then seventy-four years old, storekeeper at Hanksville during the old outlaw days, was developing a vanadium property at the foot of the Henry Mountains. On the day I visited his camp he had just returned from hunting wild cattle on the upper slopes and had packed down a fine beef. Butch Cassidy, as a seventeen-year-old boy, worked for Gibbons as cowhand when he and Dr. J. K. W. Bracken were partners in a cattle ranch near the Henrys.

Brown's Hole is now owned by a big corporation in Rock Springs and used as a wintering ground for sheep. The old 2-Bar ranch, once headquarters for scores of cowboys, is now used as a warehouse for wool. The only men I met there were former cowboys loading bales of wool on a high-powered truck. They still wore their spurs—but it was a pathetic gesture. There are no more horses to ride!

Two sons of the original settlers of Brown's Hole still remained. George Bassett owned a ranch opposite Lodore Canyon. Stanley Crouse was caretaker for the sheep corporation.

Mattie Edwards, sweetheart of Eb Bassett, who "pardoned himself" after being arrested for rustling, still lived alone on the old Bassett homestead in 1937. (The house burned a few years later.) She was a little wisp of a woman with faded blue eyes and graying hair. In one corner of her living room stood a loaded Winchester used to frighten mountain lions that came down off the mountain to investigate her chicken house. In front of the house was a tiny bed of pansies, the only flowers I saw in Brown's Hole.

Mattie was quite cordial to this intruder on her solitude when she found I was interested in Brown's Hole history. She lived entirely in the past and was able to furnish much valuable information. She pointed out the spot on Douglas Mountain where Valentine Hoy was killed by Harry Tracy. Bassett's old corral gate was gone, but in a plot of rye grass back of the house Mattie showed me the grave of Jack Bennett, hanged by settlers when the law came to Brown's Hole. Some stones had fallen down and she stooped to replace them.

"I try to keep this grave neat," she apologized. "Maybe he was only a rustler, but I guess somebody loved him."

Opposite the mouth of Beaver Creek on the south bank of the Green River stands the original Crouse cabin. On a hillside two hundred yards to the west is one of the strangest desert graves I have ever seen. Four walls of dressed red sandstone enclose a space twelve feet square filled with earth. At the head and foot stand two polished marble slabs. That at the foot is blank, but the headstone contains the following inscription:

To the
Memory of
CHARLES W. SEGER
Born Jan. 20, 1867
Died Dec. 27, 1891

"That grave is the result of a Christmas drunk," said John Muir, an old resident in Brown's Hole. "The boys were putting on a three-day spree in this cabin and started a wrestling match. Some of the witnesses were Elza Lay, Joe Davenport, and John Martin.

"Joe Tolliver, half brother to Mrs. Crouse, thought he was champion of the Hole. He had thrown all the local boys; but Charley Seger, who had just come in with his brother from Iowa, proved to be the better man and pinned Joe to the floor. That made Tolliver so mad he pulled a knife and started making mincemeat out of the man who had bested him. Seger died at 3:00 o'clock next morning. The ground was frozen so hard they could not dig a grave, so they laid him on the ground, built a wall around him, and filled the space with dirt scraped off the hillside. His brother, Al Seger, put up the markers. They were cut in Salt Lake City and packed in on horses.

"Sheriff Pope came in and took Tolliver to Vernal for trial, but he was acquitted. He was one of the toughest men in Brown's Hole. Some of the boys from here used to go into Vernal and shoot up the town. Vernal constables couldn't do anything with them, so finally the city council hired Joe Tolliver as town marshal. He knew all the boys, and they knew him. He kept pretty good order, too, but when he was drunk—which was all the time—people were more afraid of him than they were of the rustlers.

"One day Joe went into a barber shop to get a shave. He was sitting in the chair fooling with his six-shooter.

" 'Put that gun away before you hurt somebody,' warned the barber.

" 'Hell!' shouted Tolliver, 'it's perfectly safe. Look.'

"With that he pointed the gun at himself, pulled the trigger, and shot his own head off. That was the end of Joe Tolliver."

Old graves are scattered all along the river in Brown's Hole if one knows where to look. There is one just below the

Crouse cabin, occupied by the bones of a man who stood up
to Charley Crouse in the old days. Crouse was tried for that
killing but got off on a plea of self-defense, although there
are those in the Hole who believe he never waited for the
other man to draw. Near that grave is where Crouse disemboweled Albert Williams, the Speckled Nigger.

In Clay Basin is the unmarked grave of William Pigeon,
Jack Bennett's partner. He and Ike Lee were sitting in a
sheep wagon when they quarreled over a dog. Ike shot him
and he fell out of the back of the wagon. From all reports he
had already lived too long.

Near the old ferry once operated by Speck, is the ruin of
the store run by John Jarvie, whose body was set afloat on
the river by his murderer, Hood. Across the river is the grave
of Jesse Ewing, killed by Dunlap over a worthless woman.
Isom Dart lies buried at Summit Springs, where he was killed
by Tom Horn. The body of Matt Rash, killed near the same
place, was later exhumed by his father and taken to Texas.

The Hole-in-the-Wall country, scene of the famous "Invasion" of 1892, headquarters for George Curry and the
Logan brothers, has long been peaceful and quiet. Like
Brown's Hole, it is owned by a corporation, but has always
remained a cattle country. None of the old-timers who made
history there ever took their families behind the Red Wall.
None were left in 1935 to recall the stirring events of earlier
days except Bill Stubbs, who was still living in a lonely cabin
on Buffalo Creek. Stubbs was the only man in that part of
Wyoming who still wore a six-gun and retained all the old-
time flavor of pre-Invasion days. No one then in Johnson
County would say that Bill ever rustled cattle; but he was
the champion storyteller of the Powder River and spoke with
authority of the old days. Western writers missed a good bet
when they overlooked Texas Bill Stubbs.

Graves are scattered all over the Hole-in-the-Wall country.
Bill Stubbs could tell you where they are. Nearly all, how-

ever, contain the bones of men who were killed in personal fights. Bob Smith was the only man ever killed by officers at the Hole-in-the-Wall ranch.

And what of the men who made these old hideouts famous? Here is the record:

Butch Cassidy and Harry Longabaugh were killed at San Vicente, Bolivia, in 1909.

Flat Nose George Curry, leader of the Hole-in-the-Wall gang, was killed by Sheriff Jesse M. Tyler, near Thompson, Utah, on April 17, 1900.

Harvey Logan, alias Kid Curry, next to Cassidy the most hunted outlaw of his day, was finally arrested, tried, and convicted at Knoxville, Tennessee. After a spectacular jail break he tried to hold up a train near Parachute, Colorado, and was later shot by a posse. He is buried at Glenwood Springs, Colorado.

John Logan was killed by W. H. Winters, a rancher, near Landusky, Montana, January 16, 1896.

Lonny Logan was killed by officers at Dodson, Missouri, February 28, 1900.

Bill Carver was killed by Sheriff Ed Bryant at Sonora, Texas, while resisting arrest on April 2, 1901.

Ben Kilpatrick and Ole Buck attempted to hold up a train at Sanderson, Texas, on March 13, 1912, and were killed by the express messenger. Kilpatrick was hit over the head with an ice mallet; Buck was then shot with Kilpatrick's gun.

Sam Ketchum was wounded in the arm during an encounter with officers after a train holdup near Folsom, New Mexico, July 16, 1899, and died from blood poisoning. Tom "Black Jack" Ketchum, his brother, was hanged April 26, 1901, at Clayton, New Mexico.

Camilla (Comelio) Hanks was killed in a honkytonk on Utah Street, San Antonio, on April 16, 1902, by Pink Taylor and other officers while resisting arrest for passing some of the unsigned notes from the Wagner, Montana, train holdup.

Harry Tracy was sent to the pen in Oregon, escaped, killed twenty men, was surrounded by a posse, and killed himself in a wheatfield, August 5, 1902.

Patrick Lewis Johnson served a term in the Colorado pen for his part in the killing of Valentine Hoy, then returned to Iowa.

Dave Lant, with Tracy and Johnson when Hoy was killed, joined the army in 1898, served in the Philippines, was promoted for bravery in action, returned to Utah, and left the Outlaw Trail.

Tom McCarty, leader of the McCarty or Blue Mountain gang, disappeared and not even his family knows where he died. Some say he was killed near Greenriver, Utah. Matt Warner thinks he was killed in the Bitterroot country of Montana.

Bill McCarty and his son Fred were killed by W. Ray Simpson after the bank robbery at Delta, Colorado, September 7, 1893.

Joe Walker was killed on Hill Creek, forty miles from Thompson, Utah, by a posse of thirteen men, after a thirteen-day chase, on Friday, May 13, 1898. John Herron, his partner, was killed at the same time.

James F. Howells, alias Silver Tip, was killed by Arizona officers for stealing horses. John Griffith, alias Blue John, is presumed to have been drowned in the Colorado River while fleeing from a posse. Rains Lee, alias Charley Rains, disappeared after killing Chaves, a Mexican sheepherder. Jack Cottrell left the Roost after a warrant had been issued for his arrest on a statutory charge.

C. L. Maxwell, alias John Carter, was killed on the streets of Price, Utah, by "Shoot-em-up" Bill Johnson, about 1902.

Jack Moore, early resident of Robbers' Roost and at one time partner of Maxwell, is said to have been killed May 28, 1898, by a posse, either near Greenriver, Utah, or Baggs, Wyoming. His wife borrowed money from Charley Gibbons at Hanksville to bury him, went to live with J. B. Buhr on Granite ranch, and later left the country with him.

Bob Meeks was sent to the pen for his part in the Montpelier bank robbery, broke his leg in an attempted escape, and was released after the leg had been amputated.

Elza or Ellsworth Lay (William H. McGinnis), Cassidy's partner in several spectacular holdups, captured after the Folsom train robbery, was sentenced to the pen for life on October 10, 1899, at Raton, New Mexico. On July 4, 1905, his sentence was commuted to ten years and he was released on January 10, 1906. He returned to the Uintah Basin and ran a poker game for Henry Lee on the Strip. Also he visited his daughter, who was living on the upper Duchesne River. For a time he ran a saloon in Shoshoni, Wyoming. He later married Mary Calverly and was manager for her father's ranches on the Little Snake River. Many years later he was watermaster for the Imperial Valley irrigation company. He died in Los Angeles in 1933. His wife refused any information for this volume because she said her children did not know their father had been an outlaw.

Tom O'Day, captured at the time of the Belle Fourche bank robbery, escaped jail and returned to Hole-in-the-Wall. On November 23, 1903, he was captured with a band of twenty-three stolen horses by Sheriff Frank K. Webb of Casper. At his first two trials the jury disagreed, but at the third he was convicted. When pronouncing sentence, Judge Craig gave the prisoner a lecture which is well worth reproducing here. The judge said:

In the early days of Wyoming it was the custom to rustle stock, and if a list could be compiled of all the men who had gotten a start in life by this method, it would make quite a large catalog. But those days are past, and Tom, you ought to have quit when the rest of the boys did. If I were to sentence you for all the crimes you have committed, you would go to the penitentiary for the rest of your life; but your sentence shall be only for the crime upon which you have been convicted. . . . After you serve your sentence, try and lead an honest life. You will find it pays. There is but one result for those who steal.

O'Day is said to have taken Judge Craig's advice. When last heard from he was hauling coal in Shoshoni, Wyoming.

Walter Putney, who was with O'Day in the Belle Fourche bank robbery, was still living in 1949 at Pinedale, Wyoming.

Matt Warner, after serving his sentence in the Utah pen, ran a saloon in Greenriver, Utah, then moved to Price, where he was at various times peace officer, night watchman, justice of the peace, candidate for sheriff, and bootlegger.

Billy Tittsworth, who came to Brown's Hole in early days, believed Matt was really good at heart and wanted him to quit the game. One day in 1895 the two men were riding over Diamond Mountain in a buckboard on their way to Vernal. Tittsworth considered it a good opportunity to have a heart-to-heart talk.

"You can't beat this game, Matt," he explained as they rode. "It will get the best of you in the end. You can't name a single rustler or outlaw who ever made anything by it in the long run. You think you're having a good time, but it can't last. Sooner or later you will be killed or put in the pen for life. What will become of your wife and kids then? Your own children will be ashamed of you. You could make good anywhere if you'd just make up your mind to it. You're still young. Why don't you leave Brown's Hole and make a new start?"

Tittsworth talked on in the same vein for an hour. The day was warm, the trail was long; the horses slowed to a sleepy walk as their driver became absorbed in his earnest effort to "convert" the outlaw. Matt's chin dropped on his chest as if in deep thought, and Billy believed his arguments were taking effect.

Suddenly Matt came out of his brown study with a start.

Grabbing the whip he struck the horses a vicious blow which sent them galloping.

"The world owes me a living, Billy," he shouted, "and by God I'm going to get it." The following year he was sent to the pen for murder.

Matt was past seventy when I interviewed him in Price, where he was selling a superior brand of bootleg whiskey. His eyes were still sharp and his trigger finger steady. He held me spellbound for hours recounting stories of his adventures on the Outlaw Trail. He was then writing the story of his life, which was later published, but would not show me his manuscript. He was not hypocritical; he had paid for some of his foolishness and quit while the quitting was good.

"You'll never know," he said, "what it means to be hunted. You can never sleep. You've always got to listen with one ear and keep one eye open. After a while you almost go crazy. No sleep! No sleep! Even when you know you're perfectly safe you can't sleep. Every piss-ant under your pillow sounds like a posse of sheriffs coming to get you!"

Rosa, his first wife, died while he was in the pen. He married again in Price and raised a family. In 1912 he was candidate for sheriff of Carbon County on the Bull Moose ticket, under his real name of Willard Christiansen. But the legend on the posters, "Vote for Willard Christiansen for Sheriff," meant nothing to residents of Carbon County. No one knew Willard Christiansen; consequently he lost the election. If he had run under the name of Matt Warner his election would have been a landslide.

Matt Warner came to Salt Lake City shortly after the first edition of this book was published. A friend lent him a copy and he sat up all night reading it. Next morning he came to my place of business. He was the angriest man I had ever encountered.

"I have just read your book," he shouted, "and I want to say you are the God-damn'dest liar who ever lived. I'm going to sue you for libel, and if you keep on selling those books I'll burn down your establishment."

"What's the matter, Matt?" I asked. "You wouldn't give me much information when I talked to you, so I got it wherever I could. What did I say that was wrong?"

"You can call me a horse thief," Matt replied, "or a rustler or a bank robber or even a murderer, and I won't say a word. But when you say I abused my wife you are a liar and I'll sue you if I don't knock hell out of you first. Where did you get such a pack of lies as you told in that book? My wife and I never had a cross word as long as she lived!"

"I got it from the Salt Lake *Tribune*. She told the story herself."

Perhaps Matt had never seen the story; if so, he had entirely forgotten about it. This statement took the wind out of his sails, and his anger slowly ebbed away. When he was quiet I said:

"Matt, let's get together tonight and we will go through the book page by page. If I have made any misstatements, we can fix them up."

"O.K.," he said, "I'll do that. I'll come back at 5:00 o'clock."

At 4:00 o'clock Matt showed up again with an apologetic smile on his face.

"Just got a long-distance call from home," he said, "and I've got to go back to Price right away. I'll have to see you some other time."

Later I heard the rest of the story. Matt had developed kidney trouble, and doctors had ordered him to quit drinking. He had not touched a drop for over two years. But after he read my story he was so mad he bought a quart of whiskey and drank it on the way home to Price. When he got there he bought more liquor and kept on drinking heavily for ten days. Then he died, December 21, 1938.

His family says I killed him.

The picturesque, swaggering, two-gun cattle rustlers of the 1890s are gone forever. But the business of stealing cattle has recently been revived in a new streamlined pattern. Within recent years Colorado and Wyoming have experienced depredations of the new rubber-tired thief. The following news item is from a Denver newspaper, dated October 1, 1937:

> Ranchers and sheriffs from the Colorado cattle country met at the state capitol today to map a campaign against the modern "rubber-tired" cattle thief.
>
> Indignation at the kill-and-fly-by-night operations of cattle rustlers has been intense this autumn. Cool weather hardly had struck the cattle country before thieves began to shoot heifers, skin them on the spot and haul the carcasses away in trucks—this in the face of the state's new "hide and horns" law.

Old Brown's Hole, once the center of rustling operations, goes this story one better by reporting the use of refrigerator trucks!

Is Butch Cassidy
Dead?

Rumors of Cassidy's death were circulated from time to time after the killing of Joe Walker in 1898. When the story of his battle and death in South America reached old friends in Utah, it was discounted as just another of many rumors. Some believed that Cassidy himself had started the story so he could return to the States in safety under another name. He had written some of the boys in Robbers' Roost that things were getting a little too hot in the south and he might return some day. Few old-timers could be convinced that the outlaw who had out-witted so many clever officers in the United States could be killed by spiggoty cops. But as months passed without any letters being received by his old friends, and when their letters were returned unclaimed, they were forced to admit that perhaps the rumors were correct.

Most of the old Wild Bunch were either dead or safely behind the bars. A few, however, like Matt Warner and Elza Lay, could never rest until they knew the facts. Cassidy had many friends among cattlemen, scattered all over the country, who were also interested in learning his fate. Those friends decided to find out for sure whether or not he was dead or alive.

It was finally agreed to send a man to South America to ascertain the facts. None of the old gang had any money; the rustling racket had been broken up by Tom Horn, and most of the old-timers had taken up small ranches on the desert or gone into other lines of business. So funds for this trip were raised by taking up a collection of one hundred and twenty-five dollars from each one interested in the project. Matt Warner was probably the leading spirit in this undertaking. The list of those who contributed toward that fund might surprise one not acquainted with the story of Butch Cassidy. It contained many prominent names, among them Charley Gibbons, the Hanksville storekeeper, and Dr. J. W. K. Bracken, a retired capitalist who had once owned cattle in the Henry Mountains.

The emissary made a trip to the reported scene of Cassidy's last stand, interviewed surviving soldiers who had participated in the battle of San Vicente, obtained photographs taken at the time showing the two dead outlaws, and returned to Utah with his evidence. There seemed to be no question that Cassidy was dead. Queen Ann says Elza Lay told her he sent a man named Burton. Matt Warner says that when the hat was passed Walker was sent. William L. Simpson says he knows two men who investigated Cassidy's death, one being Billy Sattell.

However, as in the case of every other famous outlaw from Jesse James to John Dillinger, there are rumors to the effect that Butch Cassidy is still alive. These stories are so persistent that one may be pardoned for wondering if, after all, it was really Cassidy who was killed at San Vicente in 1909. There is a bare possibility that Longabaugh's companion in that last stand was some other American outlaw and that Cassidy was satisfied to let the world believe he had been killed.

When Dr. Bracken saw a photograph of the two dead men brought back by the emissary, he declared that the one thought to be Cassidy was actually Tom Dilley, a minor outlaw from Robbers' Roost who had gone to South America when things got too hot around Price and Greenriver.

Robert Hildebrand, an old post-office detective who says he knew Cassidy personally, declares the outlaw returned to Brown's Hole after he was reported killed, and died not many years ago.

Another story believed by many is that Butch Cassidy returned to Circleville to view the body of his dead mother. He is said to have arrived in the night and left during the following night. Friends of Mrs. Parker were not allowed to enter the house where the body lay during that day, a strange procedure in southern Utah, where neighbors always offer their services on such occasions. Mrs. Ann Campbell Parker died on May 1, 1905, three years after her outlaw son is said to have left the United States.

John Wesley Warf says that one day in Price, about 1915, he stepped into Matt Warner's saloon, where he observed a man sitting with his back to the wall. Warner and Warf were intimately acquainted. "Know who that is?" asked Matt in a whisper. "No," Warf replied, "I don't recognize him." "That's Butch Cassidy. He's staying with me for a while; but keep it under your hat." But Matt was always a great joker.

Another story generally believed by many was told by the late Anthony Ivins, first counselor to the president of the Mormon church, an old-time westerner who knew Cassidy as a boy. Mr. Ivins asserted positively that Cassidy was still living in Idaho under an assumed name which he felt under obligation of friendship not to reveal. The same story is told by an old Salt Lake barber who was raised in Circleville.

Various stories circulating in Utah are to the effect that Cassidy is still living in Mexico. One such is told by Henry Bowman, of Cedar City, Utah. It seems that Bowman, a member of the Mormon colony in Mexico, was captured by a band of Pancho Villa's soldiers during the revolution and had been lined up against a wall to be shot. As a last resort, Bowman pleaded with the officer in charge to allow him to speak with his friend, Cassidy, before the execution. Cassidy had been a resident of those parts for many years and was well known to the officer, so the request was granted. A messenger was sent and Cassidy arrived in haste. When he saw Bowman he protested the boy's innocence of any connection with the Federals, vouched for his honesty, and agreed to be responsible for his future actions. The officer was convinced and Bowman was freed, returning to Utah shortly afterward. The incident is undoubtedly true. But, according to Jim Marshall, an old-timer who knew both, the man who saved Bowman's life was Mike Cassidy, the old southern Utah bandit whose name was taken by George LeRoy Parker. Mike, says Marshall, once returned to his old haunts in Utah, dressed in broadcloth and a high silk hat. The two men met in the little store at Molan. Mike winked at Marshall and nodded to meet him outside. "You won't give me away, will you, Jim?" asked Mike. "I'm just back for a short visit." Marshall promised. Mike Cassidy then left the country, but letters were received from him later stating he had married a woman with property in Mexico and was living the life of a hidalgo. That man, says Marshall, is the Cassidy who saved Bowman's life. And Jim ought to know.

Another story comes from Harry Ogden, who as a boy met Cassidy several times in Robbers' Roost. "In 1923," says Ogden, "I was working on the international ditch just over the Mexican border. In a little Mexican saloon where the men gambled on pay days, I met Cassidy dealing in one of the games. He called me to one side and cautioned me not to mention his old name. He recalled the time we had traded horses and seemed anxious to hear all the news of his family and friends in Utah. He said he was then living on an island just off the coast. It was later reported that he died there in 1932." This was Elza Lay, not Cassidy.

In compiling her recent book, *Early Days in Wyoming*, Tacetta B. Walker was told by several old-timers near Lander that Butch Cassidy had been in that vicinity as late as 1934, had stayed several months, and had later gone to Spokane, where he was still living in 1937. This story, identical in detail, came to me from several different sources, and the evidence seemed thoroughly convincing. At last, in September, 1937, a newspaper story appeared in Utah and Wyoming announcing the death of the real Butch Cassidy in Spokane. He had lived there after coming from Lander, it was said, under the name of William Phillips. Notice of his death was given to the papers by a man in Lander who claimed to have ridden with Butch Cassidy in early days and couldn't possibly be fooled by a pretender. This old friend did not attempt to explain how Butch had survived the battle of San Vicente, but he stated positively that William Phillips of Spokane was the real Butch Cassidy and that he finally died in July, 1937.

A letter to the bureau of vital statistics of the state of Washington brought this writer a copy of the death certificate of William Phillips, the man who passed in Wyoming as Butch Cassidy. The statements therein prove positively that Phillips was not Cassidy.

A letter from Mrs. Phillips, dated October 4, 1938, says:

Wm. T. Phillips was born and raised in an eastern state until he reached the age of 14 years at which time, owing to dime novel influence, he ran away and headed for the Black Hills. There he became homesick and started to make his way back home. He finally succeeded in obtaining work on a ranch in the corn belt and in the spring again headed for the Black Hills. It was after that when he fell in with Cassidy. It was about the time of the Johnson County war, and I've heard him express himself as being entirely in sympathy with the "little fellows" instead of the stock association. He thought he knew Cassidy very well and considered he was much more sinned against than sinning.

We each knew Cassidy; I knew his family. But I can tell you little you do not already know. Both Mr. Phillips and myself came originally from the east.

Phillips, representing himself as Cassidy, searched the mountains near Fort Washakie with Bill Boyd for $70,000 supposed to have been buried there by Butch. He met Hank Bedeker of Dubois, who knew Cassidy well in the old days, but was not recognized as an impostor. He also fooled several old-timers in the vicinity of Lander and Wilcox, who swore they could not be mistaken.

Strangely enough, Mike Cassidy, the older man whose name was adopted by Butch, was still living at last reports in Los Angeles.

The preceding stories are given for what they are worth, merely to complete the record. If George LeRoy Parker, the Mormon cowboy-outlaw, is still alive, it seems strange he never returned to Circleville, Utah, to visit his old father, Maximilian Parker, who died on July 28, 1938, at the age of ninety-four.

The Speckled Nigger

Two weeks before his death—
on May 7, 1934—I visited Albert Williams, the "Speckled
Nigger," at the home of Frank Hatch, in Vernal, where he
was being cared for in his last illness. Speck was undoubtedly
one of the most interesting characters in Brown's Hole, last
survivor of the rustler era. The old black man was under the
impression I had come to write the story of his life.

"You don' need to put my picture in the book," he explained. "Nobody'd care what I looked like. I want you to
call it 'Speck Williams,' an' I want a picture of my horse on
the front cover. That'd sho' make a fine-lookin' book."

Albert Williams was born a slave in West Virginia shortly
before the Civil War. He had, of course, never learned to read
or write, and did not know his exact age. He clearly remembered soldiers returning from the war, which would make
him about eighty years old at the time of his death. He was
thin, emaciated, wrinkled, and almost toothless, but his sight
and hearing were still good. His skin was a medium brown,
bleached by poor health and covered with coal-black freckles

which gave rise to the nickname "Speck," of which he was proud.

As a young man Speck worked as mule driver in the coal mines of West Virginia. For a short time he was coachman for the "ladies and gemmen" at White Sulphur Springs, then as now a fashionable resort, and wore a fine uniform with brass buttons. But after his carriage had been held up by "Jesse James" on a lonely road, he decided it was safer to work in the mines.

In 1883, the only date he remembered definitely, Speck was shipped with a trainload of other Negro miners to break a strike at some new mines recently opened in Iowa. The Negroes had not been informed they were strike breakers, but when their train neared the mines each was given a rifle and instructed to "take the town," which they did.

Iowa was having a series of Indian scares at the time, and some Sioux warriors had been seen in the mine's vicinity. One night, when the darkies were having an exciting game of craps, Indians fired into their tent.

"There wasn't no more sevens throwed that night," said Speck. "We grabbed our rifles and started shooting into the tall grass, but didn't find any dead Injuns in the morning."

All the men in that part of Iowa belonged to the "Home Guards," a force of volunteers recruited and financed by the government. Speck and all other Negroes were organized into a company of "Black Guards," under Captain Perry, a Negro officer. The Black Guards were ordered into the field during the uprising and spent a year in an Indian campaign, chasing the Sioux as far west as the Yellowstone River.

After that experience Speck returned to Iowa, where he worked for the Whitebreast Coal company. Later he went to the mines at Bloomington, Illinois. From here he was sent with another trainload of Negroes to break a strike at Roselyn, Washington. Again the black men took the town with rifles, driving out entrenched Irish miners. From Roselyn he went to British Columbia for a short time before coming to Rock Springs to work in the Union Pacific coal mines.

Eventually the railroad imported a trainload of Chinamen to replace Welsh and Negro miners, thus starting what is locally called the "Chinese War." Speck went to Brown's Hole about that time (1895) to work for Tom Davenport, a Welsh miner who had started a cattle ranch. He worked for all the settlers at various times but always considered the Davenport place his home and spoke affectionately of "Mis' Davenpo't." He was a good worker; but his savings were invariably spent in Rock Springs on an annual spree lasting until everything he had was gone, including horse and saddle.

Speck was already in the Hole when Butch Cassidy arrived to organize the Wild Bunch. The boys camped for a while in a tent in Clear Basin. Passing that way, Speck was invited to have a drink, remained to play poker, and from that time on considered Cassidy his friend. He remembers a little cove back of that camp called the "slaughter house," where the bones of stolen cattle covered the ground so thickly one could walk a considerable distance by stepping from one skull to another.

Speck was never a bona-fide member of the Wild Bunch. Born a slave, he had early learned that to avoid trouble he must attend strictly to his own affairs. For several years he operated a ferry across the Green River and in the course of that business met every outlaw who ever passed through Brown's Hole. Many of them, including Cassidy, stopped at his cabin from time to time, and their horses were frequently left in his charge during winter months.

The old man's memory was remarkably accurate, as is often the case with one who cannot write. All the stories he told, so far as could be checked against other records, were correct. But there was a world of history hidden in his kinky old head that he would not reveal. Too well he had learned the lesson that a black man, to survive among such a crew of outlaws, must keep his mouth tightly closed at all times. He had a good word for nearly everyone in the Hole except Mike Flynn.

Flynn was the Hole's last rustler. He had once stolen Speck's horse, and the Negro was "mad at him." The 2-Bar Cattle company, another victim of Flynn's operations, hired Fred Taylor to kill him. Taylor failed, so—according to Speck—they turned the job over to "Young Tom McCarty."

Speck saw McCarty ride up the canyon to waylay Flynn. He could have warned the thief but says he "didn't feel like it." He was cutting hay with Dick Cole in Charley Crouse's field at the mouth of Crouse Canyon. McCarty tied his horse and started to crawl along a ledge commanding the narrow canyon down which Flynn must pass. Speck had spent half his life with the rustlers, who had always treated him well. He had often sent them warning of danger. It was second nature for him to side with the outlaws. As he watched McCarty climb stealthily to his high perch, like a mountain lion waiting for its prey, his instinct told him to send warning, even though he had been one of the thief's victims.

"You run and tell Flynn," he said to Cole at last. "I'm mad at him and can't do it myself." But Cole wouldn't go. Just then old man Collett started up the canyon in a wagon, on his way to Vernal. Cole told Collett, and Collett warned Flynn when they passed in the canyon above; but the rustler insisted on continuing in spite of the reported danger.

Mike Flynn was driving a team hitched to a wagon. Just as he passed under an overhanging ledge, McCarty fired. Flynn never moved. McCarty then turned the horses loose, leaving Flynn still seated on the wagon—dead. The killer threw his rifle in the river, where Speck retrieved it next day, and went on to the Park Livestock ranch, where he stayed all night.

For that job McCarty is said to have received $500. It was handled in regular Tom Horn style and put a final end to rustling in the Hole. The overhanging ledge where the rustler was killed is still called Flynn's Point.

Hood, a halfbreed Indian cowboy in Brown's Hole, sometimes worked for Mark Whalen, a former cattleman who had gone into the sheep business. He was not considered much of a cowboy. Speck says he "always broke his horses tied to a tree." Whalen owned a band of blackface bucks that he had rented out to Speck. One day in 1909 Hood came to the Negro's place with word that Whalen wanted the bucks moved to Red Creek. Speck let him have them. Hood then drove them to Rock Springs, sold the whole band, and went on a big spree. When that money was gone he returned to the Hole with a partner to rob John Jarvie, who ran the only store in the valley. Jarvie usually had several thousand dollars in cash on hand.

At 1:00 o'clock in the morning Hood and his partner forced an entrance into the store, killed Jarvie, and ransacked the place, but only obtained one hundred dollars, as the storekeeper had just paid his annual bills. They carried off everything they could pack, including a saddle belonging to Speck. Jarvie's body was sent down the river in a skiff. A year later Speck found his saddle in the sagebrush several miles from the scene. It was still in fair condition. Jarvie's body was discovered several months later by John A. Gorder and Thomas McQuillan, who had been diamond drilling in Lodore Canyon at a proposed dam site. Julius F. Stone, in *Canyon Country*, the story of his expedition down the Colorado, tells of stopping at Jarvie's cabin. In his entry for September 19, 1909, he says:

At 12 o'clock we reach Jarvie's ranch. No one is here, Jarvie having been murdered about a month ago. The ranch house is in great disorder, but we disturb nothing and go on.

Old Speck's chief contribution to this volume was his story of Tom Horn's activities in Brown's Hole. Under the name of Tom Hix, Horn camped several weeks at the Negro's cabin while studying the outlaws' movements. During Speck's recital he paused to sing a song of twenty verses telling the story of the death of Matt Rash and Isom Dart from the rustlers' angle. He had composed it himself.

While Speck was being interviewed, a doctor arrived to examine him for a "misery" in his side. When he pulled his shirt off, an ugly scar was revealed extending across his abdomen, but he would furnish no information as to how it had been acquired. Afterward the story was furnished by Mrs. William G. Tittsworth, sister of Mrs. Charley Crouse.

It seems that Speck had been working for Crouse, a big, rough, illiterate man from South Carolina with an inborn hatred for all Negroes. In his sober moments he was tolerant of his black employee, but after he had taken a few too many from the brown jug he was ugly and dangerous. One night during the latter part of September, 1900, Crouse crossed the river at the ford below his old cabin to attend a dance on Beaver Creek. During the festivities he drank too much, as usual. Mrs. Crouse sent Speck across to see that her husband got safely home. The latter resented Speck's assistance, but the black man climbed into the saddle and helped Crouse on behind. The white man rode with his arms around the Negro to keep from falling into the river.

Just as they emerged from the water on the south bank, Crouse drew his knife, reached around in front of the Negro and with one vicious slash ripped Speck's belly wide open.

"Where's Speck?" asked his wife when Crouse staggered into the cabin. "I sent him to fetch you."

"I cut the guts out of the black son of a bitch and left him dead in the willows."

Mrs. Crouse jumped on a horse and rode down to the ford, where she found the black man writhing in agony, holding his intestines in his hands. He had rolled on the ground until the wound was full of sand and leaves. With almost superhuman strength the little woman finally got him on the horse and carried him to her cabin. After sending to Rock Springs for Dr. Murray, she spent the balance of the night cleaning and dressing the wound, and did such a good job of amateur surgery that in time he recovered. During his long convalescence she nursed him as carefully as though he had been one of her own children. Speck was naturally grateful. Nothing he could say was too good for the wife of the man who had disemboweled him. . . . But he wouldn't tell me the story.

There was fun as well as tragedy in Brown's Hole in the old days. Dances were held every month, where whiskey flowed freely. Speck was driving a four-horse team one evening for Tom Davenport, on the way to a dance at Matt Warner's. The wagon was full of merrymakers who had begun the celebration before leaving home. Even Speck was feeling fine.

"What's the delay?" shouted Davenport as the wagon bumped along over the rough trail. "Why don't we go faster? Hell, Speck, you don't know how to drive. Never use the lines when you're in a hurry. Throw 'em away and use the whip!"

Speck obeyed instructions. The frightened horses tore across the valley at a mad gallop, regardless of trails, bouncing the dancers high in the air, but the wagon fortunately remained upright.

When the dance had been in progress an hour or two, one of the Wild Bunch started shooting out the lights. At the first shot, Speck made a dive for the door. He was the first one out but missed his footing and fell headlong down a short flight of steps leading to the ground. Mrs. Davenport, weighing nearly two hundred pounds, fell on top of him. The other occupants of the room all reached the door at the same instant, before the Negro could pick himself up. Most of them wore spurs. . . . Speck says he was three months getting cured of those bruises.

At such jamborees Speck was always appointed "keeper of the bottles." As each man entered the dance, he deposited his liquor with Speck, who hid it out in the sagebrush. From each bottle he extracted a toll, and was never in danger of going dry so long as he remained sober enough to remember where the stuff was hidden.

Harry Tracy, the killer, often stopped with Speck at the ferry. "But don't ever say I said *that!*" exclaimed the old man after he had let the information slip.

After having outlived his usefulness as a ranch hand, old Speck was left to shift for himself. All he had to show for a lifetime of hard work was a saddle horse, a team of mules, a wagon, a cow, and a few hens. With his possessions he moved into various abandoned cabins, where he managed to eke out an existence. When discovered by Dr. Russell G. Frazier in 1932 he was living in Little Hole, just upstream from Brown's Hole, in a cabin half a mile from the Green River. He raised a few vegetables in a little garden and his hens furnished a few eggs; but the major portion of his living came from the river.

Dr. Frazier and his crew of four men rounded a bend in the river late one afternoon on their way from Green River, Wyoming, to Boulder Dam. On a big sandstone boulder close to the bank they found the Speckled Nigger fishing in a muddy hole. It was a good place to camp, so they pulled in and spent the night on the beach. Around their campfire that evening and until the wee hours of morning the river party listened to the slow drawl of the West Virginia darkey who had elected to spend his days among the outlaws of Brown's Hole. People seldom passed that way, and the old man was glad to talk to someone interested in his story. He instantly formed a strong admiration for the jovial doctor and firmly believed at the time of his death, two years later, that Dr. Frazier could have saved him from the approaching Grim Reaper.

"When did you see Butch Cassidy last?" asked Dr. Frazier during that first interview.

"Cain't 'zactly remember the year. It was a long time ago.

Butch and some of the boys was fixin' to go on a trip somewhere, didn't say where they was headed. I says to Butch,
says I, 'Butch, will you-all be comin' back soon?' 'Sure will,'
says he, 'n' you be here when I get back. I'll be ridin' in one of
these days with my pockets full o' gold. You stay right here
till you see our dust!'

"An' I been waitin' ever since," said the old darkey. "He
ain't never come yet, but I know he will some day. He ain't
forgot old Speck. Some say he got killed in South America;
but there ain't 'ary bullet could kill Butch Cassidy. I 'spect
he'll be showin' up around here one o' these days."

"How does it happen," the doctor asked, "that you, a
colored man, lived so long among that gang of outlaws without getting killed?"

"Well, Doctor," replied Speck, "I always figgered that if a
man 'tended to his own business all the time, he'd be too
damn busy to get into trouble."

Shorty Wheelwright

No STORY of Hole-in-the-Wall would be complete without more than passing mention of Shorty Wheelwright, who was among the first to enter that famous hideout and the last to leave it. When General Crook was pursuing the Sioux in and out of the Hole in 1876, he was guided by Frank Grouard, a halfbreed South Sea Islander who as a boy had been taken captive by the Indians, had lived with them for many years, had been adopted by Sitting Bull, and later escaped to guide white soldiers against his adopted father. Grouard knew every inch of country, almost every blade of grass in Wyoming, and was particularly familiar with the Powder River country. He was allowed to choose his own assistants. One of them was John Wheelwright, whose given name was soon forgotten in favor of the more descriptive "Shorty."

In collecting notes for this volume I soon discovered that Hole-in-the-Wall was merely a legend among fiction writers, who had no definite idea of its location. Even old-timers in Utah and Wyoming could locate it only by a broad wave of the hand somewhere in Utah, Wyoming, Colorado, or Montana—which was certainly taking in plenty of territory. Among writers of history only Frederick Bechdolt appeared to know its general whereabouts. It became necessary, then, to find and visit Hole-in-the-Wall, in order to describe it accurately.

With Maurice Howe, a historically minded friend, I set out from Salt Lake City one gray morning determined to see the real outlaw hideout, even if it took a month of searching. Our first stop was at Rock Springs, where Judge David E. Thomas gave us our first clue. "It's somewhere around Buffalo," he told us. "Stop at the little town of Kaycee and make inquiries. Someone there will be able to give you definite directions."

Having lingered along the way, we did not reach Kaycee until after sundown, making camp along the roadside half a mile beyond. In the morning we drove back to the village. No one was stirring. To kill time I entered the barber shop to get a shave. During the operation of removing three days' growth, I asked if there was any old-timer in the village who might know the exact location of Hole-in-the-Wall.

"I've heard about it all my life," said the barber, "but have never been out there. The man you want to see is old Shorty Wheelwright. He's ninety years old and has been here since the first whites came in. He was scout with Crook in 1876. He can tell you anything you want to know. He lived out there until just recently. You'll have to oil him up with whiskey, but he'll be glad to take you out. I'll go hunt him up."

Taking time off from his activities he soon returned with a little, wrinkled old man who seemed too fragile to be walking the streets, to say nothing of making a long rough trip in a car. The barber sold us a quart of whiskey to sustain the old man during his journey and sandwiches for our own sustenance.

"Do you think the old man will be able to stand the trip?" I asked doubtfully.

"Hell, yes!" replied the barber. "You can't kill old Shorty. He just rode in on a horse from a ranch twelve miles north. He'll be all right."

With that assurance but some misgivings we started out. As we rode I questioned the old scout and found him to be one of the rarest historical finds I had ever made. I began by inquiring how he happened to come to Wyoming.

"I came out here first as a mule-skinner in a government freighting outfit in 1876," said Shorty. "I was born in New York State. When I was old enough I ran away from home and joined the navy. When the Civil War broke out I was working as a professional diver. Our vessel was sent to Labrador, supposedly to protect fishing vessels, but we never saw any fighting. I never heard but one gun fired while I was in the navy. I was a bit wild in those days and spent most of my time hanging by the thumbs. One day I got mad at the captain and hit him over the head with a marlinspike. They put me in the brig for that, and that's why I could never get a pension—dishonorable discharge. After the war I went in partnership with another fellow in the diving business and did well at it. But the bends got me, so I quit the sea and started west.

"There was some Indian trouble up in Canada about that time, and it wasn't long until I was acting as scout for the British army in their campaign against the Chippaways. I wasn't a professional scout, but they seemed satisfied with my work. I got a Chippaway arrow in my hip up there; that's what makes me limp now. It still hurts.

"After we pacified the Chippaways I stayed on with the British and was sent to Egypt as a canoe scout on the Nile. We had some exciting times there, I can tell you. It was hotter'n hell and the river was full of man-eating crocodiles. We couldn't get any sleep for the mosquitoes and bugs. The soldiers died like flies with fever, but as a scout I had a better chance to take care of myself and finally got back all in one piece.

"Then I started west again and got a job hauling freight to General Crook out here in Wyoming. I landed right here in 1876 and have been somewhere around here ever since. Frank Grouard hired me as a scout. Grouard was the best scout the army ever had. He spoke Sioux as good as any Indian. Calamity Jane worked with us, dressed like a man, and few of the soldiers knew the difference.

"After we made good Injuns out of the Sioux, Frank and I stayed around here until the outlaws started drifting in. We trailed them for a while. Then in 1893 we took a job surveying a route over the Big Horn Mountains so the people could get mail in the winter. We started in February, the worst month of the year. On top of Cloud Peak we got snowed in and went three days without grub. We were eight days in the mountains, and Frank went snowblind. Both of us were about dead when we got to Hyattsville, but we located a trail and the mail came in every winter after that.

"Then I went up on the mountain above Hole-in-the-Wall and found placer gold in a dry gulch. I worked it every spring while the snow was melting. For thirty years I took out between $500 and $800 a season, enough to keep me.

"Maybe I don't look tough now, but I killed a man once. He deserved to be killed too, but they gave me two years in the pen. Then I came back to my claim. Two years ago I took sick and had to come to town. Some dirty skunk jumped my claim while I was away, and by God I'm going to kill him too. Could you boys drive me up there this afternoon?"

Unfortunately we didn't have the time, which was a disappointment to the old man and to us.

After following the Powder River some distance, we came to the little settlement of Barnum, almost abandoned. Just opposite was a high, red sandstone wall, and through it appeared a narrow crevice just wide enough for our car. That was Hole-in-the-Wall, for which we had searched so long. We drove through it into a wide, beautiful valley, protected on one side by the red wall and in other directions by high, rough hills.

"Yes," said Shorty, "I've lived right here in the Hole for fifty years. I knew every outlaw who ever hid out here. Butch Cassidy was one of the best friends I ever had. He'd do anything for me. I've helped him find horses, blankets, and grub lots of times when he wanted to leave in a hurry. The last time I saw him he stopped at my cabin up yonder and borrowed a rifle and a white-handled pistol. He never came back.

"Tom McCarty and his brother Bill were in the Hole sometimes. George Curry was leader of the outlaws here until Butch Cassidy came. I remember Tom Horn very well, but we didn't know who he was when he was here. He went by the name of Tom Hale and always had an Indian boy with him. We used to see the two riding through. They never stayed two nights in the same place. We never could find out what they were doing. One day in a saloon in Buffalo, Horn had a quarrel with his Indian boy. They rode back to the Hole together. Then we saw Horn riding out alone. That was in the spring. Next fall one of the boys found the body of the Indian. We always figured Tom Horn had shot him in the back, but we couldn't prove it. Horn never killed any of the rustlers in the Hole here, but they were mighty scared he would. A lot of 'em left between sundown and sunup. They wasn't sure, but they had a good idea that Tom Hale was the mysterious killer who was sent out to pick off rustlers at $500 a head.

"Well, here we are at the old outlaw ranch. Right down there in that little meadow there used to be six cabins where the outlaws lived in the winter when it was too cold to travel. They'd bring in supplies in the fall and gamble all winter.

Nobody ever bothered them but once. That time a bunch of cattlemen came down that right-hand canyon looking for cattle and trouble. In the scrap Bob Smith was killed, about a mile up the canyon. I helped carry him back here. He died right here where this stump lays.

"Bill Stubbs lives up above here a couple of miles. He knew all the outlaws. His sister married Richardson and after he died she lived in one of the old cabins for a long time. The buildings are all gone now. You can see the remains of some of the old stone chimneys, but the logs have all rotted away. Yes, sir, this was a mighty lively spot in the old days.

"Dutch Henry used to be in here with Curry before Cassidy came. His name was Schmidt. A sheriff came in once to arrest him, got the drop on him, and told the Dutchman to stick up his hands. Dutch pulled his own gun and stuck it in the sheriff's ribs. 'Better you hold up first,' he said. The sheriff did. Then Dutch took his gun, his horse, and his boots and started him back for Buffalo afoot. Lots of sheriffs had to walk back from Hole-in-the-Wall."

On our return we had the good fortune to meet Shorty's old friend, Bill Stubbs. I recognized him from the old man's description long before he pulled up beside our car. He was typical of the old-timers who had once dominated Hole-in-the-Wall—last of the old clan who made it famous. Everything about him—his Stetson, his saddle, his gun—was perfectly in harmony with the best traditions of the old days. He was a large, muscular Texan with Roman nose and piercing eye. He was none too friendly until he spied his old friend Shorty in the back seat. Then his features softened and he dismounted to talk.

The two old-timers assisted each other's memory in recalling many exciting incidents of the good old days. Most of them had to do with killings. Stubbs remembered every shooting that ever took place there; but my pencil remained in its pocket—I knew if he saw me making notes he would close up like a clam. Bill Stubbs' memory for names and dates was uncanny. He could write a roaring good novel if he would —but he won't.

Stubbs told us about Robber's Cave, located halfway down the side of a steep canyon three miles from the Bar-C ranch. In 1897 some of the outlaws had built a cabin up on the mountain for winter quarters. Four or five of them thought the place was too dangerous, so they fixed up the cave and lived in it that winter. The old bunks and pots and pans are still there. The old cowhide that hung over the entrance was there, still in place, until last year.

Stubbs remembered old Shankersville, on the mountain, a stopping place on the Outlaw Trail just above Hole-in-the-Wall. He was there once when one of the boys rode in covered with blood. He had been shot at by a posse armed with shotguns, but the main part of the load had entered the cantle of his saddle, and this saved his life. The boys at Shankersville spent most of the night picking buckshot out of his hide.

The old Texan told us how rustlers used to work their game in the Hole. Most of them took jobs with various friendly small ranchers or nesters. On a designated day a dozen or so would take a week off, meet at an appointed place, steal a herd of cattle, sell them in Casper, and return to their jobs. When officers investigated, every man had a perfect alibi: he had been working on the ranch all the time. He could prove it by his boss. It always worked. In return for such favors, herds of the men who hired rustlers were never disturbed.

We drove carefully back to Kaycee with our fragile guide. It had been a wonderful trip. We had seen the actual Hole-in-the-Wall, basis for a thousand wild yarns. The quart bottle was empty. Next morning we called on old Shorty Wheelwright at his room in the hotel, furnished, like his drinks, meals and clothes, by the townspeople of Kaycee. He was in bed, worn out by the sixty-mile trip of the previous day. The old scout who once thought nothing of riding a hundred and fifty miles in a day and a night couldn't take it!

Sheriff
John T. Pope

THREE sheriffs of three coun-
ties lying in three different states had jurisdiction in Brown's
Hole, when they chose to exercise it—which was seldom. The
sheriff of Routt County, Colorado, apparently never entered
the hideout until 1898, when Harry Tracy killed Valentine
Hoy. The sheriff of Sweetwater County, Wyoming, was an
utter stranger to the place, although he had once sent Deputy
Jim Philbrick to arrest Isom Dart. The only officer who went
there in person previous to 1898, so far as the records show,
was Sheriff John T. Pope, of Uintah County, Utah.

Vernal, county seat of Uintah County, was fifty miles from
the Hole. Diamond Mountain, at the east end of the Uintah
range, lay between. The trail up onto the forty-mile plateau
and down again to the Hole was rough and difficult in good
weather, practically impassable in winter. Pete Dillman made
two or three trips over the mountain one winter with mail,
charging fifty dollars a trip, but gave up the job after nearly
losing his life.

Johnny Harter's store in Vernal was held up one evening

337

by a would-be outlaw named Davis, who missed killing the proprietor by a fraction of an inch. John T. Pope, who had come to the Uintah Basin in 1884 from Bear Lake, happened to be standing just outside the store at the time of the holdup. With the town marshal he started in pursuit of the robber, armed with a rifle borrowed from Harter. Having a better horse he began closing the distance between himself and Davis. They started shooting at each other, but with both horses at a gallop their shots were ineffective, although Pope had his clothes perforated with two or three bullets. Davis jumped off his horse at the mouth of Ashley Canyon and made a stand behind a big boulder, where Pope held him until other pursuers arrived.

At the next election John T. Pope was nominated—without his knowledge—and elected sheriff. He served two terms at a salary of three hundred dollars a year, all that territorial laws provided. He then served several terms as county attorney. His occupancy of public office covered those years during which the outlaws in Brown's Hole were most aggressive.

The first case tried in Vernal after its incorporation as a town was that of the Rasmussen brothers, members of Gunplay Maxwell's gang of thieves. Maxwell operated mostly in Nine Mile Canyon, south of Vernal. The cattle he stole were driven to Price, slaughtered, and sold in a butcher shop operated by his brother. Maxwell, anxious to make a reputation for himself as a big-time rustler, decided to attend the trial of his friends to intimidate the court.

Samuel R. Thurman, later a justice of the Utah supreme court, was territorial district attorney at that time. Seeing that conviction was almost a certainty, Maxwell threatened the prosecutor. When court convened next day Sheriff Pope stood at the door with a sawed-off shotgun and disarmed every man who entered, including Gunplay. When the session was over he allowed each man to retrieve his weapon from

the pile in the corner. Maxwell was last. Pope took the
cartridges from the outlaw's gun and belt, handed him the
empty weapon, and informed him that the climate of Vernal
was very unhealthy after sundown. Maxwell took the hint
and left town that night.

Pope's most celebrated coup was the transportation of
Matt Warner, Coleman, and Wall from Vernal to Ogden for
trial, recounted in a previous chapter.

The Vernal sheriff seems to have taken his office quite seriously. Through his fearlessness he merited the enmity of the
outlaw element. On one occasion he was riding along the
Green River when a shot was fired at him from the willows,
cutting his vest clear across the front. He instantly dropped
from his horse and disappeared in another handy clump of
willows. . . . Years later two skeletons were discovered at
that place and were buried at the county's expense. No one
knew how those men met their death—and John T. Pope
never told.

On another trip along the Green River, Pope heard a shot
and felt a steel-jacketed bullet pass through the calf of his
leg. Before he could dismount his horse was hit by three more
shots. As the animal fell he jumped clear and while it was still
kicking managed to pull his rifle from the saddle scabbard.
When the smoke cleared away there was one less outlaw in
Uintah County. Pope then walked three miles to a ranch,
bought another horse, and rode on to serve a warrant.

Buckskin Ed, a Brown's Hole character whose history has
been told in an earlier chapter, stole some horses while Pope
was sheriff, and Pope went in to arrest him. The officer found
his man, handcuffed him, and started back to Vernal. When
they reached the river at Crouse's place, Pope put his prisoner
in a skiff, tied his horse behind and started to row across. In
the middle of the stream, while Pope was busy with the oars,
Buckskin got out his pocket knife, jumped on the sheriff's
back, and began jabbing at his throat. Pope dropped the oars,

pulled his gun, shot back over his shoulder and killed Buckskin Ed, who fell into the river. He then pulled to shore
where he found that his windpipe had been severed. The
jugular vein had not been cut, but he was choked by the
blood running down his windpipe. He lay on the sand several
hours until the bleeding partly ceased, then mounted his
horse, rode fifty miles to Vernal, had his throat sewn up by
a doctor, and went home. He told his wife the horse had stumbled, throwing him into a sharp greasewood. Some months
later Charley Crouse asked the sheriff what had become of
Buckskin Ed.

"The last I saw of him," said Pope, "he was headed for
Arizona." But he didn't tell Crouse that Buckskin had taken
the river route. A year later Ed's body was discovered in a
pile of driftwood by Speck Williams, well down in Lodore
Canyon.

A few days after his last term expired, Pope was called
upon to join the posse from Vernal that ran down Tracy,
Johnson, and Lant for the murder of Willie Strang and Valentine Hoy, as told in an earlier chapter. If Pope had had his
way, Tracy would have been hanged beside Jack Bennett on
Bassett's gate and a score of men, later killed by Tracy,
would have been saved from sudden death.

Three years after the robbery of the Montpelier bank, Pope
received a warrant for the arrest of Butch Cassidy in connection with that job. Cassidy was then staying with the Taylor
family, several miles from Vernal. When Pope reached the
ranch Cassidy had just left. The sheriff raced back to town,
found Cassidy's horse tied in front of a saloon and entered the
front door just as Butch left the back way. It was one of the
closest calls Butch ever had after being pardoned from the
Wyoming pen. Three weeks later Pope got a postcard mailed
from a town in Arizona. It read: "Pope: God damn you. Lay
off me. I don't want to kill you. Butch."

On one of his earlier trips to Brown's Hole, Sheriff Pope met Butch Cassidy and Elza Lay. He had no warrants for them at the time, and they were both friendly. Lay wanted to cross the Green River, which was at the peak of its annual flood. He rode to the edge of a high bank and jumped his horse into the swirling water. When he came to the surface he was separated from his mount. He began struggling, threshing about, and pawing water, completely losing his head. Butch, watching proceedings from above, saw that Lay would be drowned unless he settled down to swim and conserved his strength. Drawing his six-shooter, Cassidy yelled to his partner:

"Cut out that splashing, Lay, and start swimming like a man, or by God I'll blow your fool brains out."

Lay heard the shout, looked at Butch, gathered his scattered wits and obeyed instructions. The threat had cleared his head and saved his life. He climbed out of the water half a mile below, winded but safe.

Pope went to the Hole in 1897 to arrest Joe Tolliver for the murder of Charles Seger. He also arrested Charley Crouse for murder on another occasion. Both men were acquitted. At another time Pope went to the Hole with a sheriff from Colorado to capture three Mexican horse thieves. The Mexicans were trailed to the head of Willow Creek, where the officers found them at daybreak, asleep in their blankets. Pope shouted "Hands up!" One of the men obeyed, but the other two grabbed their rifles and opened fire. In less time than it takes to tell, the two who resisted were dead. The other man then made a break, jumped on an unsaddled horse and made his escape, with both officers shooting at him. Leaving the two dead men, the sheriffs trailed the fugitive all day through the badlands east of the Hole and finally found him at the cabin of Waterhole Charley seventy miles from the scene of the shooting. He had ridden those seventy miles with a bullet through his body but died within an hour after Pope's arrival. All the hair was scalded off the horse's back by blood oozing from his wound.

Jim McKee, from near Vernal, had been arrested by Sheriff Pope for killing sheep and was convicted on August 6, 1897. Threats were circulated that the McKee brothers were going to get the sheriff. Because of many such threats, after nightfall, Pope always walked down the middle of the street. One dark night he started down town, but had forgotten the sawed-off shotgun he usually carried under his coat. Suddenly a shot rang out, and a flash of powder almost singed his hair, while the bullet tore a hole in his hat. He pulled his six-shooter and began firing, but it was too dark to see his assailant. He then ran to the front door of a saloon in time to see Jim McKee coming in the back way. Still blowing from his sprint, McKee leaned against the rear end of the bar and when accused of the shooting claimed he had not been out of the place all evening. His friends backed up his alibi, and there was nothing Pope could do about it.

Fort Duchesne had been established fifty miles west of Vernal and was occupied during Pope's term of office by several companies of colored troops, commanded by Colonel Randlett. The colonel was an old-time army man, perhaps a little more on edge than the average run of western military officers.

Armed with a warrant, Pope was one day pursuing a horse thief near the military reservation. The thief took refuge on the reservation, where he believed he was safe from civil officers. Pope rushed in and arrested his man, but in catching him he had ridden past the guards without halting and had broken a stringent post regulation against riding horses on the parade ground. The officer of the day came rushing up and ordered Pope to turn the prisoner loose. Pope refused and was promptly put under military arrest. It was one of the colonel's bad days, and when the officer of the guard appeared with Pope and the handcuffed horse thief, Randlett cursed roundly. Pope didn't like the tone of his voice and told him so. After they had measured each other a few minutes, Randlett inquired into the cause of the disturbance. When he learned the circumstance he apologized to Pope, admitted his civil authority, and ordered the officious captain of the guard to escort Pope and the prisoner back to Vernal. Randlett and Pope were always friends after that episode, and later, when the sheriff was about to take Matt Warner to Ogden for trial, the colonel offered him an escort of a full company of soldiers.

When I interviewed him in 1937, Pope was past seventy-five years old but still vigorous and keen of eye. For thirty years he had been experimenting with extraction of oil from shale deposits in Uintah County and had recently discovered a new process which promised to be a big success. He died about five years later.

Queen Ann

WHILE gathering information for the first edition of this book in Brown's Hole, Rock Springs, and Vernal, I heard many stories about Queen Ann Bassett, some complimentary and some not. From all I could learn, she was the most colorful personality in that hidden valley during its picturesque outlaw period. No one took the trouble to inform me she was still living.

It was therefore a great surprise to receive a letter from a friend in 1943 stating that Queen Ann was in Delta, Utah, and would like to see me. I drove over next day, expecting to meet a hard-bitten, wrinkled old woman, possibly profane and certainly a character. Instead, I was introduced to a well-groomed, soft-voiced, cultured lady of sixty-eight who looked as though she might have just come from a literary tea. She had been somewhat upset over statements in the early edition about herself and some of her acquaintances; but when I explained the source of such stories we soon became friends.

During the next several days she gave me her life story. And because that story contains not only history but tragedy, drama, and romance, I will attempt to tell it here just as she gave it to me. If there are discrepancies between this and other sources of information, it must be remembered that it is Queen Ann's own story.

As indicated in an earlier chapter, Uncle Sam Bassett had been in Brown's Hole as early as 1851 or 1852 in the capacity of government scout. He liked the place and was in and out of it for many years. In the early 1870s he induced his brother Herbert to locate a cattle ranch there. Herbert was a Civil War veteran who had married a woman from Virginia.

Queen Ann was born in Brown's Hole in 1875. She had an older sister, Josie, and two brothers, Eb and Sam. Herbert Bassett was an easy-going, jovial man who liked company, and his home became a center for social events. When Josie was old enough, she helped with housework; but young Ann preferred the outdoors.

Slippery Sam was handy man on the Bassett ranch, and Ann used to follow him all day as he did various chores around the place. She was at his heels one day while he was mending fence, wearing a buckskin suit given her by a friendly squaw and an ornate headdress which had already caused her to be nicknamed "Queen" Ann.

"Look'ee here, Ann," said Sam; "why are you always tagging me around all day? Why don't you stay in the house and wear dresses like a girl should? You're old enough to learn to be a lady."

"I don't want to stay in the house and wear dresses," replied Ann, who already had definite opinions of her own. "I don't want to be a lady. I want to be a cowboy."

She was only seven then, but she never gave up that ambition. She had a saddle and pony of her own, was learning to rope, and spent much of her time with other children in the valley putting on miniature rodeos. When she was born, Judge Conway, an early settler, had given her a cow and calf. Her father also gave her calves from time to time, so that when she was ten years old she already owned a small herd.

One day while riding she found a stray calf carrying the Fisher brand. It was lost, half starved and full of burs. Rather than let it die she drove it home and, unknown to her parents, added another bar to its brand, claiming it as her own. Later Fisher claimed that the calf had been stolen, and he had nearly everyone in Brown's Hole arrested on suspicion. That lone dogie, which she named Dixie, caused many hard feelings before the matter was finally settled.

Ann remembered, as a small girl, some of the old trappers who still lived in that section. Jim Baker and his brother John lived at Dixon, where Jim had built the first permanent cabin in Wyoming. Old Uncle Louie Simmons, son-in-law of Kit Carson, was there until 1890, a permanent resident since 1854. She also knew and liked all the Indians living in and around the valley.

When she was about fifteen, a friendly Indian squaw made her a beautifully beaded buckskin suit, with fringed jacket, divided skirt, and laced leggings. She wore it constantly and had others made on the same pattern when it wore out. She believed this costume, which set the style for all later rodeo cowgirls, entitled her to the honor of being "the first cowgirl."

When Ann was sixteen, she had an exciting experience which demonstrates her foolhardy courage. She and two cowboys were driving a herd of cattle from Brown's Hole to the Little Snake River, forty-five miles, for delivery to a buyer. Nearing their destination, they stopped at Longhorn Thompson's ranch, where they found two overzealous game wardens with warrants for the arrest of a young Indian who had been killing deer out of season. Since all cowmen killed deer whenever they wanted meat, she thought it was unfair to arrest the Indian and rode nine miles to warn him. Next morning Wilcox and some other deputies, guided by Thompson, went to the Indian camp. In trying to arrest the young buck, Wilcox was hit over the head with a club by the boy's mother; whereupon the officers shot both mother and son and rode back to the ranch.

Soon smoke signals were seen in the hills, and Ann knew the Indians would take revenge. She ordered Thompson to gather the neighbors and fort up at the ranch. When the officers started to leave, she grabbed a shotgun and forced them to stay to help protect the place. But she refused to help kill her Indian friends to save the foolish wardens; so she got on her horse and rode directly toward the Indian camp in order to let them know she did not approve of the killings.

Accompanying Ann on the cattle drive was another young girl from Rock Springs who had been visiting at Bassett's ranch. When Ann left, this young lady jumped on her horse and followed. Two hours later this young lady's boy friend from Rock Springs drove in to Thompson's in a buckboard. When he heard that his sweetheart had followed Ann toward the Indian camp, he unharnessed one of the horses, borrowed a saddle, and started in pursuit. His horse was not broken for riding and bucked for the first fifteen miles, but the plucky swain managed to stay aboard.

The two girls rode past the Indian camp just before sundown but saw no one. They were probably observed by the Indians, but they knew Ann's horse and let her pass. An hour later the young man passed and got a bullet through his hat. After dark the girls heard horses and hid in some brush, but it proved to be a band of range animals. It took Ann an hour to locate her friend in the dark. Then they rode on. About midnight a single horse was heard approaching from the rear. They rode off the trail to let it pass, but when Ann heard a squeaky saddle she figured the rider must be white, and she shouted. She was answered by the other girl's sweetheart. They stopped to make love while Ann fumed to get going. The boy's horse was finished, so he abandoned it and rode behind his girl friend. Just as dawn broke they arrived in

Brown's Hole to give the alarm. Both girls had been in the saddle more than twenty-four hours.

After Ann left, the whites forted up at another ranch. During the night Indians burned Thompson's place and everything in it. Thompson moved to Vernal and never went back.

The owner of one of the big ranches surrounding Brown's Hole was John Ward in Clay Basin. One fall he drove thirty head of cattle into the Hole just to see if he could get away with it. When Ann discovered these cattle she organized a roundup and with some of the younger element ran them across the Green River onto Diamond Mountain, where they strayed or mixed with Mormon herds. When no trace of these animals could be found, word got around that people in Brown's Hole were all rustlers, and there was trouble from that time on. Matt Rash got the blame for stealing those cattle; that is why he was marked for death when Tom Horn arrived.

Ann insisted there were no cattle rustlers in Brown's Hole. She claimed that neither Matt Rash, Isom Dart, nor any of the others ever stole cattle at any time. She admitted that many famous outlaws passed through at various times but said they usually behaved themselves.

When some of the big outfits tried to buy up all small ranches in the Hole, some settlers wanted to sell out and quit. But Ann called them together, argued, cajoled, and threatened until she stiffened their morale against intrusion. From then on she was considered leader of the Brown's Hole ranchers and they looked to her for advice. She knew that if one sold out, it meant the end of independent ranching in that valley.

The Middlesex cattle company north of the Hole was financed by English money and managed by an Englishman. This company tried to buy Brown's Hole but failed; they then threatened to starve the people out, but that was impossible. Eventually they ceased their effort and lived peaceably with their small neighbors. They never pulled any rough stuff, never hired gunmen.

Jack and Grif Edwards, said to have been related to English nobility, ran sheep in the vicinity and were frequent visitors at Bassett's ranch. They told Ann many entertaining stories of the outside world, particularly about Australia, where they had been in the sheep business. As a small girl, Ann was more familiar with Australia than with Vernal, fifty miles over Diamond Mountain.

Another elderly Englishman came to the valley and built himself a small cabin. He was full of interesting stories about China, where he had spent many years. But one day it was discovered he had leprosy, and children were cautioned never to go near him. From that time on, he remained alone in his cabin, fed through a hole in the door by Tommy Dowdle. After a year he died and was buried above Lodore. His cabin and everything in it were burned.

Like many western ranches owned by Englishmen, the Middlesex company was poorly managed. Many cattle were never rounded up, and within a few years thousands of un-branded two-year-olds were roaming the range. Everybody in the Hole used to gather them up. Charley Sparks, said Ann, got his start in the cattle business that way. Everybody helped himself to these mavericks; she had many of them herself. They finally became such a nuisance that settlers went on hunting expeditions to kill them off, returning with wagonloads of Middlesex beef. Gathering mavericks was a recognized custom of the range; but certain residents seem to have been overambitious and gave everyone in the valley a bad name.

In their teens Josie Bassett stayed with her mother and learned to keep house while Ann rode the range like any cow-boy. She owned a nice silk dress, but it hung unused in a closet. Finally Mrs. Bassett got tired of dusting it and gave it to Mrs. Joe Tolliver. Mrs. Tolliver wore it one day while

chasing cows through thick brush and "tore it all to hell."
Even though Ann had no use for the dress, this made her
plenty mad.

There was no church in Brown's Hole, but the Bassetts
had an organ, so on Sundays people gathered at their place to
sing gospel hymns. On such occasions young Ann, about seven
then, who hated hymns, would duck out and go to the bunk-
house, where she sang cowboy songs with the boys. She
usually got a whipping for this, but apparently her mother had
a light hand. After the Sunday songfest, neighbors would sit
in the parlor to discuss topics of the day or express their ideas
on any subject. Ann says the social tone was quite high, especially while the Englishmen were there.

When their daughters began to grow up, the Bassetts decided the girls ought to have some culture. It was difficult to
keep good teachers in the Hole, and schooling was sketchy.
Josie didn't like the idea of leaving home, but Ann thought it
might be an adventure to go back east. Since Boston was considered the cultural center of the United States, her father
took her to Boston and enrolled her in a young ladies'
seminary.

This wild young prairie flower from the wide-open spaces
didn't quite fit in with the social tone of a high-class, snobbish
girls' school.

At this school there was, of course, a class in riding, since
every real lady was supposed to be able to ride gracefully.
Only sidesaddles were used, since to ride astride was considered the height of indecency. Few of the girls had ever been
on a horse, while Ann had practically been born in a saddle.
She meekly followed instructions of her French riding master
for a few days, pretending to be afraid of her mount. But
one day when the class was ready for a gentle canter on prepared riding paths, the instructor returned to the stable for
some purpose. As soon as he was out of sight, Ann mounted
his horse and started putting it through some Wild West

maneuvers, which frightened the girls half to death. When the
Frenchman returned and caught her at it, she said, it took her
father and a United States senator to keep her from being
expelled. She stayed two years, but that was all she could
take. However, this taste of higher education gave her an
introduction to good literature, and when I knew her she was
one of the best-read women of my acquaintance.

Back in Brown's Hole, Ann took up where she left off, with
the added prestige of a Boston education. She was old enough
then to begin thinking of marriage; but none of the local
young men interested her. She had ridden with them all over
the range, eaten at their campfires, slept in the sagebrush, and
could outrope and outshoot any cowhand in the valley. They
all treated her like another man and never seemed to consider
her as a possible wife. She wanted it that way.

Then one night at a dance she met a tall, dark, handsome,
curly-haired young man with a trace of Boston accent. He
was popular with all the girls but paid special attention to Ann.
She found he had been in that country for some time, living
in Uintah Basin and at Matt Warner's cabin on Diamond
Mountain. He was Ellsworth Lay, but was better known as
Elza. He had no visible means of support, and she soon found
he was a member of the outlaw gang which was drifting
into the Hole. But he always behaved like a gentleman and
seemed to have a good education.

Ann liked him better than any young man she had met up to
that time and looked forward to his visits. Sometimes he
would be gone for weeks, then turn up with his pockets full
of money. More and more he was seen in the company of
Butch Cassidy. She never cared much for Butch, and she
insisted to me that Elza Lay was always the leader in their
exploits. Somehow Elza never quite got around to proposing
marriage.

One night Ann heard a tapping on her window and went
outside to investigate. She found Elza Lay in the shadows.

"Hello, Ann," he whispered. "I wonder if you would do something for me."

"Yes, of course," she replied. "What is it?"

"Butch and I are camped a couple of miles from here. We just got in from a long, hard ride and haven't had anything to eat. Could you fix us something to take back to camp?"

"Yes, Elza," she said. "Just wait here. It will take a little time; I'll have to be careful not to waken anyone."

She fixed a basket of grub, and he carried it back to his partner in camp. She accompanied him part of the way. When they parted he gave her a map showing where he had buried his share of the loot from the Wilcox train holdup.

"If I'm not back within a year, Ann," he told her, "I wish you would dig up that money and send it to my mother." She promised she would.

That was the last time she ever saw him until after he got out of the pen in New Mexico. About a year later he passed through and dug up his cache, but did not call on Ann. Perhaps he didn't have time.

During Butch Cassidy's operations in and around Brown's Hole, Ann met all the well-known outlaws, who frequently attended local dances. She hated Matt Warner, who was often drunk and disorderly and mistreated his wife. Butch was very quiet and paid little attention to girls. The McCarty brothers lived one winter with old man Bender at Powder Springs. They behaved themselves and were liked. Flat Nose George Curry was there at different times, also Flat Foot George and Big Nose Kelly. They were rough, ugly men but gave no trouble. Pete Neilson came in, posing as a cattle buyer. Black Jack Ketchum also spent some time in the Hole.

Jack Chew lived on Diamond Mountain with his family. Ann says he was so shiftless and lazy that his wife had to do all the farm work and even chop her own wood. One winter she had a new baby and couldn't chop wood for a few days. They ran out of fuel and the baby froze to death. When Ann heard about it she got mad and made up her mind to do something, although older heads thought it was none of their business. The Green River was running full of ice and it was almost suicide to cross. When neighbors couldn't talk her out of the idea, they went down to the river with ropes to help her in case she got into trouble. She swam her horse across safely and rode to Chew's cabin. Mrs. Chew was in bed with all her children, including the dead baby, trying to keep them warm. Ann drove Jack out and beat him with her quirt while he chopped wood. Then she returned to the house and baked bread for the hungry children. There was no other food in the house.

When the law came to Brown's Hole, Ann was attending school and was not present. But she knew the story, and her account agrees with what I have already given, except for a few additional details. While Jack Bennett was being held prisoner in the post office, seven men from the Vernal posse entered, handcuffed Deputy Farnham, tied up Herbert Bassett, and hanged Bennett on the gate. It was done so quietly that women cooking in the kitchen knew nothing of it. Ann believed that Joe Tolliver was leader of these vigilantes. When the posse returned to Bassett's ranch with Tracy, Lant, and Johnson, they wanted to hang all three. Although Longhorn Thompson was a member of the posse, his wife grabbed a shotgun and held them off, threatening to give the gun to Tracy unless they promised not to do any more hanging. They finally agreed.

When Tom Horn came to Brown's Hole under the name of Tom Hix, he stopped with various ranchers in the vicinity and finally worked for Matt Rash. Later, after Matt was found shot, she suspected Hix and wanted the sheriff of Routt County to arrest him; but there seemed to be no evidence connecting him with the killing. Three months later Isom Dart was killed in a similar manner, and she again affirmed her belief that Hix had done the job. Shortly after the Negro's death she received an anonymous letter mailed at Casper, warning her to keep her mouth shut. She still continued to voice her suspicions.

One night, as she sat by a window with the blinds pulled down, she was shot at. The bullet missed her, but she thinks it was fired by Tom Hix, who then was known to be Tom Horn. By that time the sheriff was convinced and promised to pick him up; but he was never seen again in the valley. She believed the bullet which killed Isom was intended for Jim McKnight, who later married her sister Josie.

Ann had sold some cattle to Matt Rash, which had not been paid for. After his death she rounded them up and brought them back in spite of sheriff's orders to wait until the estate was settled in court. Because of this, she says, it was reported she and Rash were sweethearts and he had remembered her in his will.

By 1910 many original pioneers of Brown's Hole had died and their children were operating their holdings. Ora Haley, a big operator on the east, thought it might be a good time to make another attempt to move in. His manager was Hi Bernard, and his foreman Frank Willis. One fall Haley organized a drive and pushed 5,000 head of cattle into the Hole at one time, intending to overrun the place. This stirred Ann's anger. She tried to get cooperation from her neighbors to resist this move, but they were apathetic and refused to do anything. So she saddled her horse, loaded some pack animals, and began driving Haley's cattle into a rough section of country where it was difficult to locate them. It took her some time, but she finally accomplished the job successfully.

According to law she had no right to move stray cattle except off her own property; she had violated the law by chasing them all over the desert. Haley was furious and had her arrested. There was a long trial in Craig, Colorado, over this affair in 1911 and 1913 but Ann was finally acquitted. Editor Lickenby of the *Steamboat Register* carried reports of the trial and always referred to Ann as "Queen of the Brown's Hole rustlers." She never forgave him for his remarks, and she was a long time in forgiving me for quoting some of them in the first edition of this book.

When this legal action failed, Haley tried to hire his foreman, Frank Willis, for a fee of $500, to go to the Hole and get legal evidence of Queen Ann's "rustling activities." He flatly refused.

During or shortly after her trial, Hi Bernard, Haley's manager, conceived a great admiration for Ann Bassett and soon was a frequent visitor to her home, although he was twenty years older. He finally proposed to her, planning to quit his job with Haley and build up a cattle ranch in the Hole. After some hesitation she accepted. She was not particularly in love with Bernard at the time, although she came to love him later. It seemed to be a good deal for both, and she hoped the arrangement would end her troubles with the big cattle barons, since Bernard was active in the Wyoming Stockgrowers association. He brought in a large herd to run with hers, and for a time everything worked out satisfactorily.

After eight years of marriage, Hi Bernard thought he knew Ann well enough to confide in her. He told her he had hired Tom Horn to kill Matt Rash and Isom Dart and had paid Horn $1,000 for the two jobs. This was too much for Ann. She left him and divided their property. He died soon after.

Some time later she met and married Frank Willis, the man who had refused to spy on her. But by that time sheep were taking over the country and cattle were no longer profitable. She sold her herds, turned the old ranch over to her brothers and left Brown's Hole. Frank became a mining engineer and together they traveled from place to place, wherever his work took him. He was developing a manganese property in Millard County when I met Ann in Delta, Utah.

Queen Ann was then sixty-eight, but life in an apartment did not appeal to her. She could not forget those years when she rode the range looking after her own cattle. She still planned to get back in the saddle some day, and wherever she went she kept looking for another hidden valley in the mountains like Brown's Hole, where she could develop a ranch.

She never found it, because all such places have long been occupied. She died at Leeds, Utah, in May, 1956.

Postscript

Most of those who will read this book are old enough to be children of pioneers who knew some of the characters described or who were familiar with some of the incidents told. They remember the political, economic, and psychological conditions prevailing in "the good old days" and will learn nothing from this chapter.

But there are millions of young people who think of Franklin D. Roosevelt as the first president of the United States and have grown up in an atmosphere of governmental regulation. They do not have a clear idea of conditions under which their great-grandparents lived or a proper understanding of pioneer psychology. Some, whose ancestors happened to travel the outlaw trail, will be ashamed of their family history. This backward glance is for their benefit.

Thousands of young men returned from the Civil War almost penniless and without definite prospects for the future. Many began wandering aimlessly around the country in search of excitement and some got into trouble. To offset this tendency, Congress issued land script entitling veterans

357

to any piece of land they chose in the public domain, hoping they would settle down and become good citizens. Later the Homestead Law was enacted, giving any man title to 160 acres of land if he would live on it for a few years and make a few simple improvements. It was the best law ever enacted by Congress and continued in effect until Roosevelt's time, when all land on which a man could make a living by farming had been occupied.

There were, of course, millions of acres in the West unsuitable for plowing, but most of it could be used for grazing. Cattle from Texas were driven or shipped to these open ranges, which were free to everyone without any restrictions whatever—first come, first served.

The great West was opened and settled under these conditions. It was a free country in every sense of the word, where every man was a law unto himself. The men who came west to occupy that free land were independent souls who loved freedom, hated restrictions of any kind, and wanted to be kings in their own little empires. They were gamblers who chanced everything on their ability to take care of themselves without assistance from anyone. Some were ruined by fire, flood, or hard winters, but they took it in their stride and started over again, certain they would make it next time. Most of them did, and laid up a competence for their old age. Whatever they had was theirs to leave to their children or do with as they pleased. That was the pioneer spirit.

While men are theoretically equal under law, they are not created equal. Some are more industrious, thrifty, or foresighted than others. Some are born lucky. Under any conditions, certain men accumulate more property than others; it has always been that way and always will be. But in the old days each man at least had an equal start. He could go anywhere he pleased, choose his own land, and operate it in his own way. If he failed it was largely because of his own bad judgment.

In any community of such fiercely independent souls there was bound to be conflict. Where each man made his own rules, many became intolerant and tried to force their rules upon others. Every man believed himself equal to, if not just a shade better than, any man living, and he lost no opportunity to demonstrate his equality and defend his individual rights. Every man went armed as a matter of course, and this naturally led to many fights and considerable bloodshed. But as time went on, certain fundamental rules of conduct became the unwritten laws of the range and most men observed them.

One of these rules was: "Possession is nine points of the law." When a man selected an unoccupied section and stocked it with cattle, latecomers were not supposed to push him off and take it for themselves. When they did, he fought for his understood rights. But certain men are born greedy, with no respect for any rights but their own. A few big western cattle barons were of this stamp, particularly after they became wealthy. When they succeeded in squeezing out or running off a homesteader or small rancher by force, as often occurred, they frequently created an outlaw. Not being able to defend himself otherwise, the victim retaliated in the only way he knew how—by turning cattle thief.

This, of course, does not account for all western outlaws. Several of those included in this story, like Harry Tracy and Harvey Logan, were naturally bad men who came west because the pickings were easier and outlaw hideouts safer. But a majority of cowboy-outlaws, particularly those born in the West, were just high-spirited young bucks who loved excitement and hated the monotony of settled communities. Their greatest joy was found in exploring new country, camping on the desert, and telling tall tales around a campfire. Sometimes they foolishly got themselves into a tight place and had to shoot their way out, but they avoided bloodshed whenever possible.

These wild, free souls saw great fortunes being made all around them by cattle kings, railroad magnates, and mining nabobs who got there first and found good pickings. Such men and corporations, almost unrestricted by law, were taking advantage of their opportunities without thought of the future, making their own rules and putting on a great display of wealth. Under pioneer conditions it was their right to do anything they could get away with, but some of them overworked that privilege.

Cowboy-outlaws resented this attitude and felt no twinges of conscience whatever in robbing railroads, mines, and banks. A good many men who lacked nerve enough to become bandits felt the same way, including some officers of the law. That was one reason why so many outlaws remained uncaught. Most of them disdained "petty larceny" and, except in rare instances, never robbed individuals. Ordinarily they observed the rules of decency and were welcome in many homes. They were generous with money when they had it and performed many charitable acts.

But times change and this period of personal liberty gradually came to an end. Beginning with Theodore Roosevelt, certain curbs were put on great corporations. National forests were set aside out of the great public domain, and new rules were established for grazing in those areas. Homesteaders began fencing off large sections, thus reducing open range land and eventually breaking up big cattle ranches. These big operations were also reduced by overgrazing. Finally sheep were introduced. They could live where a cow would starve to death, and for a time fortunes were made in wool and mutton. This automatically put an end to cattle rustling, since a sheep was not worth stealing. Good roads, telephones, and new towns made it hard for bandits to escape the law; even their hideouts had been occupied by law-abiding citizens.

With the administration of Franklin D. Roosevelt, the Homestead Law was suspended; the Taylor grazing act put all public domain under government control; stiff income taxes took the profit out of business. Subsidies were paid to farmers and stockmen for not producing. Rationing of raw materials upset laws of supply and demand.

Range lands of the West were becoming overgrazed and useless. The Taylor grazing act attempts to remedy this condition by limiting animals on the range and charging a grazing fee for use of the public domain. Under its rules each stockman is confined to a definite area and may not run his animals on any other section. Every inch of range is parceled out, and there is no opportunity for a young man to start a new ranch; he must buy grazing rights from some other rancher. Those now operating under these rules believe this change will preserve grazing lands which would otherwise have been destroyed. Homestead entries were also suspended because all land capable of cultivation had been occupied. These restrictions definitely put an end to "the good old days."

When Butch Cassidy rode the outlaw trail, no ranch house was ever locked. Every traveler was made welcome, and if owners were not at home he helped himself, taking only what was needed for his immediate necessities. If he found himself without food on the desert, he killed a beef and notified its owner later. If his horse broke a leg he caught the first horse he could find and was welcome. He camped in abandoned houses and left them as he found them, to benefit some other wayfarer.

John Dillinger and his like are not to be compared with the cowboy-outlaws who rode the range robbing trains and banks but who respected women and children.

So perhaps we old-timers may be pardoned if we heave a sigh for "the good old days" of Butch Cassidy and his Wild Bunch.

Index

362